Credo
and
Twelve Poems
A Cosmological Manifesto

Paul Monk

with images by
John Spooner

ECHO BOOKS

First published in 2015 by Barrallier Books Pty Ltd,
trading as Echo Books

Registered Office: 35-37 Gordon Avenue, West Geelong, Victoria 3220, Australia.

www.echobooks.com.au

Copyright © Paul Monk 2015
National Library of Australia cataloguing-in-publication information:

Title: Credo and twelve poems : a cosmological manifesto / Paul Monk;
John Spooner.

ISBN: 9780994418449 (hardback)

Subjects: Aphorisms and apothegms. Poetry.

Other Creators/Contributors: Spooner, John, 1946- illustrator.

Dewey Number: A821.4

Set in Garamond Premier Pro 12/17 and Fragrance.

Book and cover design, Peter Gamble, Canberra

www.echobooks.com.au

For Claudia, as a candle in the Chavista dimness of her beloved Venezuela;
for Joe Lo Bianco, in commemoration of our long, 'Steinerian' conversations
and
for all those seeking a new synthesis in a bewildering time

Portrait of the Author.

Contents

Table of Aphorisms

Credo

We Karyotes

Nutcracker Man

After the Ice

Fire and the Wheel

Circles in the Dust

The Dream

Lara

The Poet's Bell

The Bell and the Choir

Lullaby for Junius

Your Architect

Dance me on down from Toledo

Illustrations

You got me singing
Even though the world is gone
You got me thinking
I'd like to carry on

You got me singing
Even though it all looks grim
You got me singing
The Hallelujah hymn

Leonard Cohen 'You got me singing'
From the album *Popular Problems* (2014)

'Le Corbusier knew that well-placed walls could alter our mental states, that through measure
and proportion one might bring calm to the human soul ... '

Nicholas Fox Weber *Le Corbusier: A Life* (2008)

It is my belief that philosophy must return to cosmology and to a simple theory of knowledge.

Karl Popper (1958)

Preface: Why poems? Why aphorisms?

The dizzying advances of the sciences over the past century and a half have created a progressively wider and wider gulf between traditional world views and the realities evident to those absorbing the new knowledge. This is most evident with regard to religion. There is a need for a new synthesis that makes clear the human place in the cosmos and the course of human evolution and history. This book is my own attempt to outline what such a synthesis might look like. It is not, however, a systematic argument. It is, instead, a manifesto setting out a vision of what has been learned and where it now places us all.

The manifesto consists of an essay, a credo, twelve poems and 205 aphorisms. That is unusual. One has the impression that few people these days read poetry and certainly that what is read is so various and fragmented that there is no common culture of poetics or meaning. Aphorisms are, if anything, an even rarer form of reading or common coinage. Nietzsche wrote books of aphorisms, but he died well over a century ago and is a semi-mythical figure. Why write a book full of poems and aphorisms now?

The poems in question are among those I have written in recent years in an ongoing effort to create my own sense of meaning and coherence out of the jumbled mass of inherited and circulating ideas abroad in the early 21st century world. They are, like most poetry, a private articulation of felt life and a set of attempts to generate a lifeworld of my own. They are shared here purely as an offering. They arose in the context of a larger literary project which I am still at work on: a long novel about meaning, love and truth in our time. In that context, they are among 42 poems found among the unpublished papers of a deceased polymath by his literary executor. Here they will land differently and be open to various interpretations.

An aphorism is classically defined as 'a short, pithy statement or maxim, according to the *Concise Oxford Dictionary*. I think of them as anything up to a paragraph in length, but not more. The Greek root of the word—*aphorismos*—means definition. Each of the aphorisms in this book is intended to define or point to something. The overall effect is intended to be a sketch of reality and meaning. The word sketch is an approximation. This book constitutes a *position*, but not an *argument*. The aphorisms are points outlining that position.

Each can be pondered on its own; in conjunction with the poem which precedes it; in the context of the other aphorisms in that poetic setting; or in the wider ambience of the whole book. The position in question, like that of any creative writer, is where I have arrived at, after a lifetime of trying to make sense of the late 20th century and early 21st century world. It is not an 'objective' position. It is the position of a 'subject' moving across disciplines and challenges, seeking to become free of oppressive dogmas and narrow ideologies without lapsing into incoherence or solipsism.

The essay with which the book begins provides a personal, scholarly reflection on where I started, forty years ago, when I left my ancestral religion behind, and where I stood at the point when this book was being composed. Others will each have their own such story. I hope that this story and the book as a whole will stimulate others to reflect upon their own stories and perhaps see them in a fresh light. It does not require of anyone that they have had the same experiences, or have arrived at the same conclusions.

The credo and each of the poems is followed by a number of aphorisms. They are thematically related, but they are not direct explanations of the verse. They are improvisations on the themes opened up by the verse. They are intended to be read as one would listen to a jazz concert: catching the shifting moods, appreciating the various improvisations and instrumentations, reflecting on the thoughts that these things stir. They will, I hope, be read—and re-read—meditatively and enjoyably, as poems and aphorisms should be; not in an argumentative or impatient manner.

Paul Monk, PhD
Melbourne
January 2016

Getting perspective in our time: Bluebeard's Castle and the open horizon

When we are young, as a general rule, we are particularly impressionable. In my adolescence, three sets of ideas made a deep and enduring impression on me, both emotionally and intellectually. The first was reading William L. Shirer's *The Rise and Fall of the Third Reich* while still a schoolboy. The second was reading the works of Nietzsche, shortly after I had left school; most notably *Thus Spoke Zarathustra*. The third was reading, in 1975, George Steiner's 1971 *tour de force* on redefining Western culture after the Holocaust, *In Bluebeard's Castle*. Many other books influenced me, of course; but looking back these stand out as having shaped my outlook on the world; as having posed the questions to which I most urgently and seriously sought answers throughout my university education and in my private exploration of the world.

Shirer's path-breaking book filled me with horror and dread at the darkness and violence abroad in the world.[1] Though I grew up in a quiet and comfortable corner of the Earth, I have never, since reading Shirer, felt altogether at ease with my fellow human beings, or even with the idea of being human myself. Nietzsche's books, a few years later, made an explosive impact on me. I had been raised as a conservative Catholic and had contemplated a religious vocation when still at school. Reading Nietzsche changed all that forever. Though I quickly decided that his social and moral philosophy were deeply problematic, I was hooked on his

---

1. I no longer possess the old paperback edition of *The Rise and Fall of the Third Reich* that I read in 1971-72. It made an indelible impression, however; as it did on millions of my contemporaries. It was first published in 1959 and has since been reprinted scores of times in both hard cover and paperback, translated into almost every European language and many Asian ones, such is the gravity of the events it records. It has long since been surpassed as scholarship, with the combing over of massive archives and the refinement of many points of detail since the 1950s; but it remains a classic. Among the works of scholarship that have updated it in the past half century, Ian Kershaw's two volume biography of Hitler, published at the end of the 20th century, must rank high: *Hitler: 1889-1936 Hubris* (Allen Lane, Penguin, 1998) and *Hitler: 1936-1945 Nemesis* (Allen Lane, Penguin, 2000). Gitta Sereny, whose exceptional book on Albert Speer and the Third Reich is itself an inimitable contribution to the field, declared of Kershaw's work: 'What emerges is an entirely original thesis, a new insight into how this uniquely calamitous dictator managed to come so close to fulfilling his terrible aims.'

dramatic idea that the modern sciences and the inner intellectual conscience of Christianity had culminated in the 'death of God'. I was intrigued by the figure of Zarathustra and his insistence that, as human beings, we are uncertain primates who need to be faithful to the Earth and to walk a tightrope to a higher form of being.

Steiner brought all this together in his remarkable little 1971 book. Here, within just over a hundred pages, was a Western scholar—Jewish himself—pondering the implications of the Holocaust, the calamities of the 20th century, the brilliant and yet in some ways ominous achievements of the natural sciences in that same century and the ideas of Nietzsche. Though I read his book in 1975, it has taken me many years to develop a thoughtful response to it. He framed it as a critical response to T. S. Eliot's *Notes Towards a Definition of Culture* (1948), expressing puzzlement and dismay that Eliot had passed over the Holocaust, as if it had been a mere incidental sideshow in the Second World War. He went on to reflect that the humanities were dying and that the promise of progress had darkened with the possibility—embodied in the sinister enigma of nuclear weapons—that the physical sciences might be leading us all to a murderous future beyond our moral comprehension or control.

Over the decades since then, while immersed in many another study or task, I have never ceased to ponder Steiner's arguments. I have re-read *In Bluebeard's Castle* again and again, annotating it and mulling over it. I have done quite a bit of writing of my own during those years; some of which has directly addressed the large questions Steiner asked in 1971. Slowly, over a lifetime, I have arrived at opinions which differ in important respects from his, as regards precisely those questions. I have developed a worldview of my own, independent of those which made such an impression on my youthful mind. I have given expression to that worldview in this little book. But here, by way of a prelude to that expression, I want to articulate where, how and why I have come to differ with Nietzsche and Steiner, after forty years of thinking about their ideas and growing from youth to almost sixty years of age.

I differ from Nietzsche centrally as regards his assertion that all of life is simply 'the will to power and nothing else'. I do not differ with him because the implications of his doctrine are disquieting; although they are in a number of ways. I differ from him because I believe he was in error. I think his proclamation of the death of God was visionary, but I do not agree with him that this must lead to nihilism or the need for a 'revaluation of all values'. On the contrary, I think it is a poetic way of acknowledging that all tribal and anthropomorphic deities are anachronistic and that the natural sciences and the archaeologies of human history have set us free from the dogmas and delusions of the past—provided that we are willing to embrace that freedom and reinvent ourselves as emancipated beings. I still think of Nietzsche's books as enormously thought provoking, but I differ from him in many ways as regards what is true.

With George Steiner I disagree about the definition of God he offers; about what he calls the 'botched attempt to kill God'; about the role of creativity in human culture; and about the future of humanity in what he called, all those years ago, 'this cruel, late stage in Western affairs'. I still cherish his little book, but I have arrived at considered opinions which differ from his in quite fundamental ways. While leaving Shirer and Nietzsche in the deep background, I want to set out here the grounds for my disagreements with Steiner, because it is these grounds which set the stage for the poems and aphorisms which constitute *Credo and Twelve Poems*. Those who have never read *In Bluebeard's Castle*, or who have long since decided that they differed from Steiner on important things; or again those whose worldview has simply been shaped by very different readings and experiences than mine, are invited to follow my critique of Steiner simply as a pathway into my manifesto.

Steiner's God is decidedly Jewish and decidedly mystical. It is not the Trinity of the Christians and it is not Allah of the Muslims. Nor is it the Prime Mover of the Aristotelians and Deists, or the immanent wonder of Nature, as in the philosophy of Spinoza. Curiously, it is also very abstracted from the 'realities' of the deity in the Pentateuch and the bulk of the Old Testament. Moreover, he loses this God in the mists of time and shows no awareness of its mythological nature, or of the failure of modern archaeology to find the slightest trace of the tale of Moses and the Exodus. He argues that 'Western man' attempted to kill this God (not just any old God) out of resentment at its demands for an impossible standard of morality and, when this failed, turned savagely on the Jews as the messengers of this specific and intolerable God. But his argument is seriously flawed, as I shall show. He argues, at the same time, that the creative heights of Western culture are unique in human history and yet that the natural sciences have brought the whole of humanity to a precipice from which it cannot withdraw. This argument is better grounded, but also flawed in important ways.

At the end of his book, summing up his survey of the modern world, Steiner used the haunting analogy of Bartok's opera *Duke Bluebeard's Castle* to suggest that, in a collective sense, because of the scientific achievements of the West, humanity stood (by 1971) like Judith—the ill-fated woman in the opera—before 'the last door on the night' and that we shall in all probability open that door 'even if it leads, perhaps because it leads, onto realities which are beyond the reach of human comprehension and control.' He concluded that there are 'two obvious responses to this outlook:

> There is Freud's stoic acquiescence, his grimly tired supposition that human life was a cancerous anomaly, a detour between vast stages of organic repose. And there is the Nietzschean gaiety in the face of the inhuman, the tensed, ironic perception that we are, that we always have been, precarious guests in an indifferent, frequently murderous, but always fascinating world.

He expressed a preference for the Nietzschean outlook. I shall return to this presently, but simply note here in passing that there are more than two possible responses to the situation in which we find ourselves. More fundamentally, while it is thought-provoking to see ourselves as Judith in Bluebeard's castle; that is no more than a rhetorical flourish. There is vastly more going on than that operatic simile suggests and our possible futures include more options than that which confronted Bartok's Judith. Moreover, we can be aware of this and bring such options to pass chiefly because of the insights of the 'Western' sciences.

Let me bring together the first two of my critical observations about *In Bluebeard's Castle* (the definition of and the 'botched attempt to kill' God), by reflecting on Steiner's stirring, but tendentious remarks about God, the West and the Holocaust. His point of entry was the statement that:

> The failure of Eliot's *Notes Towards a Definition of Culture* to face the issue [of the Holocaust] ... is acutely disturbing. How, only three years after the event, after the publication to the world of facts and pictures that have, surely, altered our sense of the limits of human behaviour, was it possible to write a book on culture and say nothing? How was it possible to detail and plead for a Christian order when the holocaust had put in question the very nature of Christianity and of its role in European history?

These were important questions. Steiner's answer to them, however, was flawed in several ways. He insisted that the Holocaust was unlike other genocides, because it could only be understood in religious terms and as the product of a lethal philosophical intent. In defining his religious terms, he then wrote about the Hebrew God as if it had been 'revealed' once and for all—to Moses, rather than Abraham, Isaac or Jacob—without any reference to the long evolution of Jewish theology. He wrote of the intolerable burden that belief in this God is supposed to have been to 'Western man', but omitted to discuss why it was not even more intolerable to the Jews themselves. He attributed the Holocaust to an atavistic European attempt to be rid of that burden and to fall back on 'the natural savageries, intellectual torpor and material instincts of unextended man'[2]—as if the Hebrew deity had been the only thing that stood between Western civilization and such 'savageries'.

---

2.   George Steiner *In Bluebeard's Castle* (Faber & Faber, London, 1971), pp. 34-42.

Let's take these large claims one at a time. Having criticized Eliot for not reflecting on the genocide of the Jews at all, he then stated:

> It seems to me incontrovertible that the holocaust must be set in the framework of the psychology of religion, and that an understanding of this framework is vital to an argument on culture. This is a minority view. Understandably, in an effort to make this insane material susceptible and bearable to reason, sociologists, economists, political scientists, have striven to locate the topic in a rational, secular grid ... Each of these lines of inquiry is important. Together they make for an indispensable dossier of historical and sociological insight. But the phenomenon, so far as one is able to take any coherent view of it at all, lies far deeper ... We are not, I believe, dealing with some monstrous accident in modern social history. The holocaust was not the result of merely individual pathology or of the neuroses of one nation state ...

To make this case, he had then to argue (as he did) firstly that earlier or non-European cases of genocide or mass terror were not truly analogous to the Holocaust; and secondly that the 'intent' behind the Holocaust was a Pan-European, rather than a specifically pathological Nazi program.

He states, with respect to the first of these claims:

> We are not—and this is often misunderstood—considering something truly analogous to other cases of massacre, to the murder of the Gypsies or, earlier, of the Armenians. There are parallels in technique, and in the idiom of hatred; but not ontologically, not at the level of philosophic intent. That intent takes us to the heart of certain instabilities in the fabric of Western culture, in the relations between instinctual and religious life. Hitler's jibe that 'conscience is a Jewish invention' provides a clue.

But consider that the massacres of the Gypsies and the Armenians are themselves too limiting a set of case studies. Genocidal massacres span the globe and go back millennia. Tamerlane is thought to have been responsible for the slaughter of 17 million people across Central Asia and the Middle East in the 14th century, when the global human population was only about 300 million. And Tamerlane had no industrial means of extermination—no machine guns, no gas chambers, no railroads—at his disposal.[3] Mao Zedong's regime in China, after 1949, or Pol Pot's in Cambodia in the late 1970s, were responsible for the mass killing of millions with 'philosophic

---

3.   To put these numbers in statistical perspective: there are now more than seven billion human beings living on Earth. If a contemporary homicidal maniac was to conduct wars of conquest that killed the same proportion of this population as Tamerlane and his Mongols killed in the 14th century, we would witness the violent deaths of some 400 million people, which is approximately six times as many as perished in the Second World War around the world. Yet Tamerlane's depredations were confined to the Eurasian heartland, so the proportion of those dwelling there that perished at the hands of his horde was even higher than these numbers suggest. For an interesting graphic study of deaths in war see https://vimeo.com/128373915

intent', but the Jews were not the target and the intent was ideological, not religious.[4] Moreover, the intent behind the killing of the Jews in Europe under Nazism was clearly linked to a racial and nationalist program directly at odds with the emancipation and integration of Jews that had characterised Germany and the Enlightenment more generally before the catastrophe of the First World War and the Great Depression catapulted the Nazis into power.

Steiner would have had us believe, however, that the Jews were slaughtered as proxies for an unendurable God of which the collective and atavistic psyche of Europeans sought to be rid. To underwrite the scale and significance of the claim he was making, he took us back to the beginnings of monotheism, mystified it and exalted it as only someone who actually believed in religious 'revelation' would be likely to do:

> To speak of the 'invention' of monotheism is to use words in the most provisional way.

---

4.   On the general question of genocide and what to do about it, see Samantha Power *A Problem from Hell: America and the Age of Genocide* (Harper Collins, Perennial, New York, 2003). On the Armenian genocide, which the Turkish government continues to deny, see Ronald Grigor Suny *A History of the Armenian Genocide* (Princeton University Press, 2015). On the coming of the Nazi genocide of the Jews see Christopher Browning *The Origins of the Final Solution: The Evolution of Nazi Jewish Policy, September 1939-March 1942* (University of Nebraska Press, Lincoln; and Yad Vashem, Jerusalem, 2004) and Leni Yahil *The Holocaust: The Fate of European Jewry* (Oxford University Press, 1991). Hitler did not simply set out to exterminate the Jews. He launched a genocidal war against the Soviet Union in 1941 with the intention of annihilating or enslaving the Slavic populations and creating abundant *lebensraum* for the German 'master race'. See Rolf-Dieter Muller *Enemy in the East: Hitler's Secret Plans to Invade the Soviet Union* (I. B. Tauris, London and New York, 2015).

Muller remarks of Operation Barbarossa, the massive German invasion of the Soviet Union from June 1941:

> Hitler conceived of it as an ethnically ideological war of annihilation. He made sure from the German side that the campaign was fought with the utmost intensity and viciousness, and that the occupation of the conquered territories was a criminal one. It was undoubtedly the most extensive war of plunder and obliteration ever seen; one beside whose powers of destruction even the terrors of a Genghis Khan were attenuated.

Muller must be unacquainted with the depredations of Tamerlane, but his basic point is surely sound. If it was disturbing of T. S. Eliot not to mention the Holocaust in 1948, wasn't it almost as disturbing of Steiner not to dwell upon the attempted obliteration of the Slavs between 1941 and 1944? He mentions the general breakdown of civilized norms in Europe between 1933 and 1945, but he does not draw any comparison at all between the killing of some fifteen to twenty million Polish, Russian and Ukrainian people and the killing of six million Jews. Presumably, he would argue that the first was war and the second genocide. But the first was, programmatically, a genocidal war.

The cast of intellect, the social forms, the linguistic conventions which accompanied the change, maybe in the oasis at Kadesh, from polytheism to the Mosaic concept of one God, are beyond recall. We cannot feel our way into the minds and skins of the men and women who, evidently under constraint and amid frequent rebellion, passed into a new mapping of the world. The immensity of the event, its occurrence in real time, are certain, and reverberate still. But how the ancient concretions of worship, the ancient, natural reflexes of multitudinous animism were replaced, we have no way of knowing. The light curves toward us from across the remotest horizon.

Simply as a historical and theological claim this was quite tendentious. That monotheism was the exclusive invention of the Jews was and is untenable. It began to emerge piecemeal across the world over quite a few centuries and was philosophically articulated by Greek thinkers hundreds of years before the Common Era. That it was actually a revelation to Moses, as recounted in the Bible, is a fable made up by writers in Jerusalem in the 7th century BCE. There is, in fact, no evidence that the Hebrews were ever in Egypt six or seven hundred years before that (as related in the tale of Joseph and his brothers); or that a man named Moses led them out of it; or that they migrated across Sinai to then invade Canaan. The whole story is riddled with historical anachronisms and confuted by the contemporary archaeological sciences.[5]

To be sure, Steiner cannot have known in 1971 that the search for the historical and archaeological residues of the Exodus would turn up a blank by the end of the 20th century. He should, however, have known enough to have placed his theological assertion in a more historical frame of reference. But, of course, by his own account, he was seeking to 'transcend' history in the name of religion. Even so, he might at least have acknowledged that there was an ill-fated attempt in Egypt, in the 15th century BCE (after the expulsion of the Hyksos and long before the fabled Hebrew Exodus), under the Pharaoh Akhnaten, to abolish polytheism and introduce a monotheistic religion. He might have acknowledged, also, that the Persian prophet Zarathustra (Zoroaster) came

---

5.   Such a claim will come as a shock and even as a scandal to many believing Jews and Christians, but it is not a polemical excess. The argument, to be sure, was not made when Steiner was writing *In Bluebeard's Castle*; it took decades of research after that point for archaeologists and historians to be driven to this remarkable conclusion. See Israel Finkelstein and Neil Asher Silberman *The Bible Unearthed: Archaeology's New Vision of Ancient Israel and the Origin of its Sacred Texts* (Free Press, New York, 2001), pp. 48-71. Curiously, the same has happened over the same decades with regard to the origins of Islam and the identity of Muhammad. See Tom Holland *In the Shadow of the Sword: The Battle for Global Empire and the End of the Ancient World* (Abacus, London, 2013), pp. 32-63 and 329-474.

up with the idea of two rival deities—Good and Evil—in the late second millennium BCE. This was monotheism of a kind, since one was urged to take the 'side' of the Good deity against the 'dark side of the force'. During the Babylonian exile of the Jews, in the early sixth century BCE, Zoroastrian ideas began to influence Jewish theology—ultimately giving us 'the Evil One' who has literally bedevilled monotheistic religion ever since.

Steiner might have acknowledged that Xenophanes, the Greek philosopher[6], rejected the gods of the pagan pantheon as anthropomorphic and argued that if there was a God it would have to be purer and more abstract than any of the traditional deities. This was not an idea derived from the five books of Moses, but from critical thinking and scepticism about traditional religious practices. Steiner did not pause to reflect on any of these antecedents, however, before remarking:

> What we must recapture to mind, as nakedly as we can, is the singularity, the brain-hammering strangeness of the monotheistic idea. Historians of religion tell us that the emergence of the concept of the Mosaic God is a unique fact in human experience, that a genuinely comparable notion sprang up at no other place or time. The abruptness of the Mosaic revelation, the finality of the creed at Sinai tore up the human psyche by its most ancient roots. The break has never really knit.

Even assuming his assertion about the uniqueness of the God of Moses to be true; and leaving aside the awkward fact that Moses appears to be a mythological figure, invented long after the supposed events in the Pentateuch; his claim that 'the Mosaic revelation ... tore up the human psyche by its most ancient roots' makes no sense. Almost no-one was exposed to it, even after it was written down in the 7th century BCE and other human beings continued to function as they always had, more or less. His claim, clearly untrue in any literal sense, was not warranted even metaphorically.

He went on, however, to emphasize the extreme abstractness and inaccessibility of the imagined God of the 'Mosaic revelation':

> The demands made of the mind are, like God's name, unspeakable. Brain and conscience are commanded to vest belief, obedience, love in an abstraction purer, more inaccessible to ordinary sense than is the highest of mathematics. The God of the Torah not only prohibits the making of images to represent Him. He does not

---

6.   Xenophanes (570-475 BCE) is widely regarded as the founder of the Ionian school or of the Greek enlightenment. Very little of his work survives, but the most famous fragments consist of poems in which he satirized the polytheism of Homer and Hesiod and ridiculed the idea of the gods on the grounds that they were so anthropomorphic. Karl Popper revered Xenophanes, with Heraclitus and Parmenides as pioneers in critical thinking and the art of thinking in terms of 'conjectures and refutations'.

allow imagining. His attributes are, as Schoenberg concisely expressed them in *Moses und Aaron*[7]:

> *Inconceivable because invisible*
> *Because immeasurable*
> *Because everlasting*
> *Because eternal*
> *Because omnipresent*
> *Because omnipotent*

No fiercer exigence has ever pressed upon the human spirit, with its compulsive, organically determined bias towards image, towards figured presence ... It hammers at human consciousness, demanding that it transcend itself, that it reach out into a light of understanding so pure that it is itself blinding ...

Really? The God of the Old Testament seems, in fact, all too human in many respects. Even in the speaking attributed to the prophets, such as Isaiah or Micah, this deity is more a kingly figure insisting on fealty, justice and compassion than an abstruse idea impossible to conceive. In the famous scene on Mount Carmel, where Elijah seeks God, he ends up not with a baffling intellectual abstraction, but with 'a still, small voice'. And in the Psalms, we see moving appeals to a God taken to be accessible to prayerful intercession.

Steiner surely overreached in insisting that all this 'tore up the human psyche by its most ancient roots'. In fact, believers have found cognitive and moral shelter under the imagined wings of this deity for three thousand years or so. Nonetheless, he pressed his case:

> In polytheism, says Nietzsche, lay the freedom of the human spirit, its creative multiplicity. The doctrine of a single Deity, whom men cannot play off against other gods and thus win open spaces for their own aims, is 'the most monstrous of all human errors'.

Steiner did not, clearly, believe it to have been an error at all. Moreover, any good atheist

---

7.   *Moses und Aaron* is the 20th century opera by the Viennese Jewish composer Arnold Schoenberg (1874-1951). As both a musician and a composer, he was largely self-taught. He began drafting *Moses und Aaron* in 1926 and wrote the music for acts one and two between 1930 and 1932. He renounced Judaism in 1921, but in July 1933, having been sacked from the Prussian Academy of Fine Arts by the Nazi Minister of Education; he formally embraced Judaism again, in defiance of Nazism. Later that year, well ahead of the Nazi conquest of France, he sailed to the United States, where he spent the rest of his life. He was never able to compose act three of *Moses und Aaron*, whether because of religious inhibitions, distraction by the horrors of the Holocaust or composer's block in the face of the challenge is not clear.

of our time can agree that in certain respects monotheism signified progress, because it discouraged idolatry, primitive sacrifices and superstitions—at least up to a point.[8] The modern criticism of it is not that it was or is too abstract or demanding, but that it did not *finish* the work of doing away with idolatry, sacrifices and superstitions. There were, after all, still animal sacrifices at the temple in Jerusalem until the 1st century CE; and the entire Christian religion pivoted on the very strange idea that the 'Son of God' was *sacrificed* so that his blood—the 'blood of the Lamb of God'—might 'atone for' and wash away, in the 'eyes' of God 'the Father' the accumulated sins of the human world. The sins in question, of course, never ceased, but the sacrifice was ritually re-enacted in ceremonies of the 'eating of the god' in the central liturgy of Christianity.

Steiner did not address any of this. He did not, in fact, consider Christianity to be quite monotheistic enough to rank with the 'Mosaic revelation'. He wrote:

> Historically, the requirements of absolute monotheism proved all but intolerable. The Old Testament is a record of mutiny, of spasmodic, but repeated reversions to the old gods, whom the hand can touch and the imagination house. Pauline Christianity found a useful solution. While retaining something of the idiom and centralized symbolic lineaments of monotheism, it allowed scope for the pluralistic, pictorial needs of the psyche. But in their Trinitarian aspects, in their proliferation of saintly and angelic persons, or in their vividly material realization of God the Father, of Christ, of Mary, the Christian churches have, with very rare exceptions, been a hybrid of monotheistic ideals and polytheistic practices. That has been their suppleness and syncretic strength. The single, unimaginable, rigorously speaking 'unthinkable', God of the Decalogue has nothing to do with the threefold, thoroughly visualized pantheon of the churches.

If, however, the Jews were in chronic rebellion, while St Paul found 'a useful solution', how can it have transpired that the intolerable pressure built up within the Christian order, rather than within Judaism itself? In reality, Rabbinical Judaism must also have achieved some 'useful solution', since it continued to flourish as a human culture despite the catastrophic Roman destruction of Jerusalem in 70 CE and obliteration of the Jewish state altogether in 135 CE. If Jews were able to live with the Biblical God, why did it seem to Steiner so impossible that

---

8.   There is, conversely, a tradition, dating back at least to the Greek historian Polybius, in the second century BCE, which holds that popular religion is harmless and even socially necessary, whereas intellectual religion (theology) is disputatious, apt to become fanatical and a presumptuous threat to civil order. This was the view of the great Enlightenment sceptic David Hume, who held all religious belief to be inherently absurd, but allowed that ceremonies and pageantries which satisfied the popular need for such things should not be suppressed. He clearly would have drawn the line, however, at blood sacrifices, whether animal or human.

Gentiles might, in their own ways, have done so? In fact, many did.

The arcane, thoroughly rarefied God which Steiner evoked in 1971 has only ever been the mystical object of contemplation of a few religious seers and sages, whether Jewish or Christian. Curiously, he did not discuss the case of the Islamic version of God, which is also very abstract and as dependent on a supposed unique 'revelation' as Judaism—from Allah via the Archangel Gabriel to Muhammad, according to the tradition insisted upon within Islam. Having erupted out of the deserts of Arabia in the 7th century CE to overrun the old empires of the Greco-Romans and Persians as they lay prostrate after a century or so of calamitous wars, Islam has endured for almost one and a half millennia.[9] It has not exhibited more than the usual symptoms of religious neurosis or torn up psyches as a consequence of subsisting on monotheism of a much more rigorous kind than that of Christianity. How can this be, if Steiner's basic premises were sound? His answer—which was not supported by any historical data at all—was that the Pauline solution left European Christians with a bad conscience, haunted by the Jewish God, which finally triggered a savage reaction.

He wrote of the Christian order without differentiating between the ancient world, the medieval world and the modern world of scepticism and secularization:

> But that God, blank as the desert air, would not rest. The memory of His ultimatum, the presence of His Absence, have goaded Western man. The nineteenth century thought it had laid the great spectre to rest. The canonic text is Nietzsche's monologue of the madman in *La Gaia Scienza* ... Only a psychologist of Nietzsche's genius and vulnerability could experience the 'murder of God' directly, could feel at his own nerve ends its liberating doom.

We shall come to the famous passage from Nietzsche shortly, but consider that Steiner did not bother to provide any historical or textual evidence whatsoever that Christian Europe was 'goaded' by the God of Moses; as distinct from being prone to millenarian visions, fears of the Devil, large scale penitential rites and cults of the crucified Jesus and his Virgin Mother.

---

9. On the rise of Islam, see Tom Holland (2013). I refer to Islam erupting out of Arabia, but Holland has a more complex and interesting story to tell, based on quite recent scholarship. Just as with the Exodus or the historical Jesus, late 20th century archaeology and historical scholarship has delved into the origins of Islam, only to find that the tales of the Prophet, the sources of the Qur'an and the coinage of the immense body of sayings attributed to Muhammad vanished in the dry air of the Arabian peninsula, leaving large questions as to how the Arab caliphate first arose and propagated its dogmatic and sectarian religious monotheism. It appears that the tradition was pieced together well after the conquest of wide territories by the Arabs and that vast amounts of the sayings (hadith) attributed to Muhammed made their way into that tradition in the eighth and ninth centuries or even later.

This was the long epoch that the Enlightenment would recoil from, in the 18th century, as the epoch of 'barbarism and religion'.[10] Moreover, having insisted that 'God' was so rarefied as to be unnameable, invisible, more abstract than the highest mathematics, Steiner again and again referred to the deity as 'Him'. It was a striking, if wholly conventional, lapse. One could hardly be more anthropomorphic.

He also referred to the Mosaic God's 'Absence'. This always tantalized me as bordering on atheism of the Nietzschean kind, though without Nietzsche's extravagant renunciation of reason and moral restraint. It calls for an exploration that Steiner did not supply. There has long been, as he knew, a tradition of 'negative theology'—defining God by what 'He' was *not*, in order to strip away all kinds of delusional or idolatrous anthropomorphisms. The Book of Job is a very early and intriguing variation on or anticipation of this theme. We find it in Jewish and Christian thinkers alike and prominently in the writings of such great medieval Jewish thinkers as Maimonides.[11] It prefigures atheism in pointing out, in effect, that the longed for

---

10.   There is no better analysis of this process, to my knowledge, than J. G. A. Pocock's magisterial six volume study of Edward Gibbon and the downfall of the Greco-Roman world in Enlightenment historiography, *Barbarism and Religion*. The six volumes were published between 1999 and 2015 by Cambridge University Press: *The Enlightenments of Edward Gibbon 1737-1764* and *Narratives of Civil Government* (1999), *The First Decline and Fall* (2003), *Barbarians, Savages and Empires* (2005), *Religion: The First Triumph* (2010) and *Barbarism: Triumph in the West* (2015). I first read Gibbon's *The Decline and Fall of the Roman Empire* in 1972, as a schoolboy; then again in 1981 while preparing a paper for a seminar in Roman Historiography at the University of Melbourne. Pocock's remarkable work provides a greater depth of understanding of why Gibbon wrote what he did and what it means than any schoolboy's or undergraduate's reading could conceivably have conferred. It is a precious and astounding work of scholarship and a major contribution to the historiography of the modern world and of the goals and processes of enlightenment.

11.   Moshe Halbertal *Maimonides: Life and Thought* (Princeton University Press, 2014) provides an illuminating discussion of these rarefied matters, notably in chapters seven and eight, on Maimonides' famous 12th century treatise *Guide of the Perplexed*. Halbertal notes:

> *Defining anthropomorphism as the most severe religious transgression reopened the struggle against idolatry on an entirely new front ... The biblical and midrashic opposition to the worship of idols was directed toward external, plastic representation of the divinity, but Maimonides redirected it toward mental representation; henceforth, it would be necessary to shatter the internal idol. But that redirection toward the inner mental image also brought the struggle into the inner reaches of the Jewish community ... A personified image of God is created not only by painting and sculpture, but also by religious language. Moreover, the personified concept of the divinity is sustained by the very wording of Scripture, which is rife with personified images*

or feared 'Father', open to prayers, prone to take condign revenge against sinners or idolaters, laying down arcane and even absurd laws to his followers in Deuteronomy and Leviticus, inciting the Hebrews to genocide when they (supposedly) crossed the Jordan under Joshua and set about conquering Canaan[12], actually *does not exist* in any of these imagined forms. It was all a theological reading of whatever *had* taken place; which is to say a superstitious illusion turned into dogma.

It is only a short step from this negative theology to the naturalism of Baruch de Spinoza in the 17th century and the Enlightenment abandonment of the Biblical God for Aristotelian Deism, Epicurean scepticism or materialist atheism. Steiner stepped through none of this, but leapt from Mount Sinai, via St Paul to the idea of the Holocaust as the 'revenge' by Western man against Judaism and a 'botched attempt to kill God'. Since the God of Moses could not, Steiner implied, *be* killed, a more mundane expedient was resorted to—the attempt to exterminate his 'Chosen People', the bearers of the 'revelation' that had torn up the human

---

of God. On the face of it, the tradition itself, together with its sacred writings, foster the cardinal sin of imputing corporeality to God. Maimonides therefore devoted most of Part I of the Guide to clarifying the issue of religious language. The internal logic of his argument leads him to one of the most extraordinary positions to be found in the history of Jewish thought. (p. 289)

Already, in 1971, Steiner, as a learned Jew, should have been able to see in Maimonides the critique of religious language and biblical imagery which were to recur in Spinoza and open the way to the post-religious thinking (or at least religiously heterodox thought) of Immanuel Kant in the 18th century and Ludwig Wittgenstein in the 20th century. This was a path of development marked not by loathing and resentment, but by illumination and emancipation.

12.   As Robert Alter, the great scholar of Hebrew literature and religion, points out in his translation of the early 'historical' books of the Bible, the 'prevailing sense of the first half of the book [of Joshua] is ruthlessness ... Nowhere in the Bible is there a more palpable discrepancy between the values and expectations of the ancient Near Eastern era in which the book was written and those of 21st century readers.' Yet, he goes on to observe:

What the last several decades of archaeological investigation have established is that there was no sweeping conquest of Canaan by invaders from the east in the late thirteenth century BCE— which would have been the time of Joshua—and that many of the towns listed as objects of Israelite conquest were either uninhabited at this time or did not come under Israelite rule till considerably later ... The fact that this narrative does not correspond to what we can reconstruct of the actual history of Canaan offers one great consolation: the blood-curdling report of the massacre of the entire population of Canaanite towns—men, women, children and in some cases livestock as well—never happened.

Robert Alter *Ancient Israel: The Former Prophets: Joshua, Judges, Samuel and Kings* (W. W. Norton & Co., New York and London, 2013), pp. 3-4.

psyche 'by its most ancient roots':

> There was an easier vengeance to hand, a simpler way of making good the centuries
> of *mauvaise foi*, of subconscious but aching resentment against the unattainable ideal
> of the one God. By killing the Jews, Western culture would eradicate those who had
> 'invented' God, who had, however imperfectly, however restively, been the declarers of
> His unbearable Absence. The holocaust is a reflex, the more complete for being long
> inhibited, of natural sensory consciousness, of instinctual polytheistic and animist
> needs. It speaks for a world both older than Sinai and newer than Nietzsche ... [13]

The rhetoric is stirring and suggestive, but the argument for it as absent as the God of Moses
in the desert air. Moreover, Steiner shifted from the assertion that it was the active demands
of this God which had bewildered and finally angered 'Western man' to the *antithetical*
claim that it was 'His unbearable Absence' which finally triggered the 'long inhibited' reflex
destructiveness of the Holocaust. Which is to be? Was it resentment of 'His' presence, or the
agony of 'His' absence that was responsible for the great lashing out at the Jews?

Steiner did not reconcile the two claims. Instead, he pressed on to assert that the moral
demands of Judaism, while they apparently converted the Jews into an upright and ethical
people, on the whole, proved intolerable to 'Western man' and led to the Holocaust:

> But the provocation was more than metaphysical. More than 'a supreme fiction' of
> reason was being thrust on mulish humanity. The Books of the Prophets and the Sermon
> on the Mount and parables of Jesus which are so closely related to the prophetic idiom,
> constitute an unparalleled act of moral demand ... There is no salvation in the middle
> places. For the true disciple of the prophets and of Jesus, the utmost ethical commitment
> is like common breath. To become man, man must make himself new, and in so doing
> stifle the elemental desires, weaknesses and claims of the ego.

If this were truly so, we might have expected to see a greater divergence between the moral
order of the Christian era and that of the Greco-Roman world, but as the humanists in the
Renaissance realized and wrote, the great figures of the classical world were every bit as
ethical and sound as any Christian, albeit based on philosophical maxims (Platonic, Stoic or
Epicurean) and civic virtue rather than on the Bible. And the common people continued to live
much as they had always done—guided by various mixtures of folk traditions, superstitions,
civil laws and opportunistic defections from social codes.

Steiner never once paused to try to substantiate his sweeping claim with historical
evidence. In fact, he extended his sweep one daring stage further, by singling out three
Jewish figures as having, over three millennia, issued the great eschatological and moral

---

13.   Steiner (1971) pp. 38-39.

demands that 'Western man' found so intolerable as finally to turn savagely on the Jews themselves:

> The third confrontation between exigent utopia and the common pulse of Western life occurs with the rise of messianic socialism. Even where it proclaims itself to be atheist, the socialism of Marx, of Trotsky, of Ernst Bloch, is directly rooted in messianic eschatology. Three times it sounded from the same historical centre. (Some political scientists put at roughly eighty per cent the proportion of Jews in the ideological development of messianic socialism and communism). Judaism produced a summons to perfection and sought to impose it on the current and currency of Western life. Deep loathings built up in the social subconscious, murderous resentments ...

But the Western civilization he here described as full of loathing and murderous resentment had taken Jesus to its bosom as the supreme mythical hero and honoured Moses as the greatest of the Old Testament servants of the Most High.[14] And the claims

---

14.   Curiously, while emphasizing the murderous anti-Semitism of the Nazis, Steiner made no mention of the anti-Semitism—or at least anti-Judaism—of Voltaire, a key Enlightenment figure, but not an individual anyone has associated with genocidal mania or vengeful violence. In his *Essay on Morals*, ancestral, in a way, to Nietzsche's *On the Genealogy of Morals*, more than a century later, Voltaire denounced the Jews (and the Gypsies) as the detritus of corrupted and superseded religions and the seed-bed of a religion—Christianity—which he reviled as 'the most infamous superstition which has ever brutalized human beings'. This strange judgement might well occasion a bemused and critical response, but it is not aligned with Steiner's claim that 'Western man' rejected God and the Jews because of the impossible standard of morality they insisted upon. Voltaire's cause was civic virtue and good manners, politeness and commerce. In the name of these things and not intellectual torpor or natural savagery, he repudiated both Christianity and the Jews. We may differ with his argument, even where we sympathize with his cause; but we cannot find in his philosophical anti-Semitism the canker Steiner claimed was at work within Western civilization and led to the 'botched attempt to kill God'—and then in the genocidal assault on his 'messengers', the Jewish people.

Voltaire's historical works constitute a kind of sustained (and highly Eurocentric) argument that other cultures (notably China, which he saw as unchanged for thousands of years; and the Islamic world, which he saw as enlightened and tolerant compared with the Christian order) subscribed to various forms of 'natural religion' uncomplicated by Judaeo-Christian superstitions and dogmas. Europe (or at least the Latin West) by contrast, had undergone the classical experience, its downfall, the triumph of barbarism and religion and then recovery, enlightenment and progress. For a discussion of all this, see J. G. A. Pocock *Barbarism and Religion: Vol 2 Narratives of Civil Government* (Cambridge University Press, 1999), pp. 97-136. In important respects, Voltaire's rather crude argument is ancestral to the outlook on the world expressed in these pages. His errors and prejudices may be imputed chiefly to the contentious context in which he was writing—and to the ignorance which beset him at that time. In the two and a half centuries since

of Marx were rejected, when they were, not because they made intolerable moral demands, but precisely because they were incoherent, economically dubious and politically dangerous. Trotsky was no moral puritan, but a perpetrator of terror, a political failure and a man of what might be called 'emancipated' sexual and material tastes. Steiner's claims simply do not stack up.

Not content, however, with his unsubstantiated and sweeping claims about 'Western man' loathing and resenting the Biblical inheritance, he proceeded to state that the upheaval of the 1930s and 1940s, with its massive bloodshed and the Holocaust in centre frame,

> enacted a suicidal impulse in Western civilization. It was an attempt to level the future—
> or, more precisely, to make history commensurate with the natural savageries, intellectual
> torpor and material instincts of unextended man. Using theological metaphors, and there
> is no need to apologize for them in an essay on culture, one may say that the holocaust
> marks a second Fall. We can interpret it as a voluntary exit from the Garden and a
> programmatic attempt to burn the Garden behind us; lest its remembrance continue to
> infect the health of barbarism with debilitating dreams or with remorse.

Yet, if such a suicidal impulse can be imputed to Western civilization, it would surely have to be found in the First World War, which did *not* entail any kind of anti-Semitic outburst. Steiner spent some time pondering the disaster of that conflict, but then failed to see how its consequences included the destabilization and embitterment in Germany and Central Europe out of which Nazism sprang from underground. Once admit this and he would have been back into socio-economic and psychological causes of the catastrophe that subsequently befell Europe as a whole and generated the dreadful assault against Europe's Jews.

Tangential to all this, because he never raised these questions, are the considerations that, if 'Western man' in some generic sense had found the Biblical dispensation so burdensome as to resent the Jews, the Holocaust ought to have been enacted, also, in the Americas, but it was not. Moreover, if the ethical demands of the specifically Jewish deity were too great to bear and productive of murderous resentments, how can it have been that the Jews themselves did not turn brutally on their rabbis and abandon an intolerable religion along with their Gentile compatriots, whose religion, by Steiner's own account, being a quasi-polytheistic hybrid, was actually *less* intolerable? In fact, very many Jews found refuge in the United States,

---

he wrote his essay, very much in the spirit of critical inquiry with which he wrote, we have learned an enormous amount; the world has opened up to commerce and ideas beyond anything he can have imagined and secular movements have betrayed the promise of the Enlightenment in ways every bit as egregious as anything of which Voltaire ws able to accuse the Christian churches, much less the Jews.

as had many Gentiles, from religious or ethnic persecution in Europe, chiefly Eastern Europe, long before the Holocaust and again after it. And many Jews *did* defect from Judaism in the modern world, but out of scepticism and enlightenment, not in murderous resentment at 'His Absence'. Indeed, the European Enlightenment was in some respects crystallised by the Jewish heretic Spinoza, whose *Tractatus Theologico-Politicus*—upsetting to Catholics, Calvinists and orthodox Jews alike—showed how dubious traditional religious interpretations of the Bible actually were.[15]

Steiner's religious diagnosis of the Holocaust is at its most vividly suggestive in his argument that:

> It is to the ambiguous afterlife of religious feeling in Western culture that we must

---

15.   The importance of Spinoza is often overlooked in reflections on religion in the modern world and the genealogy of modern scepticism and atheism. See Steven Nadler *A Book Forged in Hell: Spinoza's Scandalous Treatise and the Birth of the Secular Age* (Princeton University Press, 2011) and Susan James *Spinoza on Philosophy, Religion and Politics: The Theological-Political Treatise* (Oxford University Press, 2012). As Nadler remarked, Spinoza's book was regarded by his contemporaries as 'the most dangerous book ever published', but in fact 'it laid the groundwork for subsequent liberal, secular and democratic thinking.' For this reason, as he remarks, it was 'one of the most important books of Western thought ever written'. Charlie Huenemann, in *Spinoza's Radical Theology: The Metaphysics of the Infinite* (Acumen, Connecticut, 2014) insists that Spinoza genuinely believed in a God and was not an atheist, as he was often accused of being, simply because he confuted so much dubious theology based on the Bible. He argued that Spinoza:

> *had a conception of God and an account of how God is responsible for the existence of all things; he had a view of human morality and politics that was grounded in his theology; and he advanced this theology not merely as an atheistic metaphysics that could be slyly promoted to the masses through duplicitous usages of religious terms, but as a genuine theology. He thought his philosophy was bringing into clarity ancient insights that were distorted through prejudice, ignorance and superstition.* (p. xv).

Yet all this was clearly a major step away from Biblical 'revelation' and towards the Deism and scepticism of the Enlightenment. Einstein was one of many modern thinkers who made clear that insofar as he believed in a God, it was Spinoza's God that he had in mind and not that of the Bible or the organized religions. And Spinoza was far more forthright in making his differences with established religion clear than was his famous contemporary, the polymath Gottfried Wilhelm Leibniz. See Matthew Stewart *The Courtier and the Heretic: Leibniz, Spinoza and the Fate of God in the Modern World* (W. W. Norton & Co., New York and London, 2006). Spinoza, needless to say, was the heretic of his title. See also Steven Nadler *The Best of all Possible Worlds: A Story of Philosophers, God and Evil* (Farrar, Straus and Giroux, New York, 2008). For a fine introduction to the importance of Spinoza in overcoming dualism and creating a foundation for a modern ethics, see Antonio Damasio *Looking for Spinoza: Joy, Sorrow and the Feeling Brain* (Harcourt, 2003).

look for the malignant energies released by the decay of natural religious forms ... *L'univers concentrationnaire* has no true counterpart in the secular mode. Its analogue is Hell. The camp embodies, often down to minutiae, the images and chronicles of Hell in European art and thought from the twelfth to the eighteenth centuries ... It is in the fantasies of the infernal, as they literally haunt Western sensibility, that we find the technology of pain without meaning, of bestiality without end, of gratuitous terror. For six hundred years, the imagination dwelt on the flaying, the racking, the mockery of the damned in a place of whips and hell-hounds, of ovens and stinking air. The literature of the camps is extensive. But nothing in it equals the fullness of Dante's observations ... The concentration and death camps of the twentieth century, wherever they exist, are Hell made immanent. They are the transference of Hell from below the earth to its surface. They are the deliberate enactment of long, precise imagining ...

He was by no means the first to see this analogy and to recoil from it in horror. But he failed to allow for the fact that *almost everyone* recoiled from the death camps in horror and that they were far from being a universal institution in Europe. Besides, if the death camps came out of the Christian imagining of Hell, why impute the Holocaust as such to rejection of the Jewish God? Why not, rather, to the specific monotheism of Christianity? Nor does he allow that the kinds of atrocities perpetrated in the death camps had ample precedent in the non-religious world, both in Europe and elsewhere, long before the Holocaust. One has only to read, for example, Bartolomeo de las Casas on Spanish atrocities in the Americas in the early 16th century to appreciate that Nazi atrocities were not new and the Jews far from being the only victims of appalling behaviour by others. Steiner did not attempt to find such antecedents, despite his evocation of what he had labelled the 'natural savageries' and 'intellectual torpor' of 'unextended man'.

I think we need to put aside Steiner's claims about the 'botched attempt to kill God' and rethink the whole idea of the 'death of God' on different lines. He referred us to the 'canonical' passage in which Nietzsche had dramatically evoked the idea that God had died and that we had killed Him. The passage in question, aphorism 125 from Book Three of *The Gay Science,* is central enough to the matter of a re-definition of (Western) culture in our time that it is well worth citing in full, as Steiner said he would, though in fact he cited it only in fragmentary part. Here is the complete aphorism:

> *The madman*—Have you not heard of that madman who lit a lantern in the bright morning hours, ran to the marketplace and cried incessantly: 'I seek God! I seek God!' As many of those who did not believe in God were standing around just then, he provoked much laughter. 'Has he got lost?' asked one. 'Did he lose his way like a

child?' asked another. 'Or is he hiding? Is he afraid of us? Has he gone on a voyage? Emigrated?' Thus they yelled and laughed.

The madman jumped into their midst and pierced them with his eyes. 'Whither is God?' he cried. 'I will tell you. We have killed him—you and I. All of us are his murderers. But how did we do this? How could we drink up the sea? Who gave us the sponge to wipe away the entire horizon? What were we doing, when we unchained this Earth from its Sun? Whither is it moving now? Whither are we moving? Away from all suns? Are we not plunging continually: backward, sideward, forward, in all directions? Is there still any up or down? Are we not straying as through an infinite nothing? Do we not feel the breath of empty space? Has it not become colder? Is not night continually closing in on us? Do we not need to light lanterns in the morning? Do we hear nothing as yet of the noise of the gravediggers who are burying God? Do we smell nothing as yet of the divine decomposition? Gods, too, decompose. God is dead. God remains dead. And we have killed him.

How shall we comfort ourselves, the murderers of all murderers? What was holiest and mightiest of all that the world has yet owned has bled to death under our knives: who will wipe this blood off us? What water is there for us to clean ourselves? What festivals of atonement, what sacred games shall we have to invent? Is not the greatness of this deed too great for us? Must we ourselves not become gods simply to appear worthy of it? There has never been a greater deed; and whoever is born after us—for the sake of this deed, he will belong to a higher history than all history hitherto.'

Here the madman fell silent and looked again at his listeners and they, too, were silent and stared at him in astonishment. At last he threw his lantern on the ground and it broke into pieces and went out. 'I have come too early,' he said then. 'My time is not yet. This tremendous event is still on its way, still wandering. It has not yet reached the ears of men. Lightning and thunder require time; the light of the stars requires time; deeds, though done, still require time to be seen and heard. This deed is still more distant from them than the most distant stars—and yet they have done it themselves.'

It has been related further that, on the same day, the madman forced his way into several churches and there struck up his *requiem aeternam deo*. Led out and called to account, he is said always to have replied nothing but: 'What, after all, are these churches now, if not the tombs and sepulchres of God?' [16]

Even the most superficial reading of this famous passage throws into relief its stark differences from Steiner's argument about God. For one thing, the madman declares that the deed has been done and *not* 'botched'. For another, he declares that it has been done by those who no longer believe in God. Far from feeling self-loathing or murderous

---

16.   Friedrich Nietzsche *The Gay Science: With a Prelude in Rhymes and an Appendix of Songs* Translated and with commentary by Walter Kaufmann (Vintage, Random House, New York, 1974) pp. 181-82.

resentments, they are oblivious to the significance of their deed and mock the madman's seriousness regarding it. Moreover, the madman himself feels reverence for the deceased deity as 'the holiest and mightiest of all that the world has yet owned', yet extols the murder of God as the beginning of 'a higher history than all history hitherto'. I submit that there is simply no way to reconcile all this with Steiner's claims.

Instead, we need to take a fresh look at how it might have been intended by Nietzsche and, more importantly, how we—'in the marketplace', like those whom the madman addressed, but also living in the shadow of the Holocaust, as Steiner pointed out—might come to terms with the religious tradition out of which 'God' arose and the very idea of 'the death of God' at our own hands. This manifesto embraces the idea of the death of God in very much the elegiac and dramatic sense that Nietzsche has his madman proclaim it. That is to say, it accepts there never was any God to kill, except in terms of a great *conceptual idol* which had arisen in various forms out of the religions of the ancient world and been toppled by modern scepticism and science. During the centuries in which 'God lived', wars and persecutions were conducted in his name; dogmas took the place of critical inquiry; prayers the place of medicine; and exorcisms or burnings the place of psychiatric care. But there were also sublime works of art, architecture, music and imagination. What now, asks the madman, will give us inspiration and coherence?

Nietzsche's response to this question was threefold: that, as his madman declared, we have somehow cut ourselves loose from our cultural moorings and are adrift; that this would almost certainly lead to outbreaks of confused nihilism; but that the immense sense of liberation and depth of perspective it afforded should be celebrated as part of 'a higher history than all history hitherto'. These, at least, are the central points I have long taken from my reading of Nietzsche almost forty years ago. He returns at various points in his writings to the question as to why the modern world had rejected the old God. On the one hand, there was growing disbelief that he existed or was of any explanatory or practical use. On the other hand, there was the intriguing idea that the ascetic ideals which had given rise to the gloomy, otherworldly visions of Christianity had finally culminated in a non-rational, psychological drive to *sacrifice* God, precisely because belief in his justice, love and providence had been so consoling. As a young man, I was strongly attracted to both lines of argument.[17]

17.   I was fascinated to hear the novice master of a religious order declare to a congregation of Catholics from the pulpit, in Sydney, in 1978, that when he had first taken up that role, in 1966, he had discovered that *none of the novices in his cohort believed in God.* They believed passionately in Jesus, in love, compassion, service and the dignity of rituals, he declared, but they believed

Consider how Nietzsche articulated each of these ideas in *Beyond Good and Evil*, in 1886. He exclaimed, regarding the rise of atheism in the 19th century:

> *Why atheism today?*—'The father' in God is thoroughly refuted; likewise 'the judge', the 'rewarder'. Likewise his 'free will': he does not hear—and if he heard, he would still not know how to help. The worst thing is, he seems incapable of making himself clearly understood: is he himself vague about what he means? These are what, in the course of many conversations, asking and listening, I found to be the causes of the decline of European theism; it seems to me that the religious instinct is indeed in vigorous growth—but that it rejects the theistic answer with profound mistrust.[18]

The nihilism which Nietzsche predicted and in some ways encouraged, seems to have persuaded quite a few people in the mid-20th century that atheism is intrinsically nihilistic and brutal. The totalitarians, Nazi and Communist alike, were atheistic after all and their appalling records made the idea of a religion of compassion, sanctuary and aesthetic refinement seem very civilized by comparison. Numerous others, however, believed that Communism represented the march of progress; in part because it was atheistic and intent on building a this-worldly utopia.

The psychological line of attack offered by Nietzsche was even more intriguing. He was an acute psychologist of deceit, hypocrisy and the arts of manoeuvre exhibited by human beings in their 'will to power'; perhaps nowhere more than in his attempts to fathom why any creature would turn ascetically on itself and renounce its natural drives in the name of a higher order of life. He wrote:

> There is a great ladder of religious cruelty with many rungs; but three of them are the most important. At one time, one sacrificed human beings to one's god, perhaps precisely those human beings one loved best—the sacrifice of the first-born, present in all prehistoric religions belongs here ... Then, in the moral epoch of mankind, one sacrificed to one's god the strongest instincts one possessed, one's 'nature';

that God was dead. It took him some time, he stated, to persuade them that if they truly wished to become Catholic priests, this would not do at all. Having decided to give up Catholicism on these very grounds, I was astonished to hear this. He went on to state that the Second Vatican Council had had a devastating effect on his order. Within a decade, he declared with unflinching candour, we lost three in five of our ordained priests and four in five of our novices. In a haunting way, it seemed, the Council had demythologized Catholicism and very many Catholics, even ordained priests, experienced this as the death of God—even calling it that. His order was, of course, fully representative in all these respects, of what happened to other religious orders in that same decade.

18.   Friedrich Nietzsche *Beyond Good and Evil: Prelude to a Philosophy of the Future* (Penguin, translated and with an introduction and commentary by R. J. Hollingdale, 1981), #53, p. 62.

the joy of this festival glitters in the cruel glance of the ascetic, the inspired 'anti-naturist'. Finally: what was left to be sacrificed? Did one not finally have to sacrifice everything comforting, holy, healing, all hope, all faith in a concealed harmony, in a future bliss and justice? Did one not have to sacrifice God himself and out of cruelty against oneself worship stone, stupidity, gravity, fate, nothingness? To sacrifice God for nothingness—this paradoxical mystery [was] the ultimate act of religious cruelty ... [19]

This is an intriguing speculative genealogy for modern atheism. Yet one could write a counter-narrative to it, in which it was less 'cruelty' that was the driving force than a fierce quest for transcendence grounded in reality. The scientifically literate person does not worship stone, stupidity, gravity, fate, nothingness, but seeks with varying degrees of Epicurean scepticism and wonder to drink in the vastness of the cosmos that the sciences have opened up, while living a fully human life.

At his better moments, Nietzsche hinted that this might be so and that the protracted 'comedy' of human manners and beliefs might be seen with 'the mocking and unconcerned eye of an Epicurean god'. He remarks, in close proximity to both of the aphorisms just quoted:

> With the strength of his spiritual sight and insight the distance and as it were the space around man continually expands: his world grows deeper, ever new stars, ever new images and enigmas come into view. Perhaps everything on which the spirit's eye has exercised its profundity and acuteness has been really but an opportunity for its exercise, a game, something for children and the childish. Perhaps the most solemn concepts which have occasioned the most strife and suffering, the concepts 'God' and 'sin', will one day seem to us of no more importance than a child's toy and a child's troubles seem to an old man—and perhaps 'old man' will then have need of another toy and other troubles—still enough of a child, an eternal child.

One sees here how Nietzsche's shifting moods and acute insights kept revolving the enigma of monotheism and the nature of human cultural history in his mind's eye. But if we connect these various perspectives of his, written the better part of a century before Steiner wrote *In Bluebeard's Castle*, to Steiner's insistence on the central dramatic role of the Jewish deity in the whole story, we can see how narrow and *cramped* Steiner's stance was compared with that of his predecessor.

Where they overlap is with regard to the 'gaiety' with which Nietzsche at times greeted the turn that human history appeared to be taking with the death of God—by which he

---

19.   Ibid. #55, p. 63.

plainly meant all versions of the phenomenon.[20] This has always seemed to me to have been best encapsulated at the end of Nietzsche's relatively early book *Daybreak*:

> *We aeronauts of the spirit!*—All those brave birds which fly out into the distance, into the farthest distance—it is certain! Somewhere or other they will be unable to go on and will perch on a mast or a bare cliff face—and they will even be thankful for this miserable accommodation! But who could venture to infer from that that there was not an immense open space before them, that they had flown as far as one could fly? All our great teachers and predecessors have at last come to a stop ... But what does that matter to you and me? Other birds will fly farther! This insight and faith of ours vies with them in flying up and away; it rises above our heads and above our impotence into the heights and from there surveys the distance and sees before it the flocks of birds which, far stronger than we, still strive whither we have striven and where everything is sea, sea, sea! And whither then would we go? Would we cross the sea? Whither does this mighty longing draw us, this longing that is worth more to us than any pleasure? Why just in this direction, thither where all the suns of humanity have hitherto gone down? Will it perhaps be said of us one day that we, too, steering westward, hoped to reach an India—but that it was our fate to be wrecked against infinity? Or, my brothers? Or? [21]

Consider the enormous contrast here between Steiner's image of mankind as Judith standing before the last door on the night in Bluebeard's castle and Nietzsche's exhilaration at the idea that we are, as a species, or at least as thinking human beings, in the position of Columbus

---

20. We need to remind ourselves that the death of gods was an ancient and universal trope in human cultures long before Nietzsche declared the death of the Biblical God in the late 19th century. In chapter XXIV of *The Golden Bough*, written long before Steiner sat down to write *In Bluebeard's Castle*, James Frazer drew attention to the mortality of the gods generally across cultures and over time:

    > *Man has created gods in his own likeness and being himself mortal he has naturally supposed his creatures to be in the same sad predicament ... In answer to the inquiries of Colonel Dodge, a North American Indian stated that the world was made by the Great Spirit. Being asked which Great Spirit he meant, the good one or the bad one, 'Oh, neither of them,' he replied, 'the Great Spirit that made the world is dead long ago. He could not possibly have lived as long as this.'* J. G. Frazer *The Golden Bough* (abridged edition, Papermac, 1987) p. 264.

    In his 'exhortation to the Greeks' in the late 2nd century CE, Clement of Alexandria wrote of the death of Zeus and how his grave was to be found in Crete. The idea of Jesus of Nazareth as a divine being who died and came back to life for the sake of humanity had very ancient roots in Middle Eastern religions long antedating Judaism and Christianity.

21. Friedrich Nietzsche *Daybreak: Thoughts on the Prejudices of Morality*, translated by R. J. Hollingdale with an introduction by Michael Tanner (Cambridge University Press, 1983) #575, pp. 228-29.

crossing the Atlantic in 1492. Steiner's is by far the darker vision. The disasters of the 20th century are the reason why. Yet, I want to argue, in truth it is Nietzsche's vision that is a better simile for where we now stand than was Steiner's.

Even Nietzsche's simile is, however, old and dated as a response to what has happened in the near century and a half since he wrote. The astounding developments in the natural sciences from the late 19th century to the beginning of the 21st century have thrown open our horizons in breathtaking ways that make the crossing of the Atlantic by Columbus and the European conquest of the Americas pale by comparison. Moreover, the rate of exploration and discovery has been increasing exponentially and fresh findings across the full spectrum of the sciences, including the reconstruction of the human past and the geological and climatic past of the Earth, are continually being made. Prosperity and the sum of human well-being and freedom have never been so great or globally distributed as they are now, for all the poverty, turmoil and environmental stress that are in evidence. Awareness of the challenges we face and of the extent of our follies has never been greater or better informed. Access to the treasure houses of what previous generations have created and to the knowledge that is now being generated has never in the past been remotely as easy, deep or widely available as it has become in our lifetimes.

Steiner concluded his little book on the rather gloomy note that the classical past of humanistic learning was vanishing and that the human future looked perilously uncertain. Despite his avowal of 'Nietzschean gaiety in the face of the inhuman', he espoused the notion— citing Ezra Pound—that our species was 'a blown husk that is finished'. 'At most one can try to get certain perplexities into focus,' he wrote. 'Hope may lie in that small exercise.' This seemed to me, as a young man, bracingly disturbing and a call to seriousness. I set about attempting to get the perplexities in question into focus. As a man of mature years, I see the matter differently. I believe that Steiner, contradicting himself, was more the Freudian stoic than the Nietzschean free spirit. I have, for my own part, found a sense of perspective that does, I think, get the central perplexities more or less sorted out. It is Nietzschean in that it posits the death of God and the exhilaration of the open horizon. But beyond that point, it leaves Nietzsche behind— drawn by the vastness of human learning, the unfinished projects of human becoming and the extraordinary challenges we have created for ourselves by setting out in this century towards the horizon of the possible.

In the final pages of his book, Steiner framed his 'Judith' argument in terms of the moral, phenomenological and epistemological challenges posed by the rigorous nature of the natural sciences. As with so much of his book, when young and for many years afterwards, I was dazzled by Steiner's show of erudition here and the high seriousness of his rhetoric. But with the passage of time, I have come to see flaws where I used fail to detect them. Having written, early in his book, of the Hebrew God as ineffable and as goading European man to a botched deicide, we find Steiner, at the far end of his reflection, declaring:

> We need no poet more urgently than Lucretius.[22]

This was a curious rhetorical move. Lucretius, famously, was an atomist and an atheist, who argued that once we understood that everything was composed of 'atoms and the void', we would be liberated from the fears and superstitions inculcated in us by religion and would actually understand the world in terms of natural philosophy. Given both what he wrote early in his book about religion and what he wrote in the paragraphs immediately following this praise of Lucretius, it is a little difficult to determine precisely what Steiner thought would be gained from reading Lucretius. He didn't pause, however, to weave his thoughts together.

The final pages of his book were, in fact, devoted to a sombre meditation on the possibility that the natural sciences were leading us to a spectacular but grim ending of the human drama—or opera. To give him his due, he wrote, regarding the prospects for scientific culture:

> This is the last question I want to touch on; and by far the most difficult. I can state it and feel its extreme pressure. But I have not been able to think it through in any clear or consequent manner.

What he wrote in the following few pages was as bracing and incisive as anything in his book, but he did need to think things through further. We can now do so, because we have almost an extra half century of data and experience on which to base our judgement. We have seen remarkable further advances in the sciences and have lived through a further forty years and more of ecological debate. We can, therefore, in principle, arrive, I think, at a clearer and more consequent set of conclusions than Steiner did.

---

22.   George Steiner *In Bluebeard's Castle* (Faber & Faber, London, 1971), p. 102. Having invoked Lucretius, it would have been helpful of Steiner to have dwelt at least a little on the Roman poet's great treatise in verse, *On the Nature of Things*. Written in six books, it was an Epicurean's perfectly serious attempt to free people from religious beliefs and superstitious fears, by explaining the workings of the world in terms of atomism and natural forces. The six books addressed the following topics: Matter and Void, The Dance of Atoms, Mortality and the Soul, The Senses, Cosmos and Civilization, Weather and the Earth. It was the contention of Stephen Greenblatt that the recovery of Lucretius and the recommitment to atomism underpinned the Renaissance and the Enlightenment; that, in effect, materialism is the enlightened alternative to religion, just as Lucretius argued long ago. Stephen Greenblatt *The Swerve: How the Renaissance Began* (Bodley Head, London, 2011).

He made three important observations in four pages:

i.   that the scientific and industrial culture of modernity had been underpinned not only by 'the immense hunger for material comfort and diversity', but by 'the conviction, centrally woven into the Western temper, at least since Athens, that mental inquiry must move forward';

ii.   that 'for the first time ... this all-governing axiom of continued advance is being questioned', both on ecological and philosophic grounds; but

iii. that 'we cannot turn back. We cannot choose the dreams of unknowing.'

Is it any wonder that a little book of just over one hundred pages concluding with these kinds of thoughts would have made a lasting impression on a young man's mind? Like much of the content of *In Bluebeard's Castle*, they were very much what young students like me *should* have been reading in the mid-1970s. They are, in one form or another, what both students and their elders should *still* be reading. But my own opinions have developed over time and, as the present book will indicate, my thinking diverges in certain respects from Steiner's, now that I am no longer so young—not even as young as *he* was when he wrote *In Bluebeard's Castle*.

To begin with, he wrote too sweepingly about 'the Western temper, at least since Athens'. Inquiry of the scientific kind can, in certain respects, be traced back to 'Athens', but it was more a diffuse product of Grecian culture, which had Ionian beginnings and flourished most clearly in the Hellenistic epoch rather than during that of the Athenian empire. This is important, because the 'conviction' of which Steiner wrote did *not* become woven into even the Grecian temper, much less the Western one. It was a tentative cultural impulse, given impetus in the 3rd century BCE by the cosmopolitan empire carved out by Alexander. It was brought to a halt by the Roman conquest of the Mediterranean basin in the second century BCE and did not revive in any systematic form until the 16th and 17th centuries CE.[23] In other words, we

---

23.   Lucio Russo *The Forgotten Revolution: How Science was Born in 300 BC and Why it Had to be Reborn* (Springer, Berlin, Heidelberg and New York, 2004) provides a deeply informative account of Hellenistic science and its lapse after the 2nd century BCE. His observations will be touched upon at a number of points within the present book. In his polemic against Christianity, *The Antichrist*, Nietzsche lamented what he saw as the Christian abandonment of the scientific methods and cultural sophistication of the Greco-Roman world. He too easily conflated scientific Greeks with the general run of Greeks and Greeks in general with Romans. This was, in important respects, a view of things that had been developed during the Renaissance and the 18th century Enlightenment, but it turns out that the problem ran far deeper. The 'Imperium Romanum' that Nietzsche extolled as the pinnacle of classical accomplishment was a good part of that problem.

are talking about a cultural phenomenon that cannot be defined in geographical or racial terms, but only in *cognitive* terms—as the achievement of a few. Our present culture, whether considered in some narrowly 'Western temper' sense or globally, is far from fully scientific and could conceivably lapse or disintegrate, as the classical one did long ago.

The 'axiom' of advance might have been called in question in the 1960s, but the advances since then, not least in terms of the 'immense hunger for material comfort and diversity' have come at a colossal pace.[24] Steiner, however, questioned whether 'certain major lines of inquiry ought to be pursued at all, whether society and the human intellect at their present level of evolution, can survive the next truths.'[25] He expressed wariness of a kind that had first surfaced with Mary Shelley's *Frankenstein*, in the very earliest years of the industrial revolution in Britain; but had become profoundly troubling after the invention of the atomic bomb in 1945:

> It may be that the truths which lie ahead wait in ambush for man, that the kinship between speculative thought and survival on which our culture has been based, will break off. The stress falls on 'our' entire culture because, as anthropologists remind us, numerous primitive societies have chosen stasis or mythological circularity over forward motion, and have endured around truths immemorially posited.[26]

---

24. Nowhere has this been more evident than in the rise of China over the decades since Steiner wrote his book. After a century and a half of inner decay and final collapse into anarchy, foreign invasion by the Japanese fascists and totalitarian poverty and oppression under Mao Zedong, China opened up to the world at the end of the 1970s, embarked systematically upon a mercantilist economic policy and began to develop at an astounding pace. It was my job, in the early to mid-1990s, to follow this development for Australia's Defence Intelligence Organization. In 1999, as an academic, I created and taught a course on modern Chinese politics. In the 2000s I wrote extensively on the continuing growth of the Chinese economy and the increasingly rapid modernization and expansion of its military power and geopolitical ambitions. Large questions presented themselves at every point.

    The ecological depletion and pollution occasioned by this breakneck industrial and commercial development, accompanied as it has been by urbanization on a scale and at a pace unprecedented in human history, have been grave. Yet there can be no denying the gains—very much the immense hunger for material comfort and diversity to which Steiner referred. In 2005, in my book, *Thunder from the Silent Zone: Rethinking China*, I argued that there was a need to think in terms of various possible scenarios about China's future and not fall into the trap of assuming an uncomplicated linear ascent. So it is, also, with the human future in general, as of 2015. On the ecological history of China, see Mark Elvin *The Retreat of the Elephants: An Environmental History of China* (Yale University Press, 2004). It is a grim history of relentless deforestation, the extinction of species, the exhaustion of natural resources and the destructive wars of humankind.

25. Steiner (1971) p. 104.

26. Ibid.

But this was a false dichotomy. Technologies had always spilled across cultures and 'truths immemorially posited' had always remained embedded within 'our' culture. The very idea of scientific and industrial advance has abounded in myths and heroic assumptions; and countless pre-scientific cultures did not survive precisely because they had become trapped in 'mythological circularity'. We need a broader vision than Steiner's to do justice to the facts.

Nowhere, I think, did Steiner press against the boundaries of philosophic and sociological speculation more sensitively than in his reflection on the possibility 'that abstract truth and the morally neutral truths of the sciences in particular, might come to paralyse or destroy Western man.' He discerned this thought arising or being 'foreshadowed' in Husserl's unfinished masterwork of the 1930s, *The Crisis of the European Sciences and Transcendental Phenomenology*; but pointed to the 'negative dialectic' of Theodor Adorno and Max Horkheimer at the Frankfurt School as having made this disturbing idea its 'dominant motif'. He wrote:

> This is one of the most challenging, though often hermetic, currents in modern feeling
> and in the modern diagnosis of the crisis of culture ... Reason itself has become repressive.
> The worship of 'truth' and of autonomous 'facts' is a cruel fetishism ... The disease of
> enlightened man is his acceptance, itself wholly superstitious, of the superiority of
> facts to ideas ... Instead of serving human ends and spontaneities, the 'positive truths'
> of science and of scientific laws have become a prison house darker than Piranesi's, *a
> carcere* to imprison the future ... As Horkheimer and Adorno emphasize in the *Dialektik
> der Aufklarung*,[27] the old obscurantisms of religious dogma and social caste have been
> replaced by the even more tyrannical obscurantism of 'rational, scientific truth'.

He did not find the argument persuasive, but neither did he delve very deeply into it, whether philosophically or sociologically.[28] Instead, he fell back on a rather sweeping claim about the

27.   Theodor Adorno and Max Horkheimer *The Dialectic of Enlightenment*, was first published in 1944, in New York, as the Second World War climaxed in the grinding down of the Axis powers by overwhelming Allied force. If any book in my library has been more heavily annotated over many years and numerous readings than *In Bluebeard's Castle*, this is probably it. Yet it is the less interesting and thought-provoking of the two books.

28.   His main point of reference was a long essay of 1969 by Tito Perlini, which he cites in the original Italian. Perlini declared eloquently:

> *Elevato ad idolo di se stesso, il fatto e un tiranno assoluto di fronte a cui il pensiero non puo
> non prosternasi in muta adorazione [Raised to the status of an autonomous idol, the fact is
> an absolute tyrant before whom thought can do nothing but bow down in silent worship];* and
>
> *In nome di un'esperienza ridotta al simulacro di se stessa, viene condannar come vuota
> fantasticheria la stessa capacita soggettiva di progettazione dell'uomo [In the name of
> experience, itself diminished to a mere figment, man's very capacity for personal, subjective
> innovation is condemned as being no more than an empty fantasy]*

In many ways, my whole book is a response to these poignant and challenging lines.

sciences as the privileged, if ominous project of 'Western man'.

Adorno and Horkheimer, Steiner charged, never spelled out how human beings should restructure their relationship with scientific or technological realities in order to recapture their imaginative freedom and critical rationality. It would have been interesting to see him apply this thought to his own lifelong preoccupation with language, poetics and translation. But he moved at once to what he declared was a more 'elemental' criticism of the critique of the natural sciences:

> The pursuit of the facts, of which the sciences merely provide the most visible, organized instance, is no contingent error embarked on by Western man at some moment of elitist or bourgeois rapacity. That pursuit is, I believe, imprinted on the fabric, on the electro-chemistry and impulse net of our cortex. Given an adequate climatic and nutritive milieu, it was bound to evolve and to augment by a constant feedback of new energy.

Note that this is a *physiological* claim, not a cognitive one. Rather oddly for someone who placed such importance on the literature of the past three millennia, Steiner did not attempt to argue that, while all human beings have certain linguistic and cognitive capacities, the development of rigorous thinking required a whole series of cultural and technological breakthroughs—and still requires them, wherever human beings seek to master truths of any kind.

He compounded this diagnostic error by imputing to Western civilization unique climatic and nutritive advantages that explained the emergence of the sciences:

> The partial absence of this questing compulsion from less-developed, dormant races and civilizations, does not represent a free choice or feat of innocence. It represents, as Montesquieu knew, the force of adverse ecological and genetic circumstance.

There has been a long debate about what precise contingencies were responsible for the scientific and industrial revolutions occurring in Western Europe rather than centuries earlier in Song China; but ecological and genetic circumstances do not appear to have been prominent among them. One major contributor may well have been the Mongol invasions, which devastated Central Asia and the Middle East and subjected China to barbarian rule at the very time when ideas were beginning to stir again in the Latin West. Economic geography may also have played a part, with the Atlantic seaboard well placed to provide a springboard for the conquest of the Americas. But there was nothing ecologically or genetically deficient about the Chinese, or for that matter the Arabs, Turks and Persians.

Steiner did not address these issues. Indeed, he did not even make the point that, as his own source, Montesquieu, argued in detail in the 18th century, institutions and the spirit of the laws of a state make a decisive difference to its liberties and creativity. We have seen this brilliantly demonstrated over the past thirty years with the shift in China from Maoism to a mercantilist and expansive economy integrated into global markets. And—though Steiner again neglected to make any mention of this—the scientific and creative genius that had blossomed in the Grecian world faded under the Roman Empire and went backwards for centuries in the medieval period. There is, in short, a lot wrong with Steiner's argument.

He concentrated his fire, however, on the ideas advanced by the counter-culture of the 1960s; derived in part from the writings of the Frankfort School and in part from various strands of older, Romantic rebellions against rationalism and the disenchantment of the world. Responding to all those who were inclined to reject science in the name of some utopian vision or other (because of the atom bomb and other monstrosities), Steiner wrote:

> The flower-child in the Western city, the neo-primitive chanting his five words of Tibetan on the highway, are performing an infantile charade—founded on the surplus wealth of that same city or highway. We cannot turn back. We cannot choose the dreams of unknowing.

But 'we' have, at intervals through historic time, 'turned back' and the 'dreams of unknowing' are the chronic condition of humanity, the overwhelming majority of whom remain scientifically, historically and archaeologically ignorant. He was far too glib, with his use of the collective first person pronoun, for a man whose life has been devoted more than anything else to the subtleties of language, the linguistic roots of individuation and dissent; the importance of the future tense and the optative mood.[29] 'We' hardly get to choose

---

29.   Steiner's most ambitious book, *After Babel: Aspects of Language and Translation*, first published in 1975, probed away at the relationship between language, thought and imagination. He has sustained an interest in this idea throughout his career, revisiting it from different angles in *Real Presences* (University of Chicago Press, 1989) and *The Poetry of Thought: From Hellenism to Celan* (New Directions, New York, 2011). He had already made the key point well before he wrote *After Babel*, however. In *Extraterritorial: Papers on Literature and the Language Revolution*, a collection of essays written between 1968 and 1972 (Penguin, 1975), he declared:

> *Man's capacity to articulate a future tense—in itself a metaphysical and logical scandal—his ability and need to 'dream forward', to hope, make him unique.* (p. 69)

In *After Babel*, his master work, written in exile from academia, he took this further. I first read this book in the late 1970s, a few years after reading *In Bluebeard's Castle* and immersing myself passionately in the moral and metaphysical acid bath of Nietzsche's writings. It fascinated me and has remained a point of reference ever since. At a crucial point in his chapter 'Word Against Object', Steiner dwells upon the very idea of the future tense in human languages and how uncanny it is (from the New Edition, Oxford University Press, 1992):

> *As in the matter of the prodigality of languages, the proper start is wonder, a tensed delight at the bare fact that there are future forms of verbs, that human beings have developed rules*

against the currents that are flowing, he might have admitted. The locus of choice is hard to pinpoint and almost impossible to govern.

Instead, he brought us all before the last door on the night, in Bluebeard's bleak castle:

> We shall, I expect, open the last door in the castle, even if it leads, perhaps because it leads, on to realities which are beyond the reach of human comprehension and control. We shall do so with that desolate clairvoyance, so marvellously rendered in Bartok's music, because opening doors is the tragic merit of our identity.

Yet how can this 'we' be sustained, given his own assertions about non-Western cultures, about the general lack of perspective characteristic of what he dubbed our 'post-culture'; and about the splintering of the sciences themselves into a mass of specializations that makes the confusion of tongues after the destruction of the Tower of Babel seem like a mere forerunner of things to come? Whose 'identity', exactly, is he including here in his 'we', who will 'open the last door in the castle'? He would, surely, have done better to have insisted that the overwhelming majority of our fellow human beings are all but oblivious to the realities he was describing and that far from there being a single door to open, we face a future in which any number of possibilities, including potentially catastrophic ones, might enter our 'castle' through any one of numerous doors or other apertures.

When the sciences have opened up so much to our vision and understanding, it seems unwarranted to use Bluebeard's castle and the last door on the night as a figurative analogy for where we stand. Far from becoming a tyranny or a new idolatry, the grasp of 'that which is the

---

> *of grammar which allow coherent utterances about tomorrow, about the last midnight of the century, about the position and luminosity of the star Vega half a billion years hence. Such supple immensity of linguistic projection and the discriminations it allows between nuances of anticipation, doubt, provisionality, probabilistic induction, fear, conditionality, hope, may well be the major achievement of the neocortex, which is that part of the brain that distinguishes man from more primitive mammals.* (p. 145).

The book as a whole is tantalizingly erudite and recondite. It is a seduction of the philosophic and linguistic imagination. And it pivots on the idea that language has given our species a capacity for counter-factual thinking which is not only unique to our species, but almost unfathomable in its implications. The programmatic statement is surely the following:

> *Future tenses are an example, though one of the most important, of the more general framework of non- and counter-factuality. They are a part of the capacity of language for the fictional and illustrate the absolutely central power of the human word to go beyond and against 'that which is the case'.*

The last phrase, a citation from Wittgenstein's *Tractatus,* situated Steiner against the positivism of the sciences.

case' has never been more within our reach and this is overwhelmingly to the good. We have, since our early ancestors mastered the uses of fire and conceived the first kinds of symbolic art, risen to extraordinary heights of technical and poetic creativity. There is an enormous amount to celebrate and feel inspired by. There are also, as there always have been, dangers and delusions that hem us in and must be faced. This is an outlook consistent with Nietzsche's 'gaiety in the face of the inhuman, the tensed, ironic perception that we are, that we always have been, precarious guests in an indifferent, frequently murderous, but always fascinating world'. The difference is that Nietzsche never even remotely anticipated the dazzling achievements of the sciences in the 20th and early 21st centuries. We are on the crest of a wave and now is not the time to deduce that we are 'a blown husk that is finished'.

Steiner had begun his book with a reflection on the idea of a 'golden age' in the past which induced nostalgia and seemed to make the present (1970s) world appear like a 'fallen' world. There have been such myths in many cultures, he observed, but in our case the point at which the perceived golden age came to an end was clear: the Great War. He allowed that scrupulous historical reflection would show the nostalgia to be selective and partial, even illusory; but he argued, all the same, that before the Great War, before 1915 at any rate, the sense that the West was ascendant and set on a course of technological and social progress was palpable. After it, the pervasive sense was one of lost promise, disillusionment, chronic crisis and, finally, disaster and looming apocalypse.[30] Hence, the second and third parts of his

---

30.   Steiner's sketch of what he dubbed 'the imagined garden of liberal culture' was characteristically rich and his historical assessment intelligently ambivalent. He wrote:

> The main features of the landscape are unmistakable. A high and gaining literacy. The rule of law. A doubtless imperfect yet actively spreading use of representative forms of government. Privacy at home and an ever-increasing measure of safety in the streets. An unforced recognition of the focal economic and civilizing role of the arts, the sciences and technology. The achievement, occasionally marred but steadily pursued, of peaceful co-existence between nation states ... A dynamic, humanely regulated interplay between social mobility and stable lines of force and custom in the community ... (p. 14)

He was able to claim without very much fear of contradiction, in 1971:

> There are still a good many alive today for whom that famous cloudless summer of 1914 extends backward, a long way, into a world more civil, more confident, more humanely articulate than any we have known since. It is against their remembrance of that great summer and our own symbolic knowledge of it, that we test the present cold. (p. 15)

However, he then contradicted the remembrance, reminding us of the underside of that golden era—or at least the metropolitan part of it:

book were titled, respectively, 'A Season in Hell' and 'In a Post-Culture'. I was born a decade after the 'season in Hell' and was a schoolboy in the 'post-culture' when Steiner was writing his book. Having read it, at the age of nineteen, I set out to find answers. I have not ceased to search since then; but at many points I have come to disagree with Steiner, as I have shown.

All this is the point of departure for the present book. It commences with a Credo which was composed to *displace* the Christian creed and all the imagined revelations of the old religions. It concludes with a poem whose refrain is:

> Dance me on down from Toledo,
> by the light on the bridge we have made,
> to a land with a non-Christian credo,
> where flamencos and tangoes are played.

Along the way, it explores or responds to the perspectives opened up in that Credo, to the realities of the Earth that have rendered all religious myths of creation and providence redundant, to the origins and accomplishments of scientific inquiry, to the long emergence of our species out of the animal kingdom, to the possibilities of human creative intentionality, the nature of gifts and the uncanny and open-ended character of human love. It comes to a rounding with the idea that song and dance are integral to our humanity, but taken for granted

---

If we listen to the historian, particularly on the radical wing, we learn quickly that the 'imagined garden' is, in crucial respects, a mere fiction. We are given to understand that the crust of high civility covered deep fissures of social exploitation; that bourgeois sexual ethics were a veneer, masking a great area of turbulent hypocrisy; that the criteria of genuine literacy were applicable only to a few; that hatred between generations and classes ran deep, if often silent; that the safety of the faubourg and of the park was based squarely on the licensed but quarantined menace of the slum ... The recognition is inescapable that the intellectual wealth and stability of middle and upper middle class life during the long liberal summer depended, directly, on economic and, ultimately military, dominion over vast portions of what is now known as the under-developed or third world ... (p. 15)

But if this was the case, why do we need a specifically religious explanation for the explosions of violence in the 20th century? Steiner provided no answer. He did not even pause to reflect upon the anomalies in his argument.

This is what Hannah Arendt had been alluding to, in 1950, when she reflected that the terrible crisis in Europe between 1914 and 1945, which remained unresolved as she wrote, had arisen from within 'the subterranean stream of Western history' and had brutally 'usurped the dignity of our tradition.' Writing a generation before Steiner—and as an emigré Jew, like him—she declared that those thirty years had generated 'an ill-defined, general agreement that the central structure of all civilizations is at the breaking point.' Hannah Arendt *The Origins of Totalitarianism* (Andre Deutsch, London, 1986), Preface to the First Edition pp. ix, vii.

almost as much as language, pointing or reasoning. The meaning of life, it claims, does not consist in preparing for an after-life—unless by that one means being remembered and cherished by others—but in the 'deep song' and intimate dance, understood as metaphors as well as realities, which become possible for us when we are fully alive and engaged in intimate communion with others. And the future stretches before us for immense vistas of time—before the Sun expands and swallows up our zone of viability; and before our galaxy collides spectacularly with our vast neighbour, Andromeda, some four billion years from now.

Credo

I believe that all deities are idols of the mind,
That blood sacrifices to them are an abomination,
That dogmas are obstacles to enlightenment.
I believe in the plurality of worlds,
But know of none that can compare with ours
In its abundance of life;
Of a kind that has arisen,
Through countless changes and catastrophes,
Out of the primal waters of the Earth.
I acknowledge that I am of this world,
Though a brief sojourner in it.
I have sprung from it and will pass back into it.
I recognize that my existence,
Both sentient body and sapient mind,
Is possible only within the natural order of things.
Capable of mimesis, metaphor and music,
Of reason and responsibility,
I believe that I am neither fated nor predestined,
But am able to live for possibilities
And move intentionally toward a horizon that is open.

1

The scandal of false beliefs: All the 'great religions' in the modern world have their roots in bygone ages and are desperately in need of revision or complete replacement for the third millennium of the Common Era. It is a scandal[31] that, a century and a half after Darwin, billions of human beings still derive their symbolic orientations in life from Hinduism, Buddhism, Christianity, Islam and many other fable-based religions. All these religions (like many a contemporary cult) make demonstrably false claims about how the world came to be, what human beings are and how we ought to behave.

2

The error of the monotheists: Long ago, in historical terms, philosophers and religious visionaries rejected polytheism, arguing that the pagan gods—Greek or Latin, Germanic or Celtic, Egyptian or Levantine—were clearly mere projections of human passions or natural forces and, therefore, not divine at all. They were idols and should not be prayed to or sacrificed to, since this was at best delusional. At worst, it entailed practices, such as the sacrificial killing of human beings or animals, which were intrinsically abominable. Those of us who seek sweeping progress in the 21ˢᵗ century agree with the monotheists about all this. We simply go one god further—that's all!

3

The tradition of negative theology: The finest and most rarefied moments in the monotheistic tradition are those in which the one god of their theology is defined negatively, which is to say in terms of what it is *not*. I write 'it', because calling the deity 'He' is the first solecism of the monotheists and the surest sign that they are as given to anthropomorphisms as the polytheists. Dubbing the deity 'She' would not solve this problem. Agreeing to strip it of gender works only if it is stripped of all human characteristics, such as temper tantrums or responsiveness to pleas (prayers) and bribes (sacrifices). Do this and you arrive, step by step, at a deity that can only be conceived as an *absence*. In that absence you will discover human freedom—and responsibility.

---

31.   The word 'scandal' tends in our time to denote tabloid copy and sexual peccadillos. Its origin, however, lies in the Greek word '*skandalon*', a snare or stumbling block. The central snare for an enlightened culture in this millennium, its stumbling block, is that billions profess belief in the old religions and many millions subscribe to the often ludicrous claims of contemporary cults.

4

No tribal favouritism: There is, in short, no great Jew in the sky petulantly demanding that one have no other gods before him; nor any great Arab overlord demanding submission; nor any triple-headed monster with a virgin queen calling for obeisance and planning an apocalypse. These are delusions and idols with whom a mature humanity must dispense. It is a long way from having done so, but there is time enough. Enlightenment is new and has only taken its first few stuttering steps since the 17th century. Besides, it is optional. It is only for those who want to be free and to shake off the fear of deities, as Lucretius suggested we do, two thousand years ago.

5

It isn't 'God' we have to invent: There is a holdover from monotheism which suggests, in the words of Voltaire, that if God did not exist we would have to invent Him. He doesn't, but we did do so. Or at least others did so and we have inherited the problem. What we do have to invent is a cosmopolitan culture after the death of God, which is to say a mode of being-in-the-world which puts the shibboleths of monotheism behind us and takes full responsibility for what our species represents on this Earth and what it is able to stand for in the Cosmos that has yawned wide before our telescopes and mathematics. The possibilities are immense.

6

There will be no Messiah: There was never going to be and there never will be a 'Messiah'; neither the one hoped for in orthodox Judaism, nor the return of Jesus as the 'Christ' prophesied in the Christian New Testament, nor the coming of the Mahdi, anticipated by Muslims. Our species has, since the end of the last Ice Age, proliferated and taken over the entire ecosphere. It has become a huge problem for itself and other species. No external supernatural power will 'save' us—or other creatures from us. Order, plenty and the culture of the future depend entirely on our collective maturity and creativity. If we are to have 'faith', it will have to be in those things prevailing over atavism, stupidity and violence. There are some grounds for such faith, but above all there is an urgent need to develop it. We are an extraordinary species, for all our flaws and errors, and we have only just begun to realize what we are and can achieve.

7

Myths and stories: Never let it be said that the poetry of monotheism should be jettisoned along with its dogmas and dubious practices. We still cherish the heroes and gods of far more ancient religions, though none of us is any longer a devotee of the ancient gods. The survival of the pagan gods long after the destruction of their temples and the disbandment of their priesthoods is a testimony to the human passions that created those gods to begin with. Similarly, in the future, we will remember the tales of the Hebrew patriarchs and prophets, the myth of Jesus as the 'Son of God', the ascetic heroes of Christianity and the heroic era of Islam as fables from the legendary past. Indeed, we will be freer than ever to draw from them whatever of enduring human value they ever contained and without fear or confusion.

8

The greatest of all stories: In a mere one hundred and sixty years since Darwin, we have reconstructed the origins of the Cosmos, the history of life on Earth and the archaeology of the human past in a way and to a depth which has confuted all the old religions and set us free—if we choose to be so. No gods haunt this story, except as fables made up by our ancestors, because they knew so little. We should be in awe of what we can now see with the mind's eye and in awe, even more, of the cognitive skills—the scientific methods—that have made it possible for us to discern all this. Pulling it together into a shared narrative of humanity is our current task—in a tradition dating back many hundreds of thousands of years around camp fires, middens and hearths.

9

A new Axial Age: Karl Jaspers dubbed the era which produced classical Judaism, Buddhism, Christianity, Confucianism and Greek philosophies such as Platonism, Stoicism, Epicureanism and Cynicism 'the Axial Age'.[32] We have entered a new Axial Age and it is

---

32.   Karl Jaspers coined the idea of the Axial Age in his 1949 book *The Origin and Goal of History*. On p. 2 of that book he wrote:

> *Confucius and Lao-Tse were living in China, all the schools of Chinese philosophy came into being, including those of Mo Ti, Chuang Tse, Lieh Tzu and a host of others; India produced the Upanishads and Buddha and, like China, ran the whole gamut of philosophical possibilities down to materialism, scepticism and nihilism; in Iran Zarathustra taught a challenging view of the world as a struggle between good and evil; in Palestine the prophets made their appearance from Elijah by way of Isaiah and Jeremiah to Deutero-Isaiah; Greece witnessed the appearance of Homer, of the philosophers—Parmenides, Heraclitus and Plato,—of the tragedians, of Thucydides and Archimedes. Everything implied by these names developed during these few centuries almost simultaneously in China, India and the West.*

Jaspers argued that the Axial Age laid the foundations for belief systems still dominant in the

time for radically reconceiving the nature of our species, its place in the Cosmos and an ethos of stewardship of the world, in the light of what the modern sciences have shown about our origins, our nature and the Cosmos itself. 'We' have learned an enormous amount in recent centuries, but especially in the past half century. It's time we took stock and created a new basis for civilization.

10

Historians and philosophers: In the 18th century, a few thoughtful individuals began to realize that the Western world had a complex and evolving story and that new ideas and possibilities were emerging which made it possible to set both the Christian religion and the classical world before it in a wholly new light. They began to conceive of history as the story of cultural evolution and progress in manners, morals and civil government. Montesquieu, a pre-eminent French aristocrat, led the way. David Hume, Adam Ferguson, Adam Smith and Edward Gibbon (all in Britain) added to the project, while continental European thinkers sought enlightenment, also, along several pathways, Immanuel Kant not least among them. They were our precursors. Now is a time for bringing global human history to a whole new level of shared comprehension—with a cosmopolitan intent.[33]

---

world at the time he was writing. He did not propose, as I do, that the late 20th century and early 21st century would constitute a new Axial Age. For an extended commentary on the ideas of Jaspers in this regard, enlarged by a more sweeping understanding of religious history, see Robert N. Bellah *Religion in Human Evolution: From the Palaeolithic to the Axial Age* (Belknap Press, Harvard University, 2011). Interestingly, he remarks:

> *Plato ... with his enormous range of interests, the living quality of his thought, and the vast corpus of his writings, which rival the Bible in length, completed an axial transition that had been long in the making and moved toward the institutionalization of an axial culture that would have enormous long-term consequences ... If one of the defining aspects of axial culture is the capacity to imagine things different from what exists, Plato would seem to be the banner bearer of all axial thinkers.* (p. 387)

But Plato was a pre-scientific thinker and did not initiate a scientific culture. That came afterwards. Even his pupil, Aristotle, would declare, 'I love Plato, but I love truth more.'

33.   The allusion is to the brilliant essay by Immanuel Kant 'Idea for a Universal History with Cosmopolitan Intent', written in 1784. This essay was a defining contribution to the European Enlightenment and in some ways the distillation of Kant's life's work. He remarked, of the nature of knowledge: 'Science is organized knowledge. Wisdom is organized life.' Few modern thinkers have been as influential as Kant in prompting both science and wisdom among thoughtful human beings.

11

It has begun: The creation and teaching of 'Big History' is an endeavour in the great tradition of Montesquieu. It is just over a decade since the publication of a book called *Maps of Time: An Introduction to Big History*, by David Christian, an Australian working in the United States. It situates human evolution and everything we normally think of as 'history' in the context of what we now know of the age and nature of the Cosmos and the geological and biological history of the Earth since it was formed, four and a half billion years ago. Montesquieu and Hume would have been astounded. It is this Big History that must serve us in generating a new 'Axial Age'. It opens up the space for informed and considered discourse and frees us, in a manner Lucretius would have applauded, from the dogmatic claims of both the old religions and modern cults.

12

No sacred scriptures: There can be no 'sacred scriptures' any more, since all the books that have been given that status, such as the Bible and the Qur'an, are riddled with historical errors, scientific ignorance, moral confusion and inducements to fanaticism in the name of 'revelation'. There is no 'revealed truth' and no 'supernatural' order of things. What *natural* order exists is cosmic and that order is full of perils and stochastic (random) processes. We have only begun to comprehend it. What complex *social* order there is has evolved by trial and error over the past ten thousand years, since we invented agriculture and began building cities. After the geopolitical earthquakes of the 20th century, it is time to rethink all this—from the ground up.

13

Rules of reason and evidence: The difference between history or science on the one hand and myth or dogma on the other lies in the openness of the first set to correction, based on close reasoning and carefully sifted evidence. The new civilization cannot be a dogmatic one or a totalitarian one. It can no more set up the writings of some demagogue or 'man on horseback' as an unquestioned authority than it can rest on the arcane tales and obscure prophecies set down long ago in the Bible or the Qur'an. It has to be based on shared principles of deliberation and workability, within which specific beliefs can be adjusted in the light of new discoveries. It will, of course, leave room for dreams, poetry and art, but it will assess any truth claims made on the basis of such things with its ingrained scepticism and circumspection.

14

Literature unbound: Once the wider narrative is grasped and the totalitarians, religious and secular alike, discredited, literature will be freer than ever to explore the countless stories of humanity at large. One can imagine a whole new theatre, both tragic and comic, based on the re-examination of the 'sacred scriptures' of the past and the lives of the prophets and seers who kept imagining themselves to be the mouthpieces of divine revelation and the messengers to mankind of retributions to come. Like the Greeks two and a half millennia ago, we could run a drama festival which would include tragedies and satire plays of immense variety designed to make global audiences weep and laugh by turns at the foibles of humanity and the dangers of feckless belief. Such theatre would transcend our current cinema, just as its audiences would have transcended the dogmas and superstitions, blood sacrifices and prayers of the old religions.

15

Burned at the stake but vindicated: Giordano Bruno was burned alive in 1600, in Rome, for espousing a heliocentric theory of the solar system, a belief in the plurality of worlds (and the infinite size of the cosmos), a belief that mathematics could unveil the workings of the natural world and an interest in reviving classical atomism. He has been vindicated. That is not to say that his specific beliefs were correct. In detail, they have long since been overtaken by the natural sciences. Rather, it is to say that his stance and his calls for open inquiry have been shown to be correct and the scriptural and theological conservatism of the Catholic Church, committed to a closed universe centred on the Earth, has long since been refuted, especially since Edwin Hubble demonstrated that even our vast galaxy, the Milky Way, is by no means the centre of the universe.

16

Darwin hesitated for years: Such was the grip of established religion even in the mid-19th century in England that Charles Darwin held back his masterpiece *On the Origin of Species* for years, fearing the firestorm it would create within that religious establishment. Even today there are Christians who refuse to accept Darwin's findings, insisting that the world was created by a deity—an 'intelligent designer'. And there are those, coming from non-Christian backgrounds, who assert vehemently that their outdated beliefs are not to be contradicted, but trump the findings of the sciences. There are even those within the scientific fraternity who declare that science and religion are based on different epistemologies and that they do not clash. This shows the same hesitancy that Darwin felt. It's time we put away such fear—in the interests of enlightenment.

17

The mythopoetic primate and the future: One of the most visionary of 20th century anthropologists, Claude Levi-Strauss, argued that myths are humanity's means of 'survival as a thinking and social species'. As George Steiner paraphrased him, in 1974: 'It is through myths that man makes sense of the world, that he experiences it in some coherent fashion, that he confronts its irremediably contradictory, divided, alien presence.'[34] But this leads into confusion and the claims of dark stories on the human imagination. The only means we have invented for actually grappling effectively with the 'contradictory, divided, alien presence' of the natural world is critical inquiry, both scientific and historical or textual. There is no contradiction between this and being able to find inspiration or enjoyment, counsel or perspective through myths and stories. But we can be free of the snares that religions and other myths set for us. The pathways to such freedom should henceforth become our governing mythopoiesis—our *autopoiesis.*

---

34.   George Steiner *Nostalgia for the Absolute*, CBC Massey Lectures, 1974, (House of Anansi Press, Toronto, 2004), p. 26. Steiner, like Levi-Strauss, is Jewish and his 'Absolute' is primarily the Hebrew god of the Old Testament and Rabbinical Judaism. He relates of the French anthropologist: 'There is an Hassidic parable which tells us that God created man so that man might tell stories. This telling of stories is, according to Levi-Strauss, the very condition of our being. The alternative would be total inertia or the eclipse of reason. The mediative, ordering capacity of myths, their ability to 'encode'—another Levi-Strauss word—to give coherent expression to reality, points to a profound harmonic accord between the inner logic of the brain and the structure of the external world.' (pp. 26-27).

But, of course, this is simply untrue. The whole of what we call knowledge consists of findings that have exposed the *lack* of 'harmonic accord' between the imaginings of the human brain and the structure of the external world. Levi-Strauss elsewhere acknowledged this, but seems to have believed that this break with our old illusions constituted a violation of our ancient 'pact' with the natural world and was set to bring on ecological catastrophe. Yet no myth could verify such a finding, even if it turned out to be true—only scrupulous inquiry that would cross-examine fears and imaginings. Our Enlightenment must, therefore, be grounded in such scrupulous inquiry and not in a reversion to unexamined myths or the 'Absolute' evoked by Steiner. This makes the history of methodologies for thinking well—and breaking with myth and superstition in the process—vital to our education as human beings. The fact that modern civilization keeps generating new myths (from political ideologies to consumer advertising to urban legends and conspiracy theories) does not lessen, but accentuates the need for critical thinking.

18

The basis for our possibilities: Our evolved capacities are the key to our future, as well as the source of our greatest dangers and confusions. But whatever happens, the fact that we evolved language and consciousness, an instinct for music and song, a capacity for art and a rudimentary and educable capacity for reasoning are 'miraculous'. Even if the 'ship' goes down, those things are the glory of our species and something all of us should wonder at and celebrate. They are what we can build upon with a sense of 'possibility', moving towards a horizon that is open—for the time being. There is plenty to build upon and abundant materials to build with.

19

Forebodings and old warnings: Plenty of people now fear that our sciences and industries, our weapons and appetites are sending us and the whole ecosphere with us over a gigantic cliff to catastrophe, in the 'sixth extinction'. There is no shortage of evidence that they may be correct. Yet so much scientific discovery and so much dialogue of concern are now going on that we should be wary of any fatalism. We should also be wary of lapsing into belief in old tales that warn against human 'hubris' and depict our divisions and confusions as the consequences of a 'fall from grace' or of divine intervention to cast down the Tower of Babel and scatter humanity abroad across the face of the Earth. We are a risen species that has achieved astonishing things and nothing can take that away from us. The future lies beckoning before us as a wilderness of choices, dilemmas and possibilities. It is, in many respects, for the time being, ours to shape.

20

Getting our cosmic bearings: That the 'horizon' is open does not mean that 'anything' is possible, or that human beings should live in fantasies, personal or collective. It means that *cultural evolution* has immense possibilities and that the closed (cyclical or predestined) universe of the classical and religious worlds has become the inconceivably vast and extraordinary Cosmos opened up not so much by Copernicus or Galileo as by Hubble and his heirs. We subsist on a small planet orbiting a perfectly ordinary star out on a spiral arm of a perfectly ordinary galaxy[35]. Yet we are already finding super-Earths within 300 light years of here that look

---

35.   Our solar system revolves around the centre of the Milky Way on an almost circular orbit, more or less within the plane of the disk that forms the core of the galaxy. To a first approximation, we are set some 30,000 light years from the centre of the galaxy (by some estimates 26 to 27,000 light years) and some 15 light years (142 trillion km) above the plane of the galactic disk. To put that in perspective, the diameter of the solar system (calculated as the diameter of Pluto's orbit

highly hospitable to life[36]; and our sciences are burgeoning in all manner of directions. This means that the horizon of the humanly possible has never been more open. Each of us can live for possibilities, whether large or small, in these rich and wondrous contexts. It requires only connection and imagination.

---

around the Sun) is only about .0015 light years. In other words, you could fit 10,000 of our solar systems end to end between the galactic plane and where we sit in the scheme of things. You could fit 20,000,000 of our solar systems between our Sun and the centre of the galaxy. Our Sun has completed 27 orbits of the heart of the Milky Way since its formation, less than five billion years ago. For several billion more years it will keep burning its huge stock of hydrogen, but after that it will morph into a red giant, swelling and consuming the zone in which the Earth orbits. Well before the planet itself is absorbed by the red giant Sun, life on it will have ended due to the overwhelming heat.

All these are fantastic numbers and considerations, when we remember that Aristarchus, in the 3rd century BCE, struggled to compute the millions of miles that he estimated was the distance between the Earth and the Sun and that both he and Copernicus, almost 1,800 years later, thought that the Sun was the centre of the universe. Just 100 years ago, Harlow Shapley concluded that the centre of the universe was the heart of the Milky Way, since he believed it *was* the universe. He was wrong. It is incomparably larger. And our search for planets has, so far, been confined to within a radius of 'only' about 300 light years from Earth—just 1% of our distance from the heart of the Milky Way. Our galactic neighbourhood—within a radius of 5 million light years—includes a number of galaxies, of which just one, Andromeda, is larger than the Milky Way. It is some 2.5 million light years away, or twenty five times the diameter of the Milky Way. Such is the nearer region of the Cosmos as we have discovered it in just the past fifty to ninety years—since Hubble's pioneering work in the 1920s.

36.   'The announcement in April 2013 that the Kepler space telescope had found two planets less than twice Earth's size, both in orbits where temperatures might permit life to survive, was one more hint that life-friendly worlds are almost certainly plentiful. So while these planets, named Kepler 62e and 62f, are too distant to study in detail, astronomers are convinced it will not be many more years before observers can look for biosignatures in the atmospheres of planets that are essentially twins of Earth.' Michael D. Lemonick 'The Dawn of Distant Skies', *Scientific American* Fall 2014 *Secrets of the Universe: Past, Present, Future*, p. 7. He went on:

> For planet hunters, business is booming. Astronomers estimate that our galaxy holds more than 100 billion planets [that is, one planet for every two stars] and are now finding several each week. The pace of discovery is accelerating: in 2014 NASA's Kepler mission announced 715 new worlds in a single day. Of those planets, 95% are smaller than Neptune and a precious few orbit in the 'habitable zone' where water could take liquid form...By far the most intense focus of observation has been concentrated on a planet known as GJ 1214b, which orbits a small, reddish M-dwarf star about 40 light years from Earth. Its proximity makes GJ 1214b relatively easy to study and its size, just 2.7 times the width of Earth, makes it far closer to being Earth-like than the hot Jupiters found in the first years of planetary hunting.

21

What, then, of social justice? One has only to take the most superficial look around to confront the reality that human beings do not inherit equal opportunity or the same menu of possibilities. Yet even the apparently most privileged, in terms of wealth and education, have continually to reinvent for themselves possibilities for self-actualization or fulfilment. And even the most downtrodden can live for possibilities, whether of emancipation or simplicity, revolution or sainthood. To live for a possibility does not mean to find one's hopes delivered on a silver platter. It means committing oneself to what is called for if such a possibility is ever to be brought into being. The emancipated human being comes to see this and to make choices, owning the difficulties and consequences, as well as the hopes and rewards of doing so.

22

Overcoming nihilism: 'Nihilism stands at the door,' wrote Nietzsche in 1885[37] and attributed the arrival of 'this uncanniest of all guests' to the fallout from the death of God and the sense that with it human existence had become meaningless and pointless and everything was permitted. Science, far from being the solution to the problem, suffered, in Nietzsche's opinion, from the same fatal flaw as ascetic religious ideals: it diminished man and cramped his style. Only art and grand schemes seemed to him to suggest sound instincts and the will to a future. We do not need to agree with him. Indeed, it would be reckless to do so. There has been a good deal of nihilism in the century and more since he wrote. The worst kind was the totalitarian plague which took as its moral compass his call for a set of 'overmen' to dominate the 'herd' and give life a meaning that it otherwise lacked. This arose in fascism, in Bolshevism, in Nazism and Maoism. We have had to fight it off. We still face the challenge of overcoming it—creatively.

23

Copernicus and X: 'Since Copernicus man has been rolling from the centre toward X'[38], Nietzsche declared. He elaborated on this with the observation: 'Since Copernicus, man seems to have got himself on an inclined plane—now he is slipping faster and faster away from the center into—what? Into nothingness? Into a penetrating sense of his nothingness?'[39]

---

37.   Friedrich Nietzsche *The Will to Power*, edited by Walter Kaufmann (Vintage Books, Random House, New York, 1968), Book One 'European Nihilism', p. 7

38.   Ibid. p. 8.

39.   Friedrich Nietzsche *On the Genealogy of Morals* and *Ecce Homo*, edited by Walter Kaufmann

When he wrote this, the natural sciences were in their infancy. Our grasp of the extent of the Cosmos has expanded enormously since 1885, as has our knowledge of our origins and history. Far from diminishing us to 'nothingness', it has enlarged the range of our vision and the evidence of how utterly extraordinary we are. It may well be that nihilism has sprung from the crises of the old religions—like the vicious savagery of Muslim terrorists in the early 21st century—and that the sciences have precipitated those crises. But, properly understood, they have set humanity free and made it possible for us, in principle, to transcend our delusions and get some perspective at last. We have taken the first few faltering steps in that direction. Now is not the time to give up—least of all on nihilistic grounds.

(Vintage Books, Random House, New York, 1969) Third Essay 'What is the Meaning of Ascetic Ideals?' Section 25, p. 155.

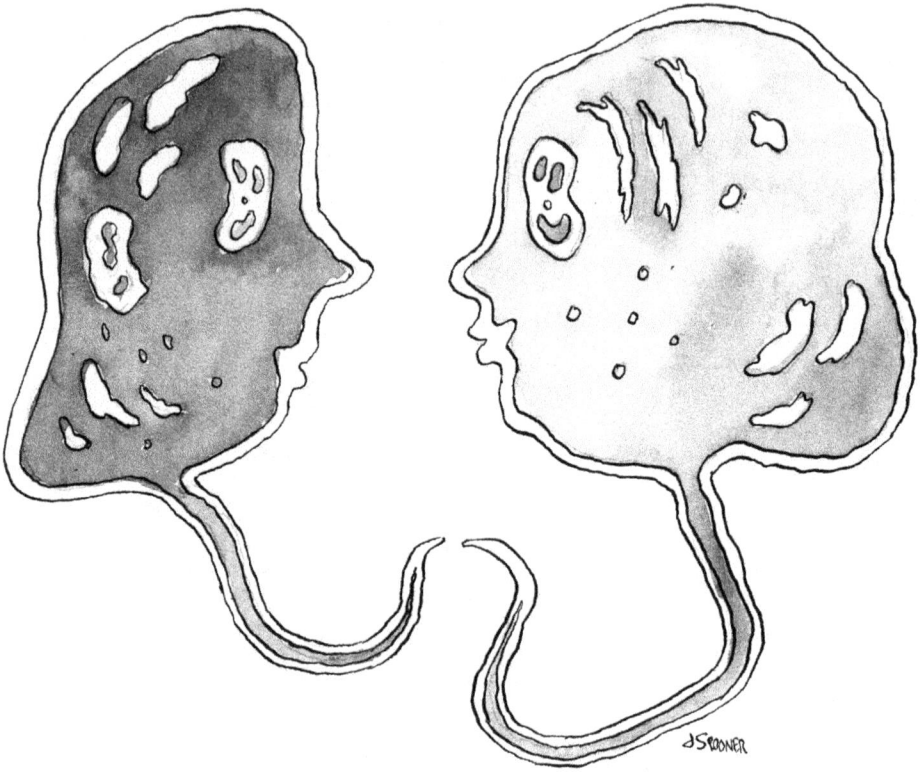

Simply prokaryotic?

We Karyotes

How would life be?
Would it still be erotic,
Had it made you and me
Simply prokaryotic?

Not very, I'd say –
Endless self-replication;
No cellular play
To exchange information

So, second my motion
As life bobs and floats
On the Archaean Ocean,
"We're eukaryotes!"

Will you carry oats,
If they come from me,
As we play wild motes
On a billion year spree?

I'd love some from eu,
If eu sent them my way,
To refresh and renew
My own DNA

24

From the primal waters of the Earth: Living organisms came into being on the Earth as far back as 3.8 billion years ago and not later than 3.5 billion years ago, in the form of single-celled bacteria—prokaryotes. They emerged from chemical processes and within a few hundred million years had proliferated widely over the Earth.[40] All other life has evolved from them. This and not any mythical process of divine 'creation' is how life began—in the primal waters of the Earth. These remarkable early beings invented photosynthesis, to draw nourishment from the overwhelming abundance of the Sun. They flourished and, over the following two billion years, transformed the atmosphere of the Earth by radically increasing its oxygen content. This opened up boundless possibilities for life to become more elaborate and ambitious—which it did.

25

Astrobiology and the cosmic sublime: We do a grave injustice to the roots of life and time if we dismiss these myriad archaic life forms as the so-called 'pre-Cambrian slime'. That epoch was not one of slime, but of the cosmic sublime: the genesis of life and the terraforming of a world through long, slow experiments in possibility. For three billion years the microbes had the Earth to themselves. It was only about 550 million years ago that the 'Cambrian explosion' changed that and only 400 million years ago that life came out of the seas onto land. Half a billion years from now, as the Sun begins to expand slowly into a red giant; the situation will begin to revert to pre-Cambrian conditions. For several billion years thereafter, there will, again, be only microbes on Earth. They will be last, as they were first; and then the end of our world will come, as the Sun's heat makes all life impossible and the Earth is finally eaten up by its expanding star. So the astrobiologists believe we can reliably calculate, based on the life-cycle of stars.

---

40.   For an illuminating discussion of the chemical origins of life, see Addy Pross *What Is Life? How Chemistry Becomes Biology* (Oxford University Press, 2012). Pross pays direct attention to the remarkable complexity of life (which has been used by creationists to insist that life could not have begun 'by chance'), in a fine passage very early in his book:

> *The simple truth is that the most basic living system, a bacterial cell, is a highly organized far-from-equilibrium functional system, which in a thermodynamic sense mimics the operation of a refrigerator, but is orders of magnitude more complex! The refrigerator involves the cooperative interaction of, at most, several dozen components, whereas a bacterial cell involves the interaction of thousands of different molecules and molecular aggregates, some of enormous complexity in themselves, all within a network of thousands of synchronized chemical reactions.* (p. xi).

26

Giving off free oxygen: It's hard to conceive of the immense periods of time it took for life to establish itself on the Earth and transform the atmosphere. Forget the 'six days of creation'. It took over a billion years of the emission of free oxygen by prokaryotes to even start the accumulation. Prior to that, it was simply reabsorbed into the Earth through chemical reactions such as the oxidization of iron. Even by two billion years ago, oxygen made up only about 3% of the atmosphere. Over the following billion years and more it rose slowly to 21%—and then it stabilized.[41] It was a deadly pollutant to many of the earliest forms of life, but the world of single celled organisms adapted to it and then some, creating multi-celled structures and a profusion of sea creatures. In bacterial, plant and animal forms, it then ingeniously colonized the shifting continents of the planet from 400 million years ago. So far, we have found nothing remotely comparable elsewhere—least of all in our own little solar system—but we are searching.

27

Eukaryotic divisions of labour: Even now, the microbes make up by far the bulk of living creatures on the face of the Earth. Each of our bodies, we have only very recently discerned, consists of a trillion eukaryotic cells working in an elaborate division of labour and ten times as many bacteria, living as symbionts or parasites within that elaborate eukaryotic cellular structure. You harbour ten trillion bacteria, of which you are oblivious. Do not scorn them. They are more purpose-built and task-oriented, in all probability, than you are as a conscious entity; and they perform vital tasks, in countless cases, without which you could not indulge in any of your frivolous activities, because you could not function as an organism. Their variety, ingenuity and complexity are staggering. They and their remote ancestors made the biosphere hospitable to complex life forms. They and their ilk will long outlast all such complex life-forms on the Earth—our own species surely included. They are life at its most fundamental and enduring.

28

The history of life on Earth: It's not strictly true that prokaryotes could not 'exchange information'. They could, but from very small genetic data banks and in limited ways.

---

41.   On the oxygenation of the atmosphere and its consequences see Donald E. Canfield *Oxygen: A Four Billion Year History* (Princeton University Press, 2014).

Eukaryotes, on the other hand, appearing for the first time about 1.7 billion years ago, exploited the oxygen that prokaryotes had long been pumping into the atmosphere, to develop a vastly greater array of metabolic skills, to grow orders of magnitude larger and to start forming multi-cellular organisms. It was 'game on'. Despite a long series of exogenous shocks and arbitrary natural catastrophes, life on Earth has never looked back. If we want to understand ourselves and our place in nature, it is this history of life that we need to study— not some theology or other about a supposed providential plan guiding the course of human history. What life is, what it has withstood, how it has reshaped itself and the marvellous, myriad forms it has taken—that is our grounding study in being alive. Simple prokaryotes began it. Eukaryotes took it to new levels.[42]

29

Exchanging information: We communicate by default, in word and gesture, but we often do it badly. If we could come to see the genesis and flourishing of life itself as rooted in the exchange of information, we might begin to look at gesture, language and sexual relations themselves in

---

42.   The question as to what life actually is goes back a long way. Immanuel Kant pointed out, in the 18th century, that the laws of physics, as articulated by Isaac Newton and his immediate successors, could not explain the existence and functionality of life. No-one before Charles Darwin came close to pinpointing an alternative set of 'laws' which might explain these things. As Addy Pross observes, 'Life's organized complexity is strange, very strange. And how it came about is even stranger'. The key characteristic calling for explanation is the self-organizing nature of life. As Pross wrote, the purposeful character of life is what seizes our attention and puzzles our intelligence:

> *That purposeful character is so well defined and unambiguous that biologists have come up with a special name for it—teleonomy. The 'teleonomy' word was introduced about half a century ago to distinguish it from the 'teleology' word with its cosmic implications ... [but] teleonomy, as a biological phenomenon is empirically irrefutable. The term simply gives a name to a pattern of behaviour that is unambiguous—all living things behave as if they have an agenda. Every living thing goes about its business of living—building nests, collecting food, protecting the young and, of course, reproducing.* (p. 9)

As he goes on to remark:

> *The notion of purpose within the inanimate world was laid to rest with the modern scientific revolution of the seventeenth century. The very existence of teleonomy however, leads us to a strange, even weird reality: in some fundamental sense we are simultaneously living in two worlds, each governed by its own set of rules—the laws of physics and chemistry within the inanimate world and the teleonomic principle that dominates the biological world.'* (p. 10)

a different light. If moreover, we could come to see ourselves as directly descended, over more than three billion years, from the prokaryotic cells that first began to terraform the Earth, we might come to appreciate our bodies, our inner complexities, our place in the biosphere and our every action and word in a different light. There was no Adam or Eve or serpent in the Garden of Eden. That is a fable made up by priests just two and half thousand years ago or so, because they had no idea how life—including human life—had evolved. We were not formed of clay in the 'image of God', only to 'fall'. We emerged, over aeons, far out on one branch of the Tree of Life (rather as our Sun is far out on one spiral arm of the Milky Way) and we rose through exchanging information. There, still, lie both our poetry and our science. There lies our future.

30

Sexuality as communication: Our sexuality is closely linked with all this. At the most obvious level, sex is linked to the exchange of *genetic* information through sexual reproduction. Yet human sexuality is about a good deal more than reproduction—both for better and for worse. Our much vaunted 'sexual revolution' put the emphasis on sexual *gratification*. But the *keys* to a dignified human sexuality are communication and empathy, intimacy and the sustained interest in the other. These things are notoriously difficult to achieve, but they are where our greatest potential for companionship, love and solace actually lie. Our problem is that we are cognitive generalists whose instincts are wayward and far too easily regress. Neither puritanical and misogynist cultures, nor pornographic and desublimated ones do justice to the emotional and communicative needs—or, indeed, the sexual needs—of human beings. Yet our stepwise increase in toleration and emancipation points to better possibilities—on the horizon!

31

Such an embarrassment: The evolution of sex is one of the great topics in biology; just as preoccupation with sex is one of the obsessions of most human cultures, our own emphatically included. While listing it among the 'ten great inventions of evolution', biochemist Nick Lane points out that the costs and disadvantages of sex are such that, analytically speaking, 'the odds seem massively loaded against sex as a mode of reproduction.'[43] It is surely not what an 'intelligent

---

43.   Nick Lane *Life Ascending: The Ten Great Inventions of Evolution* (Profile Books, London, 2009), p. 123. 'The advantages [of sexual reproduction] are surprisingly hard to gauge and made the evolution of sex the 'queen' of evolutionary problems throughout much of the twentieth century,' he comments. Set against its presumed advantages were its formidable twofold costs: the cost of finding a partner and the cost of having a partner at all (p. 122). He comments drily:

   The irate feminist, railing at the very existence of men, has a most reasonable point. On the face

designer' would have conceived as the best way to enhance life and give creatures the freedom to be themselves—if that is what the designer had in mind. They expend almost all their energies, other than what is required for ensuring nourishment, on finding a mate and reproducing. Life, as such, seems bent on propagating itself; but as a blind and overwhelming drive, not as a matter of free or conscious intent. This is why sex has become such an embarrassment to human beings and the subject of so much moral anxiety and social conflict.

32

Taking an interest: Sex long ago became the universal mode of reproduction among eukaryotic organisms. Given the extraordinary elaborations of life that sexual selection has generated, we can celebrate it as what makes the biosphere hum and dance. As Lane puts it:

> Sex makes the difference between a silent and introspective planet, full of dour self-replicating things ... and the explosion of pleasure and glory all around us. A world without sex is a world without the songs of men and women or birds or frogs, without the flamboyant colours of flowers, without gladiatorial contests, poetry, love or rapture. A world without much interest.[44]

But how did this come about? To think about it scientifically, to actually understand it, as distinct from merely re-enacting it, is a specifically human undertaking—and a very recent

---

of it, men are a heavy cost indeed, and a woman who solved the problem of virgin birth would be a worthy Madonna. While a few men seek to justify their existence by assuming the burden of childcare, or material provisioning, the same is not true of many lower creatures, human or otherwise, where the males quite literally just fuck off. Even so, the impregnated female gives birth to sons and daughters in equal measure. Fifty percent of her efforts are wasted on bringing ungrateful males into the world, where they simply perpetuate the problem.

There are variations on this theme, of course, but his point is well taken. Aristotle remarked, well over two millennia ago that a male is an animal that reproduces inside another animal. He did not pause, it seems, to elaborate on the disadvantages to 'the other animal'.

As for the compensating advantages to the animal (or plant) life as such, Charles Darwin speculated that sexual reproduction enhanced hybrid vigour, but his ignorance of genetics made it impossible for him to pin the problem down. The key to why sex works is that it shuffles the genetic deck, constantly 'experimenting', as it were, with new combinations of genes. The striking thing is that this has benefits for the population of organisms involved, but not for individual sexual organisms. Consequently, biologists had to investigate the mechanics of how it evolved from the cloning behaviour of prokaryotes and developed into a drive for elaboration embedded in the very nature of life itself and thus independent of the interests of individual organisms; in fact so dominant as to constitute their chief interest in life after eating.

44.   Lane (2009) p. 124.

one. In the interim, for thousands of years, religious efforts at transcendence have again and again led to variations on sexual renunciation or sexual extravagance; circling around the compulsion and the enigma. Enlightenment called for a more systematic inquiry.

33

The case of the mantis: Life has invented many variations on courtship, copulation and reproduction. The Elder Pliny attempted almost two thousand years ago to catalogue these, with limited knowledge or means for collecting it, in his voluminous *Natural History*, in the decades before he died during the eruption of Mount Vesuvius, attempting to rescue people fleeing the smitten towns of Herculaneum and Pompeii. One of the more notorious and lugubrious is that of the praying mantis, in which the female eats the head of the male during copulation, providing an especially dark metaphorical definition to the notion of the *femme fatale*. According to the specialists, the male appears to ignore the female's attack on his head and continue obsessively with copulation to the end; a second brain closer to the abdomen making this physically possible. It is said that some males, at least, attempt to inseminate the female and still get away, to play the same deadly game again. Talk about living dangerously! The female, for her part, knowing that the male will not provide for her or her off-spring, devours his nutritious head and sometimes other body parts, as the readiest nutriment to hand with which to feed her gravid body and her incipient off-spring.

34

The Red Queen hypothesis: After the exploration of a series of hypotheses for explaining the evolution of sex, by major biologists throughout the 20th century, Bill Hamilton, in the 1980s, came up with the idea that sexual reproduction evolved as a strategy by which organisms could keep their host parasites under control. Sexual reproduction, by generating individuals who differed genetically from their parents, made it possible for those off-spring to stay ahead of parasites that might be eating into their parents from inside. But parasites evolve rapidly, so this was an arms race with no end and locked virtually the whole eukaryotic biosphere into sexual reproduction—running very hard, like the Red Queen, in Lewis Carroll's *Through the Looking Glass*, just to stay in the same place.[45] It was an ingenious guess, but rigorous testing and computer

---

45.   The global biology of this is compelling and an overwhelming demonstration of the advantages of science over prayer and ritual sacrifices in coping with the realities of life. Lane comments of these realities:

> *Those lucky enough to live in the sterilised conditions of Europe or North America might have forgotten the full horror of parasite infestations, but the rest of the world is not so fortunate. Diseases like malaria, sleeping sickness and river blindness highlight the scale of the misery*

modelling showed by the mid-1990s that it did not really work, because most parasite infections are not serious enough to make sexual reproduction an indispensable strategy.[46]

35

Selective purges and genetic variation: Life has evolved through a long series of changes and catastrophes over billions of years. What is remarkable is that it has not merely survived these often random and exogenous shocks; it has flourished triumphantly across the Earth in countless forms. Shifts and shocks in the environment, the greatest being the mass extinction events that we have mapped so very recently, purge the biological world like Stalinists or Maoists sweeping through and conducting mass terror or causing huge famines. Sex conferred an ability to rebound from such selective purges and regain lost genetic ground. As Lane expresses it:

> Populations that reproduce clonally will lose genetic variety with every selective purge. From a population genetics point of view, large populations (in the millions) behave as if they were small (in the thousands) and this opens the door to random chance again. And so heavy selection converts even huge populations to a small 'effective' population size, rendering them vulnerable to degeneration and extinction. A series of studies has shown that exactly this kind of genetic poverty is widespread, not only in clones, but also in species that have sex only sparingly. The great advantage of sex is that it allows good genes to recombine away from the junk residing in their genetic backgrounds, while at once preserving a great deal of the hidden genetic variability in populations.

It turns out that, in the endless and blind competition for space in the biosphere, sex conferred advantages that cloning did not have—specifically a diversity that enabled populations to survive major exogenous shocks to their existence. That's why it became the dominant form of reproduction—except for bacteria.

36

The primeval sexual bottleneck: Such have been the advances in our understanding and in our taxonomic clarification of the orders of life on Earth that we can state with warranted

---

> caused by parasites. Worldwide at least 2 billion people are infected with parasites of one sort or another. We are altogether more likely to succumb to such diseases than to predators, extreme weather conditions or starvation. And, more generally, it's not uncommon for tropical animals and plants to host as many as twenty different species of parasite all at once. (p. 135).

How could any myth of 'intelligent design' conceivably explain such biological realities? Yet once we accept the compelling hypothesis of biological evolution, we are left with a bewilderingly complex world of adaptive and predatory organisms to both understand and confront.

46.   Lane (2009) p. 136.

confidence that 'the common ancestor of all eukaryotes had sex'—some 1.7 billion years ago. That's how old the game is! All the five great classes of eukaryotic organisms—protists[47], fungi, algae, plants and animals—have a number of shared characteristics and among these is sex.

> The fact that sex is so fundamental to eukaryotes is revealing. If we all descend from a sexual ancestor, which in turn descended from asexual bacteria, then there must have been a bottleneck, through which only sexual eukaryotes could squeeze. Presumably the first eukaryotes were asexual like their bacterial forebears (no bacteria have true sex), but all of them fell extinct.[48]

Just as eyes evolved via pathways we can now reconstruct—though not until eukaryotes had been around for well over a billion years—so we can reconstruct how sex may have evolved long ago, as well as why it provided advantages that have rendered it central to the strategies of all eukaryotic organisms ever since.

37

Learning from bonobos: Only slowly, as our researches became more systematic and our archives deepened, have we begun both to reconstruct the roots of our biological evolution and take a close interest in our hominid ancestors and surviving primate cousins. Following the 'sexual revolution' of the 1960s and 1970s—in which not only women, but homosexuals, male and female, pushed for emancipation from heterosexual male dominance—Franz de Waal began to look into the behaviour of bonobos, a species of primate only discovered in 1929. His central finding was that, unlike that of the chimpanzees, bonobo social order is both female centred and female dominated. Moreover, sex is engaged in by bonobos in a remarkably free manner, chiefly as a means of facilitating social bonding, reconciliation and cooperation. This included sexual encounters between adults and juveniles, males and males, females and females, as well as adult males and adult females. It had been noted as early as 1954 that, whereas chimps copulate like dogs—the male mounting his partner from behind—bonobos could be observed to copulate face to face; something until then believed to be unique to humans. Clearly, sex has not only evolved out of a prokaryotic world, but within the eukaryotic world and within the mammalian world. We have only begun to explore all this and have much to learn with a view to overhauling and revitalizing our human cultures in this new Axial Age.

---

47. Protists or Protista are the most primitive of eukaryotic life forms. The word derives from the Greek root *protos*, first. Taxonomically the term dates back almost exactly two centuries. With the enormous advances in biology it has become problematic as a sweeping categorization.

48. Lane (2009) pp. 139-40.

38

Evolution of the emotions: De Waal found that there was considerable scepticism about the 'relevance' of bonobos to humans, precisely because they were a less aggressive species than chimpanzees and the males were dominated by the females. He argued that these things are precisely what make them so interesting and potentially instructive:

> Since no-one knew what to do with them, bonobos quickly became the black sheep of the human evolutionary literature. An American anthropologist [Melvin Konner] went so far as to recommend that we simply ignore them, given that they are close to extinction anyway ... I welcome bonobos precisely because the contrast with chimpanzees enriches our view of human evolution. They show that our lineage is marked not just by male dominance and xenophobia, but also by a love of harmony and sensitivity to others.[49]

We need to reconstruct not only the physiological evolution of sex, but its emotional and social evolution. We need to do so not out of 'idle curiosity' but because we stand in need of further cultural evolution with regard to the emotions and sexual morality. Both have a very long pre-human history that we are only beginning to explore.

---

49.   Franz de Waal *The Bonobo and the Atheist: In Search of Humanism Among the Primates* (W. W. Norton & Co., New York, 2013), p. 12.

My almond shaped leaf

2
Nutcracker Man

Paranthropa went looking for Nutcracker Man,
Boisei, in the Oldowan Woods;
She hadn't in mind a particular plan;
Just to get him to give her the goods.

Her Nutcracker man, a promising youth,
Sat gazing aloft at the Sun,
Delighted and even astonished, in truth,
On account of the thing he had done.

She found him, at last, by the Olduvai stream
She cooed to him sitting alone
He turned to her slowly, as if in a dream
And showed her a curious stone

"I can see", Paranthropa then teasingly laughed,
"That I've caught you down here again knapping!
I admire, I suppose, your neat handicraft,
But you should be out hunting and trapping!"

Boisei was cut and, in some disbelief,
Exclaimed, "Oh, you're clueless, by Jimbo!
You'd be more impressed by my almond-shaped leaf
If you weren't such a Palaeobimbo!

I'd thought that the genius of my chips and cuts
Would light up your mind and connect us;
But I see all you want is fresh meat and rich nuts.
Well, look here, I'm now *Homo erectus!*"

39

Darwinian 'rules' and our freedom: It is commonly remarked that our species—*Homo sapiens*—has broken free from the Darwinian 'rules' that have governed the evolution of life from the beginning. We are the *language* animal, the *conscious* being, the *cultural* animal, the inventor and transformer. Through these unprecedented characteristics we have come to dominate the entire biosphere. Yet we have demonstrated these things only in very recent millennia. Prior to that, our hominid ancestors evolved slowly over millions of years and remained very much subject to the 'rules' of Darwinian selection pressure.[50] And we don't even understand the 'rules' well yet.

40

Rethinking our human story: Our human freedoms to think, imagine and plan emerged over long epochs which our ancestors utterly forgot, but which we have retrieved from oblivion. The paradox is that we have only begun to *rediscover* that immense genealogical past with the techniques and tools made possible by our special abilities. Before Darwin, we had none but the foggiest idea where we had come from or how we had arisen to become what we are. In the early 21st century, we now know enough to retell that story and, in its light, *completely revise* our myths and ideologies about our origins and our nature. There is a lot of work to do on this.

41

Our form and capabilities: In order truly to understand ourselves, we need to understand how we acquired upright posture and an opposable thumb; how we learned to walk and run, to point and to handle objects as tools of greater and greater sophistication; how we became largely hairless and why; how our sexuality evolved and with it our rudimentary forms of the social division

---

50.   This remained the case at the very least until as recently as 20,000 years ago. Over the period in which *Homo sapiens* gradually colonized most of Africa, Eurasia and Sahul (the ice age continent of what is now Australia, New Guinea and various island appendages of them), there were repeated climate catastrophes that sent human migration and material cultures into reverse. Again and again, it seems, the sharp changes in climate which occurred over the tens of thousands of years from 60,000 years ago, reduced wide areas that had been inhabited to freezing or otherwise arid deserts. It has been estimated that even the Levant may have been 'emptied of human settlement hundreds of times during the Late Pleistocene' in the words of John Shea. See his essay 'The Boulevard of Broken Dreams: Evolutionary Discontinuity in the Late Pleistocene Levant', in Chris Stringer et al *Rethinking the Human Revolution* (Cambridge, 2007) pp. 228-29.

of labour, with their various consequences; how our cranium and the brain within grew and changed in shape and capability[51]; how our vocal tract and larynx developed, making articulate speech physically possible. All these things are what make up our specific creaturely being.

42

Piecing ourselves together archaeologically: We need to absorb how all this came together. How did we become a creature capable of mimesis, metaphor and music; reason and moral responsibility? It is a long story. After all, our last common ancestor with the chimpanzee dates back six or seven million years, not a few millennia. Step by step, we have changed into a distinct kind of primate; breaking free of the rainforests of Africa to roam the savannah, surviving endless cycles of climate change and breaking out of Africa into the wide lands of Eurasia. That long evolutionary history, not any 'fall' in the Garden of Eden, has made us what we are now.

43

Knapping stones and awakening to consciousness: The combination of hand, eye and brain, long before segmented, grammatical speech emerged, made our remote ancestors able to fashion tools beyond any skill we can now find in other primates. There are still large gaps in our knowledge, in part because so many materials are perishable and have not left fossil traces. It is, after all, a very long time from seven million years ago, when our ancestors first discernibly began to differ from the other large primates by becoming bipeds, to the evidence of knapped stone tools in East Africa some 2.5 million years ago. And we have only begun to unearth it.

44

Seeing what is possible: Four and a half million years is a very long time to be scavenging in the savannah without fangs, claws, speed or useful tools and weapons. And, even 2.5 million years ago, the stones knapped by Mary Leakey's 'Nutcracker Man' in East Africa appear quite crude. Somewhere along the way, ever so slowly, our progenitors developed

---

51.   See Daniel E. Lieberman *The Evolution of the Human Head* (Belknap Press, Harvard University, 2011). Lieberman commences his summation (at p. 604) with a quote from *Thus Spoke Zarathustra*:

> *'Once you were apes, and even now man is more of an ape than any ape.'* As he comments: *'More than a century of concerted research has yielded a rich body of evidence showing that many of the key transformations we observe when we compare ourselves to other great apes occurred in three major stages, each of which was contingent on previous events.*' (p. 605).

If only we could induce ordinary human beings to read books such as this with the devotion they have been taught to show to the 'sacred scriptures' of their religions; not in order blindly to believe, but finally to think and begin to understand.

the cognitive ability to see *possible* tools in sticks and stones, and the manual capacity to bring them into being. That ability was more revolutionary than any of the actual tools it produced. It was the harbinger of things to come. It is, still, the cognitive capacity we most need to engage, in order to bring into being a future that actually makes sense of what we are and where we are. We must conceive it.

45

Let your 'spirituality' be creative intentionality: We had to evolve a long way physiologically and anatomically before our cognitive abilities were able to flower. Yet those abilities—the emergence within our genome of the capacity for *creative intentionality*—were more radical than any of the physical changes which preceded and prepared the way for them. The abilities are plural and only together enable the emergence of creative intentionality. We see them rise to the surface for the first time, in tantalizing and striking form, with the stone tools of *Homo erectus*, over 1.5 million years ago. Other than the fossil bones, this remarkable species has left scant material evidence of its long existence. That evidence, however, includes large numbers of enigmatic and beautifully shaped hand axes. They are the signature of a new and uncanny cognitive ability; one which other kinds of hominid would take further and then further again.[52]

46

Getting 'early' and 'late' in perspective: We pride ourselves on being 'conscious', but most of us are rather vague about what this means and even vaguer about why it should be regarded as significant. Looking back to *Homo erectus* and the creation of hand axes long ago, it is impossible not to wonder to what extent those 'early' hominids were 'conscious' of the originality and beauty of what they were doing. One writes of them as 'early' with reference

---

52.   All this has taken a very great deal of careful reconstruction by specialists in many fields. For a brilliant synthesis of the latest thinking on the cognitive capacities exhibited in Acheulian (*Homo erectus*) hand-axe making, see Gary Tomlinson's *A Million Years of Music: The Emergence of Human Modernity* (Zone Books, New York, 2015). His argument is that we do *not* yet see, in *Homo erectus* or in their hand-axes evidence of what I have called creative intentionality. Rather, we see some of its archaic *presuppositions*. His principle concern is with the evolutionary origins of music. He makes the case that tool-making, one million years ago and earlier, required rhythmic movements which were taught by mimesis rather than verbal instruction and entailed sub-conscious cognitive processes. These rhythms laid down the pathways which would later, he urges, give rise to musical syncopation and the rhythmic responsiveness of many parts of the body to music.

to our own notions of time and history, but of course they were relatively *late* in the history of human evolution, coming fully 5.5 million years after the last common ancestor with chimpanzees.

47

Knapping ourselves into shape: The makers of Acheulian hand axes can have been only very vaguely aware of the breakthrough that their skills exhibited. We know that, at least in terms of stone-knapping, they made very little further progress for well over a million years—a staggering period of time compared with the increasingly rapid cycles of our own innovations. Yet it is very difficult to accept that they were altogether 'unconscious' of what they were doing. It entailed close attention to detail in design. Our kind of mind was coming alive in them. *Hominization* was almost complete—1.5 million years ago. It is *still* almost complete; still 'coming alive'—in us.

48

Cutting to the chase: There is a theory, to which Marek Kohn bears witness, that hand axes were the product of sexual selection: that 'female hominids only mated with males who demonstrated competence in hand axe making'. He remarks:

> Hand axes need something that elemental to account for them. For the first time in hominid history, an artefact form is standardized. It is reproduced over an immense geographical range, for a period of time unrivalled by any other known artefact. Some great force must have perpetuated the hand axe and held it constant. Culture, as we know it, did not exist. What else was there but sex?

The point is that we see in these artefacts an exhibition of skill and artistry which goes 'beyond the demands of utility'. What, however, was the appeal to the female of the species? It's said that women like a man to be 'handy around the house', but those are strictly utilitarian demands. Where does the *aesthetic* element enter into the sexual selection equation? These axes were the equivalent—so Kohn argues—of a male peacock's tail. What an idea! Think of the implications.

49

Creativity and practicality: Draw a line in your own mind's eye between the symmetrical hand axes of over one million years ago and the finest creations of human craftsmanship in historical times; then extend that line to the most astonishing artefacts of modern human technology—say, a microchip or a spliced gene—and you have the *genealogy* of human creative intentionality on a spectrum. Yet we still retain an ancient prejudice in favour of the 'practical', the so-called 'bottom line'.[53] Most of us find it difficult to appreciate the

---

53.   Gary Tomlinson is particularly interesting on this point. He is at pains to denote the difference between the *archaic* human uses of technology and the *modern* human development of it—where 'modern' means the past 300,000 years and especially the past 50,000 . The implications, as he points out, take us deep into debates of long standing about the nature of (human) minds and the metaphysical implications of human thought processes. He remarks:

> *Patterned movements in the world, human or not, often lead to symmetrical patterns incised on it, even very complex ones—a fact we can savour by recalling Darwin's classic analysis of beehive design in* On the Origin of Species *... From this vantage, thinking of the hominin mind dictating symmetries has it backwards; it is the body-stone interaction from which symmetries (or perhaps even the mind) emerge. The variability of raw materials, more than varied conceptual plans, will lead to variability in tools as well as varied embodied thought. There is a rich and provocative opportunity glimpsed here of reversing our habits in conceiving early hominin experience. It is not that stone tools are proxies of mind but something closer to the reverse: mind as an outgrowth of the body-stone interface.* (pp. 67-68)

In an especially beautiful passage, he relates these lines of inquiry to Martin Heidegger's mid-20th century reflections on humanity and technology. The question of Acheulian hand-axes, he writes:

> '*requires a detour through the disclosure, revealing or unconcealing (aletheia) that Heidegger names as the forgotten essence of technology, in his famous essay on the subject. This unconcealing is a process of bringing into presence something not present. It therefore places technology under the aegis of poiesis, the broader name the Greeks gave to such bringing forth or 'presencing'. Technological unconcealing touches at the heart of Dasein, insofar as this names for Heidegger our openness to the presencing (or disclosure) that arises from our intersubjective and material connections to the world. Technological unconcealing, moreover, has a history, divided in the West into two epochs. These are distinguished especially by the increased distance, in the modern age, between technological effects and unconcealing—a distance that hides the essence of technology while capturing the energy of resources in standing reserves at human command.*
>
> *From the beginning, however, technology names a particular kind of poiesis, not a bringing forth of something in or through itself, as for instance a blossom blooming, but instead a presencing guided from without by the craftsman or artist ... Throughout its long history, in the Heideggerian account, technology is action springing from mental-template thinking ...* ' (pp. 84-85).

He points out, however, that this description does not fit what we see in the case of the makers of the Acheulean hand-axes. They were not yet Heidegger's human *Dasein*, but still pre-modern humans who did not live 'in time' and were not yet able to bring the future consciously and deliberately into being through creative intentionality.

We must, he insists, come to terms with the uncanniness and strangeness of the cognitive nature

sheer ingenuity of pure research or abstract arguments, or even of 'art for art's sake'. That is the animal in us. It requires the cultivation of particular *kind* of humanity to appreciate the transcendent insights and remodelling of the given in creative work. But those things can be seen for the first time in Acheulian hand axes. We should be in awe of them for that reason, just as of the Archaean oxygen emitters

of these ancestors of ours, so long ago and so intermediate between ourselves and the surviving primates:

> 'That an Acheulean revelation occurred, an unconcealing from the stone core of a shape replicated in countless instances, we cannot doubt. But this earliest poiesis relied on no mode of abstraction, no cognitive distance, no knowing craftsman; it was poiesis from the bottom up ... Acheulean technology stands categorically apart from Heidegger's two later technological eras, far outside the Western metaphysics of being—indeed, outside any human metaphysics at all—necessitating a third era in his poietic history: pre-sapient, primordial, non-human Dasein: Cambrian aletheia.' (pp. 87-88)

Upon which, as on unseen stairs

3
After the Ice

This book, good friend, will take your mind
Down many roads, into the past.
Allow it to and you will find
How wonderful and truly vast
The Ages were before our own:
The Age of Ice, which slowly warmed,
The immemorial Age of Stone,
When first our arts and dreams were formed.

Our arts? The ways we symbolize
The patterns that we seek and find,
With sapient, exploring eyes,
Our questing and uncanny kind.
Our dreams? Our visions and our cares;
The metaphors we make our own;
Upon which, as on unseen stairs,
Our minds ascend by thought alone.

Immerse yourself, then, in these pages,
Leaving mythic tales behind;
Explore the world's defining Ages;
Learn the truth about our kind.
For truth you'll need and insight deep
To comprehend our world in time;
And, to that end, I hope you'll keep
This slender tome and simple rhyme.

50

The world as a cooling place: Our folk 'memory' of the prehistoric past is so riddled with myths and fables as to utterly confuse what actually happened. This needs to change. Thanks to the patient work of our scientists, we can now trace the evolution not only of life, but of climate over many millions of years past. We now know, for instance, that our own *genus*—the hominids— evolved during an era of unusually rapid climatic change, characterized both by recurrent fluctuations and by a long term *cooling* trend. Over the Miocene, Pliocene and Pleistocene epochs, dating back 23 million years, the Earth cooled appreciably as the continents assumed their present configuration. The last three million years have been punctuated by recurrent ice ages.

51

Catching up with reality: The last two of these epochs, the Pliocene and the Pleistocene, were the ones in which most of our evolution away from the other primates occurred, starting just over 5 million years ago. From about 3 million years ago, a long cycle of 'ice ages' began. The most recent of these started about 100,000 years ago and ended about 15,000 years ago. Everything we think of as 'world history' has occurred since then. Generally, of course, we think of most of that period as 'prehistory'; with 'history' dating only from the invention of writing in Sumer at the earliest. That omits a huge amount. We have a lot of catching up with reality to do.

52

Past greenhouse eras not catastrophic: During the past 70 million years, the average surface temperature of the biosphere has fallen massively, from 24 degrees C to 14 degrees C and at times as low as 10 degrees C (during the ice ages). Prior to that, there were long greenhouse eras, such as the Cambrian and the age of the dinosaurs, in which the temperature hovered around 24 degrees C for tens of millions of years at a time.[54] Our concern that anthropogenic

---

54.   David Christian *Maps of Time: An Introduction to Big History* (University of California Press, 2004), p. 132. The overall trend in global temperatures has been one of cooling, since the Archaean epoch billions of years ago. Since the Cambrian era, some 540 million years ago, there have been three major greenhouse eras, each lasting for many tens of millions of years. There was an extended period of cold from the Devonian to the end of the Permian, in which surface temperatures were similar to those which have prevailed in the relatively recent past—hovering between 10 and 14 degrees Celsius. But during the long era in which primates have evolved (the past sixty five million years or so), temperatures have been falling from the high 24 C to 14 or 15 C in the hominid

global warming will ruin the biosphere by increasing its temperature some 2 to 4 degrees C is, therefore, in error. What is in possible jeopardy is not the biosphere, but conditions congenial to us.

53

Climate and human settlement: A *runaway* greenhouse effect would, of course, be immensely and perhaps fatally destructive; but an increase of two or three degrees would *not* be. The challenge such increases would represent, should they occur, is to the patterns of *human settlement*. That challenge could be quite radical, given the current extent and nature of human settlement, but we must keep it in long term perspective when alarms are sounded. We must see it against the background of actual climate changes going back many tens and even hundreds of millions of years and acknowledge that some warming is not necessarily or totally a bad thing.

54

Ancient and time-honed instincts: When we utter any kind of sound, much less articulate speech; when we 'ape' others with mimetic clowning; when we listen and respond to the rhythms and haunting sounds of music; when we point at objects or otherwise gesture meaningfully; when we stride or run with coordination and balance; when we throw stones, balls or missiles with intent and at least some precision; when we gaze into the flickering surreal of flames in an open fire; when we groom or stroke others; tease and taunt them; share food with them; cooperate in teams; enjoy camping out in the bush or the mountains; coo or babble with infants; or take things in hand and puzzle about how to make best use of them, we are *re-enacting ancient modes of being* that take us back somatically to our earliest hominid

---

period; between 10 and 14 C during the past million years or so.

During much of the past 100 million years, as is shown at Harvard University's Peabody Museum of Natural History Climate Change Exhibition, surface ocean temperatures were between 4 and 8 C higher than they are now. Deep ocean temperatures, near freezing in our time, hovered around 12 C. Tropical trees flourished far northward and southward of current limits. There were Arctic forests of redwoods, palms, fig and magnolia trees, tiny primates, cat sized horses and crocodiles in the warm waters off the coast of what is now Greenland. There were lush pine forests in what is now Antarctica. All this has only been learned in very recent years, using highly sensitive instruments and advanced chemical tests. We would know precisely nothing about it had it not been for the advances in the natural sciences in the late 20th century. Religious belief never, at any point, gave access to such knowledge, but left us 'flying blind' regarding the climate history of our environment.

ancestors and beyond into the primeval primate world. We should remember this. It needs to become foundational to our new religion for the 21ˢᵗ century and as far into the future as our species endures.

55

The most ancient art: We have no record of human art before the beginning of the most recent ice age, about 100,000 years ago and even that is exiguous—the traces of ochre pigment making in the Blombos Cave, in South Africa.[55] The finest cave art we have recovered from the Pleistocene dates back less than half as far, most notably the Chauvet Cave, in southern France, whose murals have been dated back to just 32,000 years ago. Yet we have evidence of human ancestors fashioning complex tools far earlier than that. We have, for example, long thrusting spears made by Neanderthals as far back as 400,000 years ago. What we almost entirely lack are all the *perishable* materials which may have borne witness, had they been preserved, to the evolution of the human capacities for technological prowess and innovative thought. The two are surely related, since inventiveness requires not only manual dexterity and the coordination of eye, hand and brain; but the capacity to conceive new ideas and possibilities. We know that this occurred. We are left to infer from still fragmentary evidence precisely *how* it evolved.

56

Mythology, the Moon and our new outlook: The English poet and novelist Robert Graves postulated, in *The White Goddess*, that the Moon was the primordial deity of humankind and the eternal Muse of poetry. He went so far as to write, in a 1960 Postscript to the book: 'A prophet like Moses, or John the Baptist or Mohammed, speaks in the name of a male deity, saying 'Thus saith the Lord!' I am no prophet of the White Goddess and would never presume to say, 'Thus saith the Goddess!'. A simple loving declaration: 'None greater in the universe than the Triple Goddess!' has been made implicitly or explicitly by all true Muse-poets since poetry began.'[56]

---

55.   The Blombos site yielded 100,000 year old 'paint pots' indicating multiple possible uses of ochre. These materials are clearly indicative of the kinds of perishable artefacts that have generally not shown up in the archaeological record. In reconstructing the past, consequently, we have again and again to carefully calibrate and reset our judgments.

56.   Robert Graves *The White Goddess: A Historical Grammar of Poetic Myth* (Faber & Faber, London, 1999) p. 483. Graves was a late Romantic and seems to have had only the most tenuous knowledge of human evolution and the archaeology of the Eurasian heartland. His reflections

57

Transcending Moon calendars: It *is* the case that Moon mythologies are universal across human cultures and that the Moon long ago became associated with the female because of the coincidence between lunar and menstrual cycles. The most ancient human markings we have are Moon calendars scratched into stone and bone. The Moon's cycles of renewal, endlessly repeated, were even more arresting to our ancestors than the daily passage of the Sun. Metaphors drawn from both are deeply embedded in our poetries and old religions. It is time for us, knowing more than our ancestors, to build deeper cycles and greater realities into our poetries, our religions, our annual feast days and our *dies nefasti*—our days of solemnity and counter-festivity, our days of remembrance and reflective foreboding. This is what overhauling our religions requires of us.

58

The Moon, the Sun and a vast new reckoning: Jules Cashford reminds us that the Moon's role in the evolution of the human mind is older and more pervasive than anyone in the era of the Sun had recognized. 'Moon worship', she points out, 'preceded Sun worship in most if not all parts of the world.' The Moon, not the Sun, prompted measurement of multiple days and monthly cycles. The very word 'measurement' has the same etymological root as 'Moon' in many languages.[57] The Moon's endless cycles of brightness, dying away,

---

are a fabulous illustration of the imaginative and poetic uses of mythology, but an unreliable guide to ontology—the knowledge of what actually exists—or to secular history. His writing was done in the wake of the Great War and in large part as a reaction against it, beginning with his war memoir, *Goodbye To All That* (1929) and climaxing with his two volume edition of the Greek myths and his three best known novels of the classical world: *I, Claudius* (1934), *Claudius the God* (1934), and *Count Belisarius* (1938). He also wrote a life of Jesus of Nazareth, *King Jesus* (1946), which was written as a pioneering inquiry and took the point of view that Jesus was a sworn enemy of the White Goddess who was, in the end, defeated by her. That it was published two years before *The White Goddess* (1948) puts the latter in an interesting light. Graves revised *The White Goddess* extensively in 1960 and, re-issuing the book in 1997, its editor Grevel Lindop described it as 'complex and capricious in argument' and a 'confusing palimpsest of a book'. It launched him into the 1960s 'counter culture' and, while a tantalizingly labyrinthine read, is not to be relied upon as a guide to either historical reality or religious history.

57.   Jules Cashford *The Moon: Myth and Image* (Cassell Illustrated, London, 2003). Cashford blots her copy book at one point, in remarking: 'This way of seeing the Moon in Egypt lasted for over three thousand years, entering the Greek and Roman worlds and only ended in the second

eclipse and renewal stirred thoughts about being and time. Following its cycles slowly gave a *transcendent* focus to human consciousness. How far back we do not know. But our ancestors stood upright, became bipedal and begun to venture out into wide new spaces some 7 million years ago. Once upright and in the open, we were freer to gaze at the sky, by night and day. So we began to wonder at what we were seeing. With agrarian civilizations, the worship of the Moon began to recede into the background. But we now, so very recently, have opened up the cosmos itself to our gaze; and, rather than worship Sun or Moon, or abstractions from them in the form of deities, we need to fill our minds with a suitable and informed awe at all that is the case. It is a vast new reckoning.

59

Becoming what we are: Both music and language came to those early ancestors of ours. We are only slowly and tentatively reconstructing how. Before we could *name*, we could *point*. Before we could *sing*, we could *tap, whistle* and perhaps *hum*. This is still true of each of us as individuals. Yet, as a species and as cultures, we have developed elaborate taxonomies, theories of knowledge, fabulous reservoirs of poetry, music and song. How have we become what we are? That is the single most important inquiry in which we should be engaged. That is the subject for new songs.

60

The task of humane education: Understanding the evolution of our species should form the basis of our education in being human: our philosophy and our religion on the far side of all deities. The task of education, in other words, is not and cannot be merely equipping individuals to perform some productive and remunerated role within the vast engine of agrarian, industrial and specialized technical production we have collectively created. It is to enable and foster the development of human beings aware of what they *are* and capable of enacting the greatest possible range of human potentiality in their lives. Our finest academies used to do something along these lines, in the name of the old religion and the classical tradition. An authentically advanced civilization would make such an upgraded education its systematic goal.

---

century AD, when the temples of Isis were closed on the orders of the Christian emperor Theophrastus.' (p. 34). There was, of course, no Christian emperor in the second century and there never was one called Theophrastus. She should have written 'ended in the late *fourth* century AD, when the temples of Isis were closed on the orders of the Christian emperor *Theodosius.*' It is curious, also, to see a scholar working on cosmopolitan terms still using the term AD (Anno Domini) instead of CE (Common Era).

Your playing to me on bones flutes

4
Fire and the Wheel

I've loved you from the beginning,
With the simplest of gestures;
With inarticulate cries;
With unself-conscious mimicry.

I've loved you since the first fire-wielding,
When we yelled together at encircling beasts;
Feasted on fire-roasted insects and nuts;
Huddled round the flames in awe.

Was that Eden, that long ago aeon;
As the hand formed and the inner eye,
The larynx and Broca's brain;
Before ever we sang to one another?

Or was Eden the time of hand-axes,
As all this came together
In our hearths and hunting
From old Andalusia to the Chinese rivers?

What years those were of wide-exploring!
Eurasia was ours with new spears!
Exulting in our uncanny craft,
We wondered at what we were.

Our long days fell like forest leaves;
They endured like evergreens.
Our fire-circles lit the long nights;
Changing our dreams.

Were those shimmering years,
Those many hundred millennia
Before our love made music,
Truly our Golden Age?

Did you feel loved then,
As the wide seas rose and fell?
As the ice advanced and retreated?
As the giant forests shifted, again and again?

Or was it only later, only later
That sentiment came and crooning;
Coaxed by oxytocin out of the flicker
Of long light under the waxing Moon?

Was I a caricature to your mind
Of all that was possible—possible –
For a singing hominid under the Sun?
Was I stone in need of shaping?

Ah! We buried each other many times,
Again and again with grief and ochre,
Over ages under the ageless stars,
From Jebel Qafzeh to Beringia.

Remember the times, sheltered from
The harsh climate shift in the north,
When we relished our little piece of Africa
In Andalusia? Those idyllic coasts and caves?

But your love transformed me:
Your call for songs and stories;
Your playing to me on bone flutes;
Your vivid art of changing forms.

We shook the shackles of the ancient trees,
Hailed the Sky God with high hands;
We took to the open horizon;
Pitched bold camp on the stark steppe.

There, at last, you carved me into shape!
Your love cut antler into a figurine;
And I, deer hunter, roamed forth Gravettian,
Making long lasting legends on the plains.

You wove me a coat of wool,
Dyed in wondrous new colours,
Finer than any cured skin and
I revelled in your homespun beauty.

Even that was a long age of ardour
Under the high wheeling stars;
Rich with rumour of far mountains,
With mammoth hunts and possibilities.

Then the revolution came at last: the Wheel,
The mastery and mustering of horses,
The making of wains and war chariots,
The being of bright burnished bronze.

Ah, sky gods! The Wheel and the horse
Brought an end to our long cycles!
Ah! My lover with golden hair,
The Wheel set us rolling, riding, racing

In the chariot of the Sun, did it not?
Since then, everything has gone in a flash:
A riotous blur of songs and innovations;
A nightmare of blood and terror.

I've loved you from the beginning.
Let's not now go under the Wheel.
All our myths are confused.
I long only for your beauty.

61

The fire continent and the hearth: 'I think the very act of associating with fire was the turning point in human evolution ... ' wrote Frances Burton, in *Fire: The Spark That Ignited Human Evolution*. She dated our use of fire—that is to say the opportunistic use of fire by our ancestors in Africa, the 'fire continent'—back almost to the divergence between our first biped forebears and the chimpanzees, some seven million years ago. Is it any wonder that we still find the sight of flickering flames, in a hearth or a bonfire, mesmerizing? The dance of such flames has accompanied our evolution for the longest time, stimulating changes in our endocrine system, our cortical brain development and our social habits. It may not have been until the classical Greek world that the myth emerged of Prometheus stealing fire from heaven and making of it a gift to human beings, which transformed their condition (to the anger of the old gods), but the truth is far older and vastly more interesting than the myth. So it is with many of our new truths.

62

Firing up humanity: 'My view of human evolution', Burton wrote, 'is that the acquisition of fire was the engine that propelled the incredibly fast evolution of humans. Directly or indirectly, it affected cognitive processes, social processes, genetic systems, reproduction, the immune system and digestion, among others. It may even have enhanced hair loss.' She emphasized the sense of speed and trajectory, as well as their link with the use of fire. By six million years ago, our ancestors were moderately bipedal; by four million years ago, there had been rapid advances in facial and dental development; by 2.5 million years ago, our ancestors were shaping stone tools.[58]

63

Looking into the dancing flames: As she expressed it, our ancestors were, no later than this epochal development, 'taking the direction of their own change into their own hands'— literally. By 1.5 million years ago, our *Homo erectus* forebears had become 'cosmopolitan', fanning out right across Africa and Eurasia, having radically differentiated themselves from all other primates. All this we need to acknowledge, as we gaze into the fire with awe, as having

---

58.   In fact, new findings suggest that the making of stone tools may date back much earlier. In May 2015, in *Nature*, it was reported that anvils, hammer stones and worked cobbles dating back 3.3 million years had been found by the shores of a Kenyan lake. John Ross 'Archaeology rocked by ancient stone tools', *The Australian* 21/05/15 p. 8.

been lived by our forebears, as being embodied in our genome, as being our lineage and our authentic identity. This past is what we should now see, whenever we gaze into the dancing flames of a hearth or a field fire lit for our warmth and pleasure.

64

Little upright creatures: 'With a brain no larger than a chimp's, but a mind accelerating genetically, anatomically and behaviourally by leaps and bounds, *these little creatures altered the face of the earth*,' wrote Burton. 'They did so because they were more interested in delicacies found at a smouldering fire than they were afraid of heat or flame; they were playful and social and dared to pick up firebrands; they saw the advantage of brandishing these sticks at predators that came too close; and they found comfort in fire's warmth and perceived that putting twigs into it kept it going. They changed the timetable of growth, development and reproduction because sitting by the fire altered the night's flow of melatonin and the cascade of hormones that follow it.' [59] How electrifying this finding is! One might say it fires the imagination. These were our beginnings. An informed mind would incorporate commemoration of them into new rites and festivals.

65

Our ancestors in Deep Time: Just as there were tens of different species of ape across Africa and Eurasia during the Pliocene and Miocene (between 23 and 5 million years ago), there were numerous different species of hominid across Africa and Eurasia during the Miocene and Pleistocene. We have so far identified the fossil remains of at least fifteen of them. By the time we reach the Holocene (ten thousand years ago), however, most species of ape and all species of hominid other than our own had become extinct. Only in this past century, have we gradually rediscovered them and only through the use of highly disciplined and sensitive scientific inquiry.

66

Remembering the extinct humans: We are only at the beginning of determining whether our ancestors played a direct role in the extinction of the two other hominid species that had survived into the late Pleistocene—*Homo erectus* and *Homo Neanderthalensis*.[60] Climate

---

59.   All these citations are from Frances D. Burton *Fire: The Spark That Ignited Human Evolution*, (University of New Mexico, Albuquerque, 2009).

60.   There may have been a third such species, but marooned in the archipelago of what is now Indonesia: *Homo floresiensis*, dubbed 'the hobbit' in folk palaeoanthropology, because of its

change may well have been the chief cause of the extinction of earlier species over time and, indeed, of those two species. Or perhaps, in those two cases, we were simply too voracious a competitor in the same ecological niches. They had been around for more than one and a half million years and 300,000 years, respectively, before we appeared on the scene. Our ancestors emerged among them from out of Africa. Their terrestrial existences were, also, epochs of exploring and altering the face of the Earth. This we should now work into our collective memories and into new, scientific folk traditions. Not to do so, while persisting with our old myths, would be sheer denial of reality.[61]

67

Music—the supreme mystery of humanity: 'The propensity to make music is the most mysterious, wonderful and neglected feature of humankind', wrote Steven Mithen, in *The Singing Neanderthals.*[62] The great French anthropologist, Claude Levi-Strauss, perhaps expressed the same thought more portentously and poetically, when he remarked that 'Music is the supreme mystery of man.' Nietzsche went further in declaring 'Without music, life would be a mistake.' Daniel Levitin has recently gone so far as to assert that the 'musical brain created human nature.'[63] But how did we get from the earliest whistling or crooning to bone flutes, skin drums and ultimately the orchestra and the saxophone? There has been an extraordinary cultural evolution here.

---

diminutive size. See Mike Morwood and Penny Oosterzee *The Discovery of the Hobbit: The Scientific Breakthrough that Changed the Face of Human History* (Random House, Australia, 2007).

61.   Research in to the Neanderthals has burgeoned in recent decades. See Clive Finlayson *The Humans Who Went Extinct: Why Neanderthals Died Out and we Survived* (Oxford University Press, 2009) and Dimitra Papagianni and Michael A. Morse *The Neanderthals Rediscovered: How Modern Science is Rewriting Their Story* (Thames & Hudson, London, 2013). On the broader question of the evolution of our species see Ian Tattersall *Masters of the Planet: The Search for Human Origins* (Palgrave Macmillan, 2012), Kim Sterelny *The Evolved Apprentice: How Evolution Made Humans Unique* (Bradford Books, MIT Press, Cambridge and London, 2012) and Clive Finlayson *The Improbable Primate: How Water Shaped Human Evolution* (Oxford University Press, 2014). By water here, Finlayson chiefly means rain and the patterns of changing rainfall coincident with cycles of climate change throughout the last million years and more, especially over the past half million years.

62.   Steve Mithen *The Singing Neanderthals: The Origins of Music, Language, Mind and Body* (Weidenfeld and Nicolson, London, 2005), p. vii.

63.   Daniel Levitin *The World in Six Songs: How the Musical Brain Created Human Nature* (Dutton, New York, 2008)

68

The saxophone and a new piety: As Steven Cottrell remarks:

> The saxophone was developed to address specific problems that Adolphe Sax had identified among low wind instruments and his solution to these was made possible, in part, because of nineteenth century advances in engineering ... and through increased understanding of acoustics and the musical possibilities such understanding afforded. From its inception, therefore, the instrument has been identified with modernity, innovation and a sense of exploration and enquiry ... [64]

But what was it like, long ago, to *commence* this process of musical innovation, exploration and enquiry, in the vast and untamed natural world in which our ancestors roamed?[65] Our *piety* should now include a felt sense of the immense antiquity, mystery and slow evolutionary development of *music*—and the way it has subtly reshaped our humanity. For it *has* done so.[66]

69

The evolution of love: The great French writer Stendhal wrote, some two hundred years ago, that 'in true love the soul envelops the body'. But how did what we call 'love' develop in reality, during the long aeons of our evolution? Like music, it has required endless refinement and reinvention with regard to the comprehension of and regard for the other, the rituals of courtship, the expression of and enactment of sexual desire; such that it generated intimacy as well as and even instead of simply generating progeny; much less mere 'possession'.

70

Retracing the evolutionary pathway: Just as our bodies, *in utero*, retrace the stages of our evolutionary past before morphologically becoming recognizably human and individuated, so our sexual and emotional behaviour requires development to become fully human. It remains all too prone to regression or psychological disarray, unless it is both disciplined

---

64.   Stephen Cottrell *The Saxophone* (Yale University Press, New Haven, 2012), p. 306.

65.   Gary Tomlinson and others have very recently broken new ground in this regard. His work, referred to above, *A Million Years of Music* (2015) takes the inquiry deeper than ever before and throws new light on the complex evolutionary origins of the human capacity for rhythm, syncopation and what he calls 'musicking' as distinct from 'speaking'—or for that matter 'singing'.

66.   Plato was very much concerned with music and devoted considerable discussion to it, especially in his late and severe treatise *The Laws*. He believed that music helped to form or deform character and public decorum and should be taught with some discrimination and considerable rigour, both to the guardians of his utopian polity and to its citizens, with different kinds of melodies being taught to men and women.

and cultivated. Music, song and ritual are clearly bound up with all this—and have been for the longest time. We need to deepen our grasp of this aspect of our humanity, if we are to become genuinely 'civilized', not merely in a few impressive individual cases, but generally—as contemporary humans.

71

The 'ancient world' was merely yesterday: We are overwhelmingly accustomed to thinking of the pre-classical world and the Neolithic, or even the classical world, as being 'long ago', as being 'ancient times'. But they were as yesterday! We simply have to readjust our sense of perspective to see that everything that has happened since the end of the last Ice Age is very *recent* in the actual history of our species. In fact, *our* species is very recent in the evolutionary history of humanity and only dates back a couple of Ice Ages (perhaps to 200,000 years ago). Throughout our authentic past, as distinct from our muddled folkloric memory of it, immensely significant developments in our genetic form and cognitive abilities occurred over *millions* of years.

72

The flaming chariot of innovation: Then suddenly, a mere five to seven thousand years ago, things began to *accelerate*. Innovation became cumulatively faster and faster in culture, in technology, in weapons, in strategies and what had been a deep, if uncanny presence in the world became—with the invention of the wheel and war chariots, metals and arms in Eurasia—more and more akin to Phaeton's wild ride in the chariot of the Sun, in the Greek legend, which ended in a fiery crash.[67] That's where we now stand: having to gain greater

---

67.   According to *Brewer's Dictionary of Phrase and Fable* (Centenary Edition, revised by Ivor H. Evans, Cassell, London, 1970): in classical myth, Phaeton, the son of Phoebus (the Sun) undertook to drive his father's chariot and was upset, so that he lost control of the chariot and crashed to earth ruinously; thereby causing Libya to be parched into barren sands, and all Africa to be more or less injured, the inhabitants blackened and vegetation nearly destroyed. His fall would have set the world itself on fire had not Zeus transfixed Phaeton with a thunderbolt. (p. 826). Centuries after the myth arose in Greece, it became conflated with the myth of the fall of Lucifer the archangel, after his rebellion against God, remarked Jean Seznec, in *The Survival of the Pagan Gods: The Mythological Tradition and its Place in Renaissance Humanism and Art* (Bollingen, Princeton University Press, 1972), p. 93.

Of course the myth of Lucifer itself had deep roots. The name was originally that of the morning star, Venus. It was then taken up by Isaiah and applied to the King of Babylon—'How art thou fallen from heaven, O Lucifer, son of the morning'. St Jerome, centuries after Isaiah, then picked

steering control over the speeding chariot in which we find ourselves rushing towards an unknown future. The momentum is overwhelming and there is no way to get off the chariot now, because we have made the whole Earth our chariot. We must steer well—or we may crash in fiery ruin, very much as in the Grecian fable.

---

the name up as an epithet for Satan, the Great Enemy and Evil One. Thereafter, poets took as read that Lucifer had been the name of Satan before he fell and was cast out of heaven. In Book Ten of *Paradise Lost*, Milton makes the borrowing explicit: 'Of Lucifer so by allusion called of that bright star to Satan paragoned'. Such are the modes of mythic and poetic transmission and invention—by allusion.

The contrast, on the other hand, between the Phaeton fable and what we now know regarding the nature of desertification and the evolution of human beings in Africa, skin pigmentation and patterns of vegetation is a perfect illustration of the immense advantages of science over confabulation in enhancing the understanding. Little by little, in patient and exacting work, we have reconstructed the climatic history of Africa, just as we mapped and surveyed it. Of course, to say 'we' here is a gross liberty. The undertaking was that of very small numbers of scientists and surveyors, to begin with under the auspices of the British and French empires. Yet the vividness of myth and fable has long ensured its durability. A revitalized cosmopolitan civilization will need to take this into account in shaping stories that are taught to the young and the credulous.

How could you think that a Latin sword ... ?

5
Circles in the Dust

You went under the wheel, Archimedes;
Pondering spheres and a theory of gravity;
Absorbed in the beauties of geometry;
Drawing fine circles in the dust.

Did you forget yourself, old man?
How could you think that a Latin sword,
Fired with rage at your machines
Would be withheld from your circles?

Or had you given up on the City,
Now swarming with the legions of Marcellus?
Had you given yourself over to pure thought –
Drawing those perfect circles in the dust?

You'd made mockery of Rome's big ships
And elaborately prepared siege engines:
With your artillery and hydraulic tricks,
You used its vessels to ladle the sea into your wine-cups.

You transcended the factions of Syracuse;
In the chaos of the Punic War;
Your mind was elsewhere, deep thinker;
Divining the workings of the real world.

Had you high hopes of Alexandria at that point:
Remembering conversations with Ctesibius,
Knowing the catalogues of Callimachus;
Reckoning with Aristarchus regarding the Sun?

You went under the wheel, Archimedes;
Pondering spheres and a theory of gravity;
Absorbed in the beauties of geometry;
Drawing fine circles in the dust.

73

The original downfall of science: Science, as we understand the term today; and as it has been broadly understood since the time of Galileo and Newton, began not in the 17th century, but in the 3rd century BCE.[68] It lasted roughly one hundred and fifty years, from Euclid (around 300 BCE) to the expulsion from Alexandria of the Greek intellectuals by Ptolemy VIII (145 BCE).[69] After that it stagnated for several centuries and then went into decline in the late classical era, not recovering its vitality until the late Renaissance. Given the dangers in

---

68.   Lucio Russo's *The Forgotten Revolution: How Science was Born in 300 BC and Why it had to be Reborn* (Springer, New York, 2004) is indispensable in understanding all this. His historical thesis, richly developed in a book which runs to over 400 pages, rests on three primary claims:

–   *the method that we have called 'scientific' was not fully present in the ancient empires, nor yet in fifth century (BCE) Greece, or in the works of Plato and Aristotle;*

–   *The boom in scientific theories took place during the third century (BCE) and was an essential feature of Hellenistic civilization;*

–   *If one must identify a turning point in the process of formation of the new method, the best candidate seems to be the foundation of Alexander's empire.*

He points out that this has been almost entirely overlooked by scientists and historians alike and this has grossly distorted our understanding of the history of science:

Usually the comparison between modern and ancient scientific thought is established primarily in terms of modern physics and the ideas of the Greeks, most often presented as a conceptual evolution that, starting with the Ionian school, seems to essentially end with Aristotle ... Even a scientist of vast learning like Heisenberg, in sketching a comparison between Greek thought and modern physics, after having dwelt at length on pre-Socratic thinkers (with interesting things to say) jumps from Aristotle to modern science, without devoting a single word to the development of ancient exact science, which took place chiefly after Euclid. (p. 22)

Though Russo does not mention him, the same can be said regarding the great philosopher of science Karl Popper, whose last book, published posthumously, dwelt on the pre-Socratics as the pioneers of 'conjectures and refutations' and ignored the great Hellenistic scientists of the 3rd century BCE.

69.   Russo makes precisely this point:

Starting with the year 212 (BCE), which witnessed the plunder of Syracuse and the killing of Archimedes, Hellenistic centres were defeated and conquered by the Romans. During the second century (BCE) scientific studies declined rapidly. Alexandria's scientific activity, in particular, stopped abruptly in 145-144 (BCE), when Ptolemy VIII (Euergetes II), who had just ascended the throne, initiated a policy of brutal persecution against the city's Greek ruling class. (p. 11)

Yet the history of this whole century has been all but eliminated from Western cultural memory.

our world, this is vital to understand: science and true understanding began once and were aborted. It could happen again.

74

We, too, could regress scientifically: We don't learn about this first scientific era, even in our studies of history or of science. We are given, at best, a vague and largely condescending nod to the Pre-Socratics and to Plato and Aristotle as pre-scientific thinkers, while the Hellenistic epoch is all but erased from the record. This has to be rectified. Its significance is that science as we know it began once before and then was abandoned. We may have advanced far beyond where the Hellenes got to, but we should not assume that scientific civilization can never regress to superstition, ideological narrowness and theological conservatism. The Hellenistic epoch is, from this point of view, crucial to our self-understanding and ought to be a core part of our humanistic curriculum in the 21st century.

75

A greater scientist than Aristotle: Archimedes (287-212 BCE) lived a century after Aristotle (who died in 322 BCE) and was killed by a Roman soldier during the sack of Syracuse, at the height of the Second Punic War (218-202 BCE). He lived through the middle period or golden age of Hellenistic science and was one of its most notable practitioners. Whereas Aristotle was a 'natural philosopher', Archimedes was a scientist as we would recognize that term in the modern world—one given to theory and experiment, leading to engineering and invention.[70] His death marks the collision between the nascent scientific culture of

---

70.   Armand Marie Leroi, in a fine recent book, *The Lagoon: How Aristotle Invented Science* (Bloomsbury Circus, London, 2014) has attributed the invention of science to Aristotle himself and less because of his treatises on analytics and logic, metaphysics and physics than because of his work in the area of biology. The book centres overwhelmingly on his time on the island of Lesbos and his interest in marine biology. In a moving passage at the end of his book, Leroi remarks:

> *Of the whole vast natural world, the Academy deemed only the stars worthy of study. But, and this is Aristotle's point, we do not live among the stars; we live here, on Earth. Nor do we live just anywhere on Earth ... Lesbos and the lagoon at Pyrrha gave to Aristotle a place, calm and lovely, where he could be among natural things. Lesbos was for him what Chimborazo was for Humboldt, the Malay archipelago for Wallace, the Amazon for Bates, and a Berkshire wood for Hamilton. It was what the Atlantic rainforest of Brazil, the bleak pampas of Patagonia, the black volcanic rocks of the Galapagos and a field in Kent were for Darwin. Biologists often have such places. They need them, for ideas do not come from nothing, they come from nature herself.* (p. 376).

the Greek world and the pre-scientific, pragmatic culture of the Roman world. It is iconic of the death of ancient science.

76

Pre-scientific Romans: Over a period of almost 200 years, ending with the seizure of Alexandria in 30 BCE, the Romans conquered and plundered the Greek world. In doing so, they unwittingly all but obliterated the institutional and cultural underpinnings of Greek science. They admired the products of Greek culture, but they had no appreciation of theory or experiment and neglected the greatest works of Greek thinking. Even the most learned Romans, such as Varro and Vitruvius, exhibited no understanding of theory. It has been wryly remarked that the closest any Roman came to serious mathematics was the soldier who killed Archimedes. This is the root of the poem 'Circles in the Dust': the fate of Archimedes and its significance.

77

The scientists vs the philosopher: Aristotle's erroneous idea that the Earth is the centre of the universe, that all heavy objects are drawn towards its centre and that light objects naturally move up and away from that centre, was refuted by Archimedes, who developed a theory of sphericity and gravity in the late 3rd century BCE. Yet it was Aristotle's *errors*, not the great insights of Archimedes, which were to become the received wisdom and supposed truth throughout late antiquity and the Middle Ages. For centuries, before the 17th century breakthroughs in physics and astronomy, Aristotle was touted as 'the master of those who know'. Why? To understand why, we must see this problem in the context of many others. To begin with, we have to rediscover the lost history of the Hellenistic era. It should be central to our education.

There is, however, no mention in Leroi of the experiments and accomplishments of the Hellenistic scientists or the relationship methodologically between their diverse work and Aristotle's biology. He should, at the very least, have reflected on the work of Euclid not only in geometry, for which he is best known, but in optics; since Euclid's thought formed a bridge between the Platonist preoccupations with mathematics, geometry and the stars, on the one hand, and Hellenistic science's work in mechanics, urban design, geodesy, physiology, astronomy, physics and the whole conceptual art of scientific method. Above all, he failed to make mention of the contrast between Aristotle's erroneous ideas about the cosmos and the Hellenistic conjecture that the Earth revolved around the Sun and that the cosmos was infinite and not centred on the Earth at all. All this and very much more is addressed by Lucio Russo in *The Forgotten Revolution*, published a decade or more before *The Lagoon*. Yet Leroi entirely overlooked Russo's work—and, with it, that of the Hellenes.

78

The Sun, the human body and intuition: Aristarchus (310-230 BCE) had postulated that the Earth revolved around the Sun, not the Sun around the Earth; and had also correctly estimated the relative distances from the Sun of the other planets. Yet his theory, like the work of Archimedes and many others, went under the wheel for almost two millennia. Herophilus (335-280 BCE) had initiated a true science of anatomy and physiology, based on dissection and careful mapping of the brain, the eye, the circulatory and nervous systems and the reproductive organs. Yet his work, too, was halted and neglected, not to be resumed until the work of Harvey and Vesalius in the 16ᵗʰ and 17ᵗʰ centuries. Aristotle's ideas conformed with intuitive notions. Science was hard and counter-intuitive. It required intellectual discipline and a culture of inquiry which largely ceased to exist from about the end of the second century BCE. Even now, the hold of discipline and culture are tenuous.

79

An erasure of scientific knowledge: In his masterful and neglected work *The Forgotten Revolution*, Lucio Russo remarks:

> there remains no sustained historical account of the period between 301 BCE ... and 221 BCE ... Not only do we have no historical works dating from the Hellenistic period, but even the subsequent work of Livy is missing its second ten books, which contained the period from 292 to 219 BCE. The tradition preserved the history of classical Greece and that of the rise of Rome—the periods that remained cultural reference points in the late Empire and in the Middle Ages, whereas the history of the century of scientific revolution was forgotten with the return of civilization to a prescientific stage.[71]

As he added, 'almost all writings of the time have been lost.[72] The civilization that handed

---

71. Russo (2004), p. 7. The likelihood that Livy would have covered the work of the scientists, it must be said, is low. Livy was a 'captains and kings' kind of historian and would, based on the surviving portions of his history of Rome, have concentrated on the speeches and battles involved in Rome's wars in the West, rather than on the important thinking that was going on in the Hellenistic East at that time. Even his account of battles was notoriously uninformed and characterized more by dramatic rhetoric than military science.

72. Russo points out that among these losses were much of the work of Euclid and crucially his predecessors in laying the foundations for geometry. Of Euclid himself, he remarks, we know nothing, though we have biographies of countless lesser figures. Such is the selection process in cultural history. David Berlinski, a philosopher of mathematics, has written a delightful little book about Euclid—*The King of Infinite Space: Euclid and His Elements* (Basic

down to us, among so many intellectual achievements, the very idea of libraries and of the zealous preservation of the thinking of the past, was erased together with its works. We have a few scientific works transmitted through Byzantium and the Arabs, but Europe preserved none.' We have almost nothing of the work of Chrysippus (279-206 BCE), considered to have been the greatest thinker of his age. We have nothing at all of the work of Strato of Lampsacus (335-269 BCE), who may have originated natural science in the true sense of the term. The killing of Archimedes stands for all this loss and what it signifies even now regarding the vulnerability of scientific culture in a turbulent and irrational world.[73] How could *you* think that a Latin sword ...

Books, New York, 2013). His closing tribute to Euclid might be offered up to the Hellenistic scientists more generally, but Euclid was one of their founding figures:

> *The slow and painful undertaking by which the theorems of Euclidean geometry are derived from its axioms is an unfolding. The world of the senses recedes. The mind expands. A complex new figure emerges in thought, one expressing the relationship between the axioms of a system, its theorems and its illustrations. The relationship cannot be seen at once: it must be understood. It is not immediate; it must be acquired. An axiomatic system is like the sonata or the nineteenth century novel. Where the listener first hears a succession of melodies, the mathematician hears a theme and its development. A sense of coherence must be earned. It cannot be granted. And it does not come easy.* (pp. 149-50)

There is a famous story (which Berlinski inevitably recounts) to the effect that when asked by the Hellenistic king of Egypt, Ptolemy Soter, was there not an easier way to learn geometry, Euclid responded: 'There is no royal road to geometry'. As Berlinski magisterially comments: 'No work, nothing gained; no work, nothing learned; no work, nothing. This, too, is a part of the Euclidean tradition, its moral urgency.' (p. 58). The same may be said—and should be imported into our general culture—with regard to Hellenistic science as a whole and, by deduction, or derivation, the mastery that the modern sciences have begun to give us—to the extent that we do the necessary work.

73.   To these two reasons, Russo added two others: the lack of systematic excavation of the centres of Ptolemaic Egypt, which was clearly a centre of learning from around 300 BCE, when Ptolemy I founded the Library and Museum of Alexandria, with its famous collection of the knowledge of the known world; and our virtually complete ignorance of the Hellenistic states *other* than Egypt. He comments specifically:

> *Our lack of information about the Seleucid kingdom, which included Mesopotamia, is particularly jarring, because there are several indications that its contribution to scientific development may have been comparable to Ptolemaic Egypt's.* (pp. 8-9)

This is not, he adds, only a matter of complete loss of the relevant materials, but of the scandalous neglect of even that which *has* survived.

80

A great library that vanished: The Library and Museum of Alexandria are legendary, but their history is fragmentary. There are some indications that the idea of the Library was derived from the private library that Aristotle had assembled in Athens before he died in 322 BCE.[74] The city of Alexandria had been founded in 331 BCE by Alexander the Great himself, but it was his general Ptolemy who built it, within a generation, into the largest and most prosperous city in the Mediterranean, rivalling Carthage and, for two hundred years, far outstripping Rome. As for the Library, it was said to contain half a million books—a modest collection by the standards of our era, but unprecedented in the ancient world. One must assume that all the books whose loss we only now lament will have been in that collection by the late 3rd century BCE (the death of Archimedes). There was also, by then, a great catalogue of the collection, prepared by Callimachus (310-240 BCE), itself 120 volumes in length; but it has vanished, also; along with the overwhelming bulk of the books that once existed in that fabulous library.

81

Alexandria—petri-dish of science: Callimachus, having catalogued the collection, was able to draw upon it in writing his numerous erudite literary works. Eratosthenes, the curator of the Library and Museum in the second quarter of the third century BCE, performed prodigies of scholarship there; among them the correct calculation, based on experiment and sound mathematics, of the circumference of the Earth to within about 200 km. The crucial function of the Library and Museum complex, however, was the magnetic attraction it exerted on pioneering thinkers in a variety of fields. It was not the mere *bulk* of books that existed there, but their cumulative cross-fertilization: the inter-disciplinary and scientific thinking that took place there—until it was curtailed in the mid-second century BCE. That is the true lost treasure of Alexandria.

---

74.   The geographer Strabo, writing in the age of Augustus, some three hundred years after the time of Aristotle and Ptolemy, stated that Aristotle was 'the first to have put together a collection of books' and 'taught the kings in Egypt how to arrange a library.' In reality, Aristotle died almost two decades before Ptolemy took over Egypt and well before he created the Library there. However, Demetrius Phalareus, the governor of Athens until 317 BCE, was familiar with Aristotle's library and it may have been he who, having fled to Alexandria in 317, introduced the idea of the Library to Ptolemy. On the history of the Library, see Lionel Casson *Libraries in the Ancient World* (Yale University Press, New Haven and London, 2001), Ch 3 'The Library of Alexandria' and Luciano Canfora *The Vanished Library* (Vintage, 1991).

82

Three Hellenistic scientists and the Sun: Few scientific theories are more iconic of the breakthrough to modernity than Copernicus's heliocentric theory of the cosmos, in the 16th century. Yet such a theory was developed in the early 3rd century BCE by Aristarchus of Samos. It is widely claimed that his theory was disavowed by his contemporaries very quickly, but this seems to be untrue. Rather, it endured as long as scientific Hellenistic culture, well into the 2nd century BCE. Archimedes is said to have built a planetarium modelled on the heliocentric theory. There are, in fact, grounds for believing that both the heliocentric theory and the concept that the Earth itself moves, rotating on its axis, were common to the Hellenistic scientists.

83

A lost proof of heliocentrism: According to an obscure passage in Plutarch, who wrote about three hundred years later, the 2nd century BCE astronomer Seleucus of Babylon actually 'proved' the heliocentric theory.[75] It was only as science ground to a halt that the retrograde doctrines of Aristotle—that the Sun revolves around a stationary Earth, as do the planets and the 'fixed stars'—took hold and was then elaborated in the work of the 2nd century CE astronomer Claudius Ptolemy. This is an index of what we lost with the abortion of ancient science. We lost an intellectual culture that was getting beyond metaphysical and vague naturalistic speculation to theory, experiment and demonstration. It was reaching out to actually map the cosmos.

84

Likewise with medicine: Roy Porter titled his two major works on the history of medicine *The Greatest Benefit to Mankind* and *Flesh in the Age of Reason*.[76] Both benefit and reason can be discerned in Hellenistic anatomy and physiology, with the dissection and close understanding of the human body. The key figures are Praxagoras, Herophilus and Erasistratus. Herophilus (335-260 BCE) is the stand out figure and should, far more than Hippocrates, be known as

---

75.　Russo (2004). p. 311. He goes on to remark:

　　Ptolemy not only did not use gravity (or any other dynamical idea) in astronomy; he also
　　approached the Earth's sphericity in a purely geometric and descriptive way, seemingly
　　unaware of the explanation for it that was well known in Hellenistic times. (p. 318)

76.　Roy Porter *The Greatest Benefit to Mankind: A Medical History of Humanity from Antiquity to the Present* (Harper Collins, 1997) and *Flesh in the Age of Reason* (Allen Land 2003).

the 'Father of Western medicine'.[77] He wrote a treatise on the eye, which has been lost. He concluded, moreover, that the brain was the seat of intelligence, whereas Aristotle had had the erroneous notion that the brain was simply an organ for cooling the blood.

85

The erasure of physiology: Herophilus also described the heart's cavities and valves and accepted the distinction of his teacher Praxagoras between veins and arteries. He made significant contributions to respiratory and reproductive anatomy, discovering the ovaries and the Fallopian tubes, as well as providing an accurate description of the sperm ducts. He was also the first physician to describe the symptoms of mental illness. Yet his work was abandoned and lost in late antiquity and throughout the Middle Ages. Galen, in Roman times, so often described as the doyen of classical masters of medicine, made no discoveries or innovations that can be compared to those by the Hellenes before him. What an erasure! What cultural amnesia!

---

77. The only study of Herophilus specifically of which I am aware is Heinrich von Staden *Herophilus: The Art of Medicine in Early Alexandria* (Cambridge University Press, 1989), but it is Russo who places Herophilus in the context in which he truly belongs: that of Hellenistic science and its erasure, both in the ancient world and in modern memory. He draws attention, for example, to 'the unity of Hellenistic culture, which has never been recovered since' (p. 146), in which the discoveries of thinkers in different fields began to lend not only technical support to the endeavours of others, but suggested to them, by analogy and insight, further lines of investigation in their own work.

And then, above my fevered form, there swept

6
The Dream

Shadows, gloom, a red and white veined dark;
Muffled voices, murmurings, running, fear;
Horses gallop on a sunless plain; stark
Clash of angers; then—ah! ah!—the spear!

A wounded leg, a pallet and a chill;
Fevered tossing, winter heart and hut;
Lamed and lingering, flickering hope and will;
The limb and life-force fester quickly. Cut

To memories of a settled hearthside scene:
The eye, by fire, enlivening the hand
To carve from unknown bone a figurine –
A likeness hoped and longed for more than planned

And then, above my fevered form, there swept
The kiss, the breast, the eyes—but—glassy stone;
Mute, I watched agape as those eyes wept,
For I was gone. The kiss stood there alone

Thought, sharper than spear thrust; start –
Dream died and woke a succoured heart.

86

Erasure, amnesia and the awakening of 'memory': The erasure of Hellenistic science and its achievements may be the single most poignant case of erasure in the long history of the species, given its implications. Yet erasure and amnesia have been the fate of so *many* species, so *many* peoples and so *much* of civilization over the fifteen millennia since the end of the last Ice Age. 'Memory' of what came before has only, with any reliability, been painstakingly reconstructed by our archaeological sciences in the very recent past. Little by little, we have exhumed the fossil record, also, and rediscovered the countless species and genera of flora and fauna that inhabited the Earth long before us and had been erased by time and natural catastrophe. It is a grand paradox that this is happening amidst the present 'sixth extinction.'[78]

87

Even our personal genealogies: This is all very recent and very hard won knowledge. But there are, also, our own personal genealogies and fates. For the overwhelming majority of us, the genealogical line of our forebears dips into darkness once we go back a mere three or four generations.[79] Even of what we can see, there is little that is clear or detailed. Memories and

---

78.   The 'sixth extinction' is a term used recently to refer to the obliteration of other species by the rampant growth in human numbers and the overwhelming human dominance of and consumption of everything on offer within the biosphere. This dominance dates back many millennia, but has come to a crescendo in our time. See Richard Leakey and Roger Lewin *The Sixth Extinction: Biodiversity and its Survival* (Weidenfeld and Nicolson, London, 1996) and Elizabeth Kolbert *The Sixth Extinction: An Unnatural History* (Bloomsbury, London, 2014). It is called the *sixth* because we have, in very recent times, discovered that, over the past five hundred million years, there have been five previous mass extinctions, each of which has drastically reshaped the ecology of life on Earth.

The most radical of these was 250 million years ago, at the end of the Permian. See Douglas H. Erwin *Extinction: How Life on Earth Nearly Ended 250 Million Years Ago* (Princeton University Press, 2006). More generally, it has only been in the past two centuries, but especially in the past half century, that the earth sciences have begun to really open up reality before the eyes of those of us paying attention. See James Lawrence Powell *Four Revolutions in the Earth Sciences: From Heresy to Truth* (Columbia University Press, New York, 2015). The four revolutions to which he refers have been the discovery of deep geological time, the discovery of continental drift and plate tectonics, the discovery of meteorite impacts and their significance; and, finally, the realization that human material activity in the biosphere, especially the massive emission of industrial gases into the atmosphere, is having ominous consequences, such as global warming.

79.   There are, of course, exceptions. A notable illustration of lineage is Ranulph Fiennes *Agincourt: My Family, the Battle and the Fight for France* (Hodder & Stoughton, London, 2014). Fiennes is

records are fragmentary and vague. Crowning all this is the fact of our own personal mortality and the swift passing of our years, to be followed inexorably by debility, death and oblivion. We are, existentially, 'thrown' toward death and oblivion from the moment we become fully conscious that we are alive. All our questions about meaning and truth arise in that context.

88

Now we know of the Younger Dryas: The 'last'—which is to say the most recent—Ice Age finished some 15,000 years ago. The ice sheets began to melt and warmer, wetter weather than any seen in tens of thousands of years came to the part of the world we call the Fertile Crescent. For two thousand years sedentary, proto-agrarian life began in villages scattered across that wide zone from the Nile, via the Jordan Valley to the Tigris. Trade, handicrafts and elaborate burial rites for village chieftains became customary. Then came the Younger Dryas: suddenly, the climate flipped back into Ice Age temperatures *within a decade*. The consequence was a thousand years of cold, dry conditions, aborting the quasi-settled life and throwing our ancestors back into hunting and gathering. It was the most recent in a long pattern of such flips—all news to us!

89

So recent and tenuous: That millennium long drought ended with an abrupt flip back to warm and wet conditions roughly 12,000 years ago.[80] Villages sprang up again and the seeds of agriculture

---

able to trace his direct ancestry back to Charles Martel, the Frankish King who, in the early eighth century CE defeated the invading Moors at Tours (732 CE) and so checked the advance of Islam in Western Europe. He had four male ancestors who fought on the English side at the famous battle of Agincourt, in 1415, six hundred years ago now and seven hundred years after the time of Charles Martel. He also had four males ancestors fighting on the French side in that same battle. His fabulous story is not unique. Other aristocratic lineages have such stories to tell. But the thing to understand here is that our new discoveries have made it possible for us each and all to comprehend the past as one of lineage and to find added value in the reconstruction not only of the immediate past of our families, but of the deep past of our species.

80. According to Steven Mithen, at 9600 BCE (some 11,600 years ago), global temperatures rose by 7 degrees C in less than a decade. *After the Ice: A Global Human History 20,000-5,000 BC* (Weidenfeld & Nicolson, London, 2003), p. 54. This is a phenomenal increase, dwarfing even the most alarmist climate scenarios advanced in our time, which predict a 4C rise over the next century, if nothing is done to curtail our prodigal generation of greenhouse gases through the use of fossil fuels. The consequence in the tenth millennium BCE of that 7C rise in temperatures was not a global catastrophe, but a new period of abundance and human flourishing—the beginning of what we now know as the Holocene. It was to be a further six thousand years before the invention

were planted. Yet all of this had been forgotten utterly until our archaeologists unearthed it and dated it over just the past twenty years. Our knowledge of our own history is, in other words, very recent. It is similar in character to the beginnings of science in the Hellenistic epoch and as little appreciated by the mass of 21ˢᵗ century people. Currently, that precious knowledge is no better established within our general culture than was the heliocentric theory of the cosmos in Hellenistic and Roman culture, in the 2ⁿᵈ century BCE. We need to entrench it.

90

The truth about Jericho: In the sixth chapter of the Book of Joshua it is recounted that the Hebrews laid siege to Jericho, blew their trumpets as they marched around its walls and the walls came tumbling down. In the tenth chapter of the Book of Joshua, we are told that the Sun and the Moon stood still a whole day. Neither statement is true. Jericho was founded in the tenth millennium BCE, but at the time of the supposed conquest of Canaan by Joshua, it did not exist; it was in ruins and abandoned.[81] As for the Sun and Moon standing still, it was this very passage that Galileo brought before the Roman Inquisition as evidence that the Bible could not be used as a source of information about the natural world.[82] The cardinals recoiled, but Galileo was right.

---

of writing, but from the end of the Younger Dryas until now there has been no turning back the tide of human cultural evolution and the conquest of the biosphere, for better or worse, by our species. Nor has there been either a new Ice Age or a recurrence of the kind of climate flip-flop that created the Younger Dryas.

81.   Robert Alter's new translation of the books of Joshua, Judges, Samuel and Kings—*Ancient Israel* (W. W. Norton & Co., New York and London, 2013)—is a remarkable offering and invaluable for its linguistic and historical commentaries. He notes:

> *... the extensive archaeological exploration of Jericho indicates that its conquest by Joshua could not have taken place. There was a very old town on this site, but it was destroyed by the Middle Bronze Age and at the putative time of Joshua's conquest, in the Late Bronze Age, toward the end of the thirteenth century BCE, there had been no walled town on this site for at least a couple of centuries. The writer [of the Book of Joshua] no doubt had in mind Jericho's antiquity—it is one of the oldest cities in the world—and its role as eastern gateway to Canaan, but historically it could not have been an object of Joshua's conquest.* (p. 33 n20)

The writer of the Book of Joshua was at work many centuries later, when Jericho was again a flourishing town, and, being ignorant of the archaeology of the site, invented a tale of Hebrew siege and conquest.

82.   The matter of Galileo and the interpretation by the Catholic Church of Joshua 10: 12-14 is ably covered by J. L. Heilbron in *Galileo* (Oxford University Press, 2010), chapter 6 'Miscalculated Risks', pp. 200-212. The presumption of the inerrancy of the Bible as 'holy scripture' was the problem. Galileo took the plausible line that what had been written more than two thousand

91

We are probing at the foundations: It was the excavations in the 1950s by Kathleen Kenyon that first brought to light the immense antiquity of Jericho. For a while it was believed to be the oldest urban settlement anywhere in the world. By 9,000 BCE, it was a walled town with perhaps a thousand inhabitants, having a wall some ten feet high and a tower 25 feet high with an internal staircase of twenty two steps leading to its summit. As Steven Mithen remarks, 'Such architecture was completely unprecedented in human history.' Yet, until the second half of the 20th century, all this had long since been forgotten. It is emblematic of how very recently and tenuously we have recovered our human past from oblivion. There is a great deal of work still to be done.

92

We embody our non-mythological past: 'When you look in the mirror,' wrote David Anthony, in *The Horse, the Wheel and Language*, just a few years ago:

> you see not just your face but a museum ... We carry the past around with us all the time, and not just in our bodies. It lives also in our customs, including the way we speak. The past is a set of invisible lenses we wear constantly and, through these, we perceive the world and the world perceives us. We stand always on the shoulders of our ancestors, whether or not we look down to acknowledge them. [83]

His principal concern was to pull together the many lines of inquiry which, especially

---

years before had, of necessity, 'accommodated its message to the limited capacities of an ignorant people.' It made no sense, he argued, to assume that the Bible provided an adequate account of natural history and the cosmos, when God had given us the senses, language, reason and scientific instruments with which to discern what was actually so in the natural world.

The Catholic censors, on the other hand, took doggedly to the line that Scripture could not be argued with and that it would hardly have described the Sun as standing still if the Sun did not ordinarily move. The Copernican theory, of course, held that the Sun was fixed and it was the Earth which moved. It is one of the wonders of Western civilization that this struggle over the supposed primacy of a book of 'holy writ' over the findings of reason and science lasted far beyond Galileo's time and encompassed, also, the whole exploration of biological and human evolution in the 19th and 20th centuries. Even now, there are 'creationists' and other religious believers who insist that their old fables trump evolutionary biology as explanations for how the world and life came to exist. They had their counterparts in the classical world which saw the abortion of Hellenistic science.

83.   David W. Anthony *The Horse, the Wheel and Language: How Bronze-Age Riders from the Eurasian Steppes Shaped the Modern World* (Princeton University Press, 2007) p. 3.

since the collapse of the Soviet Union, in 1991, had opened up the heartland of Eurasia to cosmopolitan scholarship and made possible an unprecedented understanding of the origins of the Indo-European languages and the material cultures that went with them thousands of years ago.

93

Beginning to recognize our great language families: Today, Anthony pointed out, at the beginning of the 21st century, more than three billion people speak Indo-European languages—more than speak the off-shoots of any other language family. And all those languages can be traced back to a language spoken in the steppes of southern Russia, north of the Black and Caspian Seas and at the foot of the Urals, some 5,000 to 6,000 years ago. *There* is ancestry![84] But how are we to 'look down' to acknowledge it? Doing so requires delving into a world of scholarship that is very intricate and so recent that few of us are aware of it. And this is only one piece of the puzzle. The other great language families—in Asia, in Africa, in the Americas—beckon us back even further into our common human ancestry. The whole science is both specialized and relatively speaking in its infancy. Our counterpart to the Library and Museum of Alexandria, in the 21st century should bring all of this together, cataloguing it for universal access. There is a dream for civilization! Can the world wide web fulfil such a dream in our time?

---

84.   The hunt for ethnic and linguistic ancestry has a complex and not always fortunate history in the modern world. Michael Kulikowski points out that, in the 18th, 19th and 20th centuries, Romanticism in Europe led to a search for the origins of the Germanic peoples as supposedly a pure 'race' existing prior to and struggling heroically against the oppression and ultimate decadence of the Greeks and Romans. He shows that the recovery of the *Germania*, by the classical Roman historian Tacitus, during the late 15th century and the uncritical acceptance of the Gothic history of the Byzantine historian Jordanes, written in the sixth century CE, seriously distorted both scholarly and popular understanding of German ancestry in the 19th century. This was especially so as Germany became a unified modern state. It fed fatefully into Nazi racial fantasies and ideology in the first half of the 20th century. See Kulikowski *Rome's Gothic Wars* (Cambridge University Press, 2007).

It is notable that both Tacitus and Jordanes drew upon longer, more detailed historical works, long since lost. Tacitus, as he acknowledged drew upon a twelve volume *History of the Germanic Wars* by Pliny the Elder; while Jordanes, as he also acknowledged, drew upon at least vague memories of a twelve volume history of the Goths written by Cassiodorus, who had been a close counsellor to King Theodoric the Ostrogoth, in Ravenna, in the early sixth century CE. Chiefly, however, as Kulikowski argues, it is only very recent scholarship that has slowly begun to peg back the deeply misleading fables of Jordanes and establish with greater clarity how and when the barbarian peoples federated and migrated in the Roman era.

94

Our languages are archaeological sites: 'The Sanskrit language, whatever be its antiquity, is of a wonderful structure' declared William Jones to the Asia Society of Bengal in 1786:

> more perfect than the Greek, more copious than the Latin and more exquisitely refined than either; yet bearing to both of them a stronger affinity, both in the roots of verbs and in the forms of grammar, than could possibly have been produced by accident; so strong indeed, that no philologer could examine them all three, without believing them to have sprung from some common source, which, perhaps, no longer exists.[85]

Little by little, in the very recent past, linguists have reconstructed that common source. It is known as Proto-Indo-European. It turns out that languages change over time according to identifiable rules of syntax and phonology. By putting these rules into reverse, we can recover the elements of an ancient grammar and vocabulary that takes us back thousands of years.[86]

95

Old words and decimal numbers: The numerals 1, 10, 100 and 1,000, for example, can be traced back linguistically in this manner; showing that the ancient Indo-Europeans used a decimal numbering system. Another set of words that has been reconstructed is that to do with wheels, wagons, axles and riding. The word 'wheel' emerges as a Proto-Indo-European word sounding something like '*kwekwelos*', whence the Greek *kyklos* from which we derive words like cyclical. For thousands of years after the Indo-Europeans tamed horses and made wains and war chariots on the steppes, long *cycles* of barbarian invasion and crises of civilization south of the Caspian and south of the Danube, or west of the Rhine, marked the course of European history; but also the histories of Central Asia, Iran and India and the dynastic history of China.[87] Properly understood, this is our common history—though separate from the histories of our

---

85.   Quoted in Anthony (2007) p. 7.

86.   The specific constellation of grammatical categories, structures, transformations and endings that characterize the Indo-European languages, David Anthony pointed out:

> *is not at all necessary or universal in human language. It is unique as a system and is found only in the Indo-European languages. The languages that share this grammatical system certainly are daughters of a single language from which that system was inherited.* (p. 37.)

87.   On the collision between China and the horsed nomads of the Eurasian and Mongolian steppes, see Nicola Di Cosmo *Ancient China and its Enemies: The Rise of Nomadic Power in East Asian History* (Cambridge University Press, 2002).

human kin in Africa, Oceania and the Americas, all of which were safe from those cycles of invasion.

96

Indo-Europeans—the centaurs of Eurasia: Proto-Indo-European did not spread into Europe, where it was to colonize the linguistic landscape right down to our own time, until after 4,000 BCE. By then, non-Indo-European farmers had been in Europe for two or three thousand years and it is estimated that they spoke hundreds of different languages—all long since vanished. Those farmers, coming it is thought out of Anatolia, had migrated into lands that had been the hunting grounds of yet older peoples for thousands of years, since the end of the Ice Age and in many cases, surely, long before that. But the farmers developed a material culture which has been dubbed that of 'Old Europe'. Then the 'centaurs' came: the men on horseback from the east.

97

The quest for the old goddesses: Marija Gimbutas and others have argued that this old culture was matriarchal and that it centred on a Goddess of Life, Death and Regeneration, not unlike the 'Triple-headed' White Goddess acclaimed by Robert Graves.[88] Both associated this goddess

---

88.   Robert Graves claimed that in Old Europe there were 'at first no male gods contemporary with the Goddess to challenge her prestige or power'; but that this changed when 'the revolutionary institution of fatherhood, imported into Europe from the East, brought with it the institution of individual marriage.' He went on to assert that a third stage in this line of development consisted in the abolition of the Goddess and goddesses in general altogether. This was the 'purely patriarchal' stage and was to be found in the monotheistic religions—the religions rooted in the Bible. *The White Goddess: A Historical Grammar of Poetic Myth*, first published in 1948. It was reissued by Faber & Faber in 1997. The citations are taken from the 1997 edition, pp. 378-80.

Marija Gimbutas took up this idea and sought to lend it greater historical and archaeological credibility. Her central focus was on what she described as:

> *... the persistence of the Goddess worship for more than 20,000 years, from the Palaeolithic to the Neolithic and beyond*

the culture to which this gave rise in 'Old Europe' (centring on Greece, the Aegean, the Balkans and southern Italy); and the way in which:

> *the increasing cultural momentum of European societies was ... cut short by the aggressive infiltration and settlement of semi-nomadic pastoralists, ancestors of the Indo-Europeans, who disturbed most of central and eastern Europe during the fourth millennium BCE.*

The Goddesses and Gods of Old Europe: Myths and Cult Images (Thames and Hudson, London, 1982) pp. 9-18.

with the Moon. Both argued that it was the Indo-European invaders who destroyed this ancient culture, replacing it with a patriarchal culture of war and conquest. The key to the advance of the Indo-Europeans was the mastery and riding of horses, which seems to have begun early in the fourth millennium BCE. Organized and sophisticated armies of horsemen would take a further two millennia to emerge, but the Indo-Europeans came out of the steppes—and swept across the steppes—on horseback and in horse-drawn wagons or chariots. So, too, did the old conquerors of ancient Iran and India—Indo-Europeans or 'Aryans' all of them.

98

A tale of grave goods and linguistic afterlives: The increased mobility that came with the taming of horses was accompanied, among the Proto-Indo-Europeans, by growing long distance trade, the rise of warrior leaders, the appearance of status goods in graves (especially copper and even gold ornaments) and escalating raiding and chronic warfare against settled agrarian communities in the lands to the west. But the story gradually unearthed and reconstructed by archaeologists is more complex than any mythic tale of Indo-Europeans sweeping into Old Europe would suggest. It is in the complex detail of shifting changes over many centuries that the beauty of the reconstruction is to be found. Our task is to master the complexities of the story and thus equip ourselves to understand our old myths and religions in a whole new light.

99

The European promontory and the goods of Asia: Old Europe collapsed early in the fourth millennium BCE and the peoples of the steppe turned their trade and attentions increasingly southeast to the urban civilizations of Anatolia and Mesopotamia, which existed beyond the rim of their known world—over the horizon, as it were. Grave goods began to feature luxuries from afar, such as gold covered clothing, gold and silver staffs and great quantities of bronze weapons.[89] Only in recent decades, after millennia of interment, have these been coming to light. Yet out on the little jutting out promontory of Asia that is Europe, as Friedrich Nietzsche once put it, henges in wood and stone began to be built and the early religions of our specifically European ancestors began to take root during these same millennia—the era of the Druids.

100

All this is our common heritage: Our longing to understand and to recover our collective memories now works back across that rim and lost horizon from the centres of urban civilization into the steppe; literally into the graves of the primeval past. Through exiguous

---

89.   Anthony (2007) p. 263.

buried fragments of material culture, the ceremonially interred bones of old chieftains and primitive kings and the traces of language that have wended their way across six millennia, we are recovering a wider and deeper sense of our common humanity—and of the stages of evolution which went before our own era of hectic innovation and scientific warfare. Little by little, also, this is being woven into an informed understanding of the other linguistic and ethnic branches of humanity, by then already widely dispersed across Africa, Oceania and the Americas.

Above all, do not vanish somewhere ...

7
Lara

Is it you who stands over the table of my years,
Flanked by masses of white lilac, cyclamen and cineraria?

Is it you who stands out for her casual beauty,
Among a crowd drawn dimly by my poetry and science?

Is it you whose presence fills the unceremonied silence,
In which only the flowers stand for singing and for psalms?

You are conversing with my brother, the watcher,
Learning of the long, coincidental meanings of our lives.

Ah! You exclaim in wonder at that late learning:
Is that really true? How astounding! How foreordained!

But have you guessed how my candle burned –
How my candle burned on the table of our winter's night?

Kiss me with that last kiss prescribed in the ritual!
Kiss me amid the white lilac, the cyclamen and cineraria!

Lean over me, shielding me with your whole being:
With your head, your breast, your heart, your loving hands.

Feel what a love ours was: how free, how pure,
How true to song and void of mere passionate necessity.

It transcended all around us in soaring scope:
Trees, clouds, sky, crowded streets—the wide world.

We made everything high and ravishing our own:
The open horizon, the myriad forms of beauty, the very Sun.

Cry freely now—abundantly—for the riddle of life;
The riddle of death, the beauty of genius, the winter of love;

But don't stand over me unable to live, in pitiful misery,
Thinking you can't go on, with your hair standing on end.

Above all, do not vanish somewhere, forgotten as
A nameless number on a list that has been mislaid.

This I want for you after flowers and psalms:
A long life, rounded with the joy that I have been yours.

101

Blow upon the candle: There is a passage towards the end of Ivan Turgenev's novel *Fathers and Sons* (1861), in which he describes the death of Yevgeny Bazarov. The woman Bazarov loves comes to his bedside as he lies stricken. He says to her:

> Ah, Anna Sergeyevna, let us speak the truth. It's all over with me. I've fallen under the wheel ... Death is an old jest, but it comes new to everyone ... Well, I must say my farewell! Live long, that's best of all, and make the most of it while there's time. Farewell. Listen, you know I never kissed you then ... Breathe on the dying flame and let it go out ...

She touches his forehead with her lips. 'Enough!' he murmurs and sinks back on his pillow, saying 'Now, darkness ... '. It is one of the most poignant death scenes in our literature; one that etches itself on the memory—Bazarov as the sputtering candle.

102

Conceiving the figure of Zhivago: In *Doctor Zhivago*, Boris Pasternak's description of the death of Yuri Zhivago—and the last reflections by Larissa Guichard (Lara) over his body—build a kind of literary cairn over Turgenev's description of the death of Bazarov, a century earlier. Between the publication of *Fathers and Sons* and that of *Doctor Zhivago* had come the First World War, the Russian Revolution and Civil War, the Red Terror of Lenin, the forced collectivization and terrible famine under Stalin, Stalin's Great Terror and the mushrooming of the Communist GULAG, the Second World War and the beginnings of the nuclear arms race. The amount of killing and suffering that had happened in Russia in that century was colossal. The figure of Zhivago—doctor of medicine and poet, natural philosopher and humanist—was conceived by Pasternak in opposition to all that tyranny and slaughter. He brings this to completion with his rendering of Lara's reflections on the aspirations that had given meaning to her life and that of the poet of life, love and science, Yuri Zhivago; even as Zhivago, like Bazarov and Archimedes, went 'under the wheel'. Unlike Bazarov's, Zhivago's death—under conditions of poverty and abandonment—*defied* darkness, rather than lapsing into it.

103

A garden strewn with blossom: When Pasternak died, in 1960, the Soviet press barely reported his passing; even though it was headline news all around the world, where

Doctor Zhivago was being read by great numbers of people.[90] His funeral took place at the beginning of summer. The apple and lilac trees in his garden, we are told, were a riot of pink, white and purple blossom, while the ground was covered with wildflowers. The funeral of Zhivago in David Lean's famous film of the novel pales by comparison. People came by their hundreds—even thousands by some accounts—and filled to overflowing the garden of Pasternak's dacha at Peredelkino.[91] His coffin was banked with wildflowers, cherry and apple blossoms, tulips and lilac: heaped with life.

<h2 style="text-align:center">104</h2>

Hallowing Pasternak against oppression: Olga Ivinskaya, unlike Lara, for whom she was the life-model, was unable to linger in solitude for a while with the body of her beloved, because the press of the crowd was too great. Speaking over Pasternak's grave, his friend Valentin Asmus, a philosopher, remarked that the dead writer had had 'the ability to express humanity in the highest terms.' Before the coffin was lowered into the grave, a young man, nervous and stammering, recited aloud the poem 'Hamlet', from the unpublished manuscript of *Doctor Zhivago*. It is said that hundreds of pairs of lips began to move in silent unison with the young man's recital. The KGB, instruments of the authorities, dispersed the crowd, but some fifty people remained by the graveside reciting Pasternak's poetry.[92]

---

90. Pasternak's description of the passing away of Yuri Zhivago almost eerily anticipates his own, though his own was on a larger and more poignant scale:

> The news of the death of a man almost without name had spread all around their circle with miraculous speed. A good number of people turned up who had known the dead man at various periods of his life and at various times had lost track of or forgotten him. His scientific thought and his muse were found to have a still greater number of unknown friends, who had never seen the man they were drawn to, and who came to look at him for the first time and to give him a last parting glance.

91. Peredelkino was the Soviet writers' colony outside Moscow. Pasternak long had a dacha there. Over time, several of his neighbours were taken away from their dachas by Stalin's secret police. When he himself died, several of his neighbours hid in their dachas and did not attend his funeral, for fear of being unfavourably noted by the same secret police, though it was by then 1960 and Stalin had been dead seven years.

92. Peter Finn and Petra Couvée *The Zhivago Affair: The Kremlin, the CIA and the Battle Over a Forbidden Book*, (Harvill Secker, London, 2014), pp. 234-241. Pasternak's poem 'Hamlet' begins with the verse:

> The hum dies down. I step out on the stage. Leaning against a doorpost, I try to catch the echoes from far off of what my age is bringing.

That was the poet's vocation, from his youth down to his great novel and his passing away.

Few graves in the long history of the Russian steppe had been so hallowed.[93] Pasternak, like his avatar Zhivago, had stood for humanity against tyranny, for healing against violence and for poetry against brutal social engineering. He merits a place in the 21st century's Hall of Remembrance—unlike any of the Bolsheviks who sacked Russia and desecrated its culture.[94]

105

Ancient raiders and modern barbarians: We recall the ancient history of the steppe, in which, from as far back as six thousand years ago, men on horseback or in chariots, came raiding the settled lands of farmers and city-dwellers, whether in Old Europe, Anatolia and Mesopotamia, Persia or the Indian sub-continent and later China. Little by little, we have been piecing that long story together again in recent decades. Yet our efforts to do so have been undertaken in the shadow of the colossal depredations by totalitarian regimes across those very lands of Eurasia in the 20th century. 'You,' declared Peter Stolypin, the last great prime minister of Tsarist Russia, to the Leftists in the Duma, in 1907, 'want a great upheaval.

---

93.   One such funeral was that of the great Romantic poet Alexander Pushkin, in 1837, which had some of the same characteristics, except that it was an urban funeral and not at a rural dacha. See T. J. Binyon *Pushkin: A Biography* (Alfred A. Knopf, New York, 2003) pp. 606-612.

94.   The extent of the Bolshevik ransacking of Russia from 1917 onwards has seldom been appreciated. It began as soon as Lenin had violently seized power from the Provisional Revolutionary Government and proceeded throughout the years in which Lenin remained alive, gutting the Russian economy and demonstrating an utter incapacity to understand money or markets. See Sean McMeekin *History's Greatest Heist: The Looting of Russia by the Bolsheviks* (Yale University Press, New Haven and London, 2009). The damage, however, was more than economic and social. Untold numbers of Russia's most highly educated and creative people were either driven into exile, executed or hounded to death by the Communist regime over the decades after 1917.

   It was computed as early as 1962 that 'the average age of death since the Revolution of those who had meanwhile lived in exile was 72, of those who remained in or returned to the USSR it was 45.' An estimated 1,500 writers perished at the hands of the regime, among them several close friends of Boris Pasternak. See Vitaly Shentalinsky *Arrested Voices: Resurrecting the Disappeared Writers of the Soviet Regime* (Martin Kessler Books, The Free Press, New York, 1996). Among the endless victims of this nightmare regime was the great genius Pavel Florensky, who was shipped off to the GULAG and shot in October 1937. See Avril Pyman *Pavel Florensky: A Quiet Genius—The Tragic and Extraordinary Life of Russia's Unknown Da Vinci* (Continuum, New York and London, 2010). Florensky was a remarkable figure in the Russian tradition of Tolstoy and Soloviev, who prefigured in some respects the fictional figure of Zhivago, created by Pasternak many years after the death of the visionary at the hands of Stalin's executioners.

We want a great Russia. Give me twenty five years of peace and you will not recognize Russia!' There was no such peace in Russia for the following forty five years and when they ended Russia was unrecognizable for other reasons than Stolypin had had in mind when he addressed the Duma.[95]

106

A book of literature against the terror: Russia suffered the First World War, the Bolshevik seizure of power, the Civil War, forced collectivization, the Great Terror the Second World War and the final years of Stalin's remorseless tyranny in relentless succession. The climax came in the years 1936-45, with first Stalin's Great Terror and then Barbarossa, the colossal Nazi invasion of the steppe-lands in an effort to enslave them and create a new, racist 'Aryan' Empire. In its wake, Stalin carved out a new totalitarian empire in Eastern Europe[96] and then the nuclear arms race commenced and the world came to live under the threat of genocide on an unprecedented scale. These were the years in which Boris Pasternak grew to adulthood and sought to make a life as a poet, as a translator and finally as a novelist. Tens of millions perished in those years from violence, famine and destructive incarceration. Yet, coming out of all that, Pasternak wrote *Doctor Zhivago*. He saw it as the culmination of his life's work— more important than all the poetry and translations of Shakespeare and Goethe for which he had long been celebrated. It was his testament to life.

107

A creative and well-connected family: Pasternak came from a deeply cultured background and considered becoming, by turns, a painter, a pianist and a philosopher, before deciding, in 1913, that his true vocation was poetry. His father, Leonid Osipovich Pasternak, was a painter and illustrator. His mother, Rozalia Isidorovna Kaufman, was a concert pianist. They were Jewish and lived for years in Odessa, on the Black Sea coast; moving to Moscow shortly before Boris was born. The family knew Leo Tolstoy (of whom Leonid did several portraits) and the composer Alexander Scriabin. Scriabin encouraged Boris to think of a career as a composer, but it was at just that time, when he was nineteen years old, that he discovered the poetry of Rainer Maria Rilke and began to write his own poetry. Such were the origins of *Doctor Zhivago*.

---

95.   On Stolypin, see Abraham Ascher *P. A. Stolypin: The Search for Stability in Late Imperial Russia* (Stanford University Press, 2001).

96.   See Anne Applebaum *Iron Curtain: The Crushing of Eastern Europe 1944-1956* (Allen Lane, London, 2012).

108

Marburg—philosophy or poetry? Pasternak began studying law at Moscow University, but then switched to philosophy, which he studied seriously until 1913. During that time, he spent a semester in Marburg, studying philosophy under the great Neo-Kantian teachers Hermann Cohen and Paul Natorp.[97] Cohen, a formidable figure, thought Boris had the makings of a great philosopher; but it was in Marburg, paradoxically, that the young Pasternak finally decided his true vocation was poetry. This rich and varied background lay behind his later development into a creative writer who never could embrace the narrow, oppressive and philistine cultural policies of the Communist regime—or its 'dialectical materialism'. His was a true and rounded humanism, sensitive to all that could make human life meaningful and dignified. For decades, through his poetry, he strove to give this humanism its appropriate expression. He succeeded, in his own eyes, only at the end of his life—with *Doctor Zhivago*.[98] Everything led up to that creative work.

---

97.   Pasternak's biographer Ronald Hingley points out that the sojourn in Marburg made a profound impression on the young man:

> *Bypassing Bergsonism and Husserlianism, both of which had their advocates at Moscow University, Pasternak the philosopher became an adherent of neo-Kantianism, as expounded by the illustrious Professor Hermann Cohen in the lecture halls of Marburg in western Germany. The Marburg school was well entrenched in Moscow and it had become customary to send the best Muscovite Philosophy students to receive part of their education in Marburg itself. Pasternak had heard so much about the German city's intellectual and topographical charms that he could not wait to go west.*

> In his autobiographical story, *Safe Conduct*, in the 1920s, Pasternak described Marburg in detail as 'one of Germany's smallest and most picturesque university cities' with its assembly hall, its eight hundred year old medieval castle and 'its streets clinging to steep slopes like Gothic dwarfs'. Cohen was very impressed by the young student and encouraged him to study for a doctorate in philosophy, just as Scriabin had encouraged him to think of a career as a composer. He spurned the invitation, however, and committed himself to poetry, left Marburg and went on a tour of Italy. *Pasternak: A Biography* (Weidenfeld & Nicolson, London, 1983) pp. 27-29.

98.   As early as 1918, Pasternak contemplated writing 'a long work in prose'. He actually began writing that year a novel set in the Urals. Throughout the 1920s and 1930s he experimented with prose fiction and autobiography. In 1936-39, during the Great Terror, he drafted a novel which clearly foreshadowed *Doctor Zhivago* even in some of its characters' names and details of the plot. His main character was called Patrick, not Yuri, but was an orphan who, like the later Zhivago, grew up in the home of a family named Gromeko and married their daughter, Tonya. There was a female character who anticipated the later Lara and whose husband, like Pasha Antipov in *Doctor Zhivago*, became a teacher at Yuriatin, in the Urals.

109

Love—disease of the psyche or source of transcendence? One of the most famous books about love is that by Stendhal—Marie Henri Beyle (1783-1842)—which was written between 1819 and 1821. It is an agonized and incomplete book, filled with the author's attempts to understand and come to terms with an unrequited love for a beautiful woman called Mathilde Viscontini Dembowksi. There is an overlap with Pasternak's account of the love between Yuri Zhivago and Larissa Guichard, but the key difference is that *that* love (the fictional one, in *Doctor Zhivago*) was mutual and consummated. It is worth pondering which book is more instructive.

110

An adorable sensibility and sublime actions: Stendhal was a man of the world and a flamboyant, versatile writer. He had had a number of lovers before he met Mathilde Dembowksi, but she came to obsess him as no other woman had done. She was twenty eight when he first encountered her and was to die at the age of thirty five. She was an ardent Italian patriot and

---

Patrick became torn between Tonya and this other woman, as Zhivago later would—all of which is interesting in that Pasternak had not, at that point, encountered Olga Ivinskaya, on whom Lara was later to be modelled. The manuscript of this early novel was destroyed in a fire, however, in 1941. Throughout the 1930s, he lamented the abandonment of the 'age-old gracious tradition that breathes with transformations and anticipations' in favour of a brutalized and mechanistic pseudo-culture. It was central to such reflections that his key character would have a name, Zhivago, which was based on the stem *zhiv*, meaning 'alive'.

In 1939, he was asked by the great theatrical director Vsevolod Meyerhold (1874-1940) to produce a translation of *Hamlet*. Not very long after engaging Pasternak, Meyerhold was arrested, tortured and executed by the Stalin regime as a spy for the British and the Japanese. But Pasternak became deeply immersed in Shakespeare and above all in *Hamlet*. It is reported that twelve versions of the play were found among his papers when he died in 1960.

It was out of this work that the poem 'Hamlet', which appears first among the poems attributed to Zhivago, and which was recited by the nervous young man at Pasternak's funeral, was first written. It was revised in 1946, when Pasternak came to realize that even the catastrophe of the war was not going to induce the regime to free Russia and allow its natural culture to flower. It was then and for that reason that he finally began work on *Doctor Zhivago*. Writing it consumed him for a decade. Seeing it published in the West and acclaimed around the world outside the Soviet Union, filled him with an exalted sense that he had, at last, been expressed and fulfilled his vocation as a Russian cultural figure. On all this, see Richard Pevear's Introduction to his and Larissa Volokhonsky's translation of *Doctor Zhivago* (Pantheon Books, New York, 2010) pp. xii-xx.

active in the revolutionary movement in northern Italy against foreign occupation. She was described by one of her great female friends as an 'angelic woman in whom were united all the perfections of an adorable sensibility with the energy that makes one capable of the most sublime actions.' How could such a man as Stendhal not have fallen hard for such a woman?

111

A model for literary heroines: Stendhal was fascinated by her, but she neither loved nor understood him. She was coolly indifferent towards him and over several years rejected his persistent courtship. She died in 1825, but he remained preoccupied by thoughts of her for the rest of his life. The heroines of his great novels (most notably Mathilde de la Mole in *Scarlet and Black*) were modelled on her. In *Love*, he sought to articulate a whole theory of happiness, passionate freedom and the emancipation of women—all inspired by Mathilde Dembowski.[99]

112

A real and transcendent love: In Pasternak we see something similar happening, but with the difference that the love is fulfilled, rather than becoming a matter only of romantic obsession verging on solipsism. Stendhal went so far as to describe *Love* as a diagnostic analysis of the 'disease of the soul' that goes by the name of love. Pasternak, conversely, depicted the love of Yuri and Lara as something transcendent and remarkable. Stendhal's book is a classic, but who would not prefer the love described by Pasternak, even amidst the grim repression of Stalinism, to the obsessive and unrequited passion analysed by Stendhal, who suffered no such things?

113

Science, art and subjectivity: There are passages in *Doctor Zhivago* which bring to the foreground Pasternak's whole, rich education and above all his early interest in philosophy. They articulate his wonderful appreciation of the natural world and the human place within it. Several of these occur in the chapter 'Forest Army', in Book Two, covering the period in which Zhivago is held captive by the Red partisans, as their medical officer. In one, he bitterly rebukes Liberius Mikulitsyn for talking about how the revolution will remake life. This, to Yuri, is complete heresy.

114

Alive in the autumn forest: Life, he declares (and we must recall that his own name is based on the root *zhiv*, meaning 'alive'), is not some crude clump of raw material that you can remake:

---

99.   Stendhal *Love*, translated by Gilbert and Suzanne Sale, with an Introduction by Jean Stewart and B. C. J. G. Knight (Penguin Classics, 1975).

It is, if you want to know, a continually self-renewing, eternally self-recreating principle, it eternally alters and transforms itself, it is far above your and my dim-witted theories.[100]

Later in the chapter, Pasternak describes, through Zhivago's eyes, the wonderful colours of the forest in autumn; how the undersides of leaves 'burned with the green fire of transparent bottle glass' and how ripe berries of all kinds festooned the forest with colour: 'lady's-smock, brick-brown, flabby elderberries' and 'the shimmering white-crimson clusters of the guilder rose'; while dragonflies, 'their glassy wings tinkling, floated slowly through the air, speckled and transparent, like the fire and the forest.'[101] All this was miles away from the 'heroics' of Leninist class warfare.

115

The butterfly and creativity: But above all, there is a passage, a little further on again, in which Zhivago, reflecting on the sight of a brown speckled butterfly camouflaged against the bark of a pine tree, muses on the relationship between evolution and consciousness.

> What is a subject? What is an object? How give a definition of their identity? In the doctor's reflections, Darwin met with Schelling and the passing butterfly with modern painting, with impressionist art. He thought of creation, the creature, creativity and mimicry.[102]

This is the poetry of life and its stunning *autopoiesis* which Pasternak championed against the crudities and cruelties of the 'revolution', with its arrogant pretensions and ruthless censorship.

116

Love—free and unprecedented: Into all Zhivago's meditations on the natural world and its relationship to consciousness and creativity, comes the exalted and tormented reality of his love for Lara, whom he fears he will never see again.

> Oh, how he loved her! How beautiful she was! Just as he had always thought and dreamed, as he had needed! But in what, in which side of her? In anything that could be named or singled out by examination? Oh, no, no! But in that incomparably simple and impetuous line with which the Creator had outlined her entirely at one stroke, from top to bottom, and in that divine contour had handed her to his soul, like a just-bathed child tightly wrapped in linen ... Like a poster on an enormous length of fabric stretched over a city street, there hung in the air from one side of the forest clearing to the other the diffuse, greatly magnified phantom of an astonishing, adored head. And the head wept, and the increasing rain kissed it and poured over it.

---

100.   Boris Pasternak *Doctor Zhivago* (Translated by Richard Pevear and Larissa Volokhonsky, Pantheon Books, New York, 2010) p. 303.

101.   Ibid. pp. 307-08.

102.   Ibid. p. 310.

Later, in the room on Kamergersky Lane, standing over Yuri's coffin, Lara will unconsciously echo all of this, in her lament for his passing:

> Oh, what love this was, free, unprecedented, unlike anything else! They thought the way other people sing ... Ah, it was this, this was the chief thing that united them and made them akin! Never, never, even in moments of the most gratuitous, self-forgetful happiness, did that most lofty and thrilling thing abandon them: delight in the general mold of the world, the feeling of their relation to the whole picture, the sense of belonging to the beauty of the whole spectacle, to the whole universe.[103]

Those lines were the culmination of Pasternak's life journey, through art and music, philosophy and poetry, translation and brooding reflection on the fate of Russia under Lenin and Stalin.

---

103.   Ibid. pp. 329-30, 445-46.

Needless to say, Pasternak's personal life was considerably more complicated than his novel. His personal relationships with two of the leading female poets of his time, Marina Tsvetayeva and Anna Akhmatova were complex and psychologically fraught. He three times proposed to Akhmatova, even though each of them was already married. He was twice married, but in 1946, while still living with his second wife, Zinaida Neygauz, he met and fell in love with Olga Ivinskaya, twenty two years his junior.

She was, as Ronald Hingley remarked in his biography of the poet: 'to become the beloved companion of his last years' and was to leave behind 'a record of her life with him in her memoir, *A Captive of Time.*' She had herself already been married twice, before she met Pasternak; and both her husbands had died. She 'had worshipped Pasternak's poetry since adolescence' and, 'as a student of literature in the early 1930s she had been taken by her first lover to a recital by Pasternak.'

When they met, she was working as a junior editor at the literary journal *Novy Mir.* She was introduced to him as one of his 'ardent admirers' and his own, reciprocal attraction was instant and unqualified. His love affair with her coincided with his writing of *Doctor Zhivago,* but was itself more complicated than the tale of Yuri and Lara in the novel. Anna Akhmatova, though she had rejected Pasternak's three proposals, was rather scornful of his affair with Olga and of Olga's intellectual pretensions. Such are the endless complications of life and of being *zhiv*—alive. See Hingley *Pasternak: A Biography* (Weidenfeld & Nicolson, London, 1983) pp. 159-63. See, also, Roberta Reeder *Anna Akhmatova: Poet and Prophet* (St Martin's Press, New York, 1994) pp. 355-68.

Reeder wrote that 'Akhmatova had nothing but contempt for Ivinskaya.' (p. 357). But then again, she was rather contemptuous of all the women in Pasternak's life, starting with his first wife, Yevgeniya, who 'was sweet and intelligent, but, but but'; and his second wife, Zinaida, 'a dragon on eight paws, crude, vulgar, the embodiment of anti-art.' (p. 360). She was also sceptical about his novel. She thought it an artistic failure, because it was too preachy (p. 364). Yet those who knew her well saw much of this as a kind of love/hate passion for Pasternak. Akhmatova grieved over his death and the circumstances in which it occurred.

Might, like a poet's bell, then toll

8
The Poet's Bell

My love for you does not disperse
The virtues of my self or soul,
But rather the entire reverse:

It prompts me to express in verse,
My spirit's heartbeat, with the goal,
That thus my love will not disperse.

In doing so, I must rehearse
Both rhyme and metrical control,
Or bring about the mere reverse

Of music beauty and, what's worse,
Disordering the part or whole,
Imply my love could thus disperse.

In these brief stanzas, then, immerse
Your self and play the critic's role;
Then turn—and play the charmed reverse.

This simple villanelle, though terse,
Might, like a poet's bell, then toll
Of love that, rather than disperse,
Regathers sound from each reverse.

117

What is a villanelle? To ask 'Why write a villanelle?' is tantamount to asking, 'Why write poetry at all?' Good poetry is its own argument and it either works its way upon the psyche of the recipient or stands outside his or her experience. A villanelle, however, is an unusually strict form of poem, tighter in construction than a sonnet and with more insistent repetition. It consists, as we see here, of nineteen lines, including five tercets (three line stanzas) and a quatrain (a four line stanza). The first and third lines of the first tercet, or the rhymes at the ends of them, must be alternately repeated in the following four tercets and must both appear in the quatrain.

118

From rustic dances: The form seems to have evolved from rustic dance songs, hence the name, which derives from the Italian, French and English words for a peasant or farmhand. The repetitions (often of whole lines and not only of rhymes) suggest choral dance songs. But in the 19th and 20th centuries, the villanelle was practised by a succession of poets who were anything but rustic and did not write for choruses. Among them, famously, was Dylan Thomas, whose villanelle 'Do not go gently into that good night' is widely famous and much cited. 'A Poet's Bell' addresses the beloved within a meditative context in which the integrity of love and the writing of poetry itself are at stake. The subject matter is the capacity of a human being to generate both beauty and order in life—and an affirmation that this is possible, as shown by the poem itself.

119

Life as autopoiesis: Life itself—contrary to the laws of physics—is a process of the organic and self-organizing *creation of order* through the use of energy. This begins with the simplest prokaryotes. As Zhivago declares, in Pasternak's great 'artistic failure' of a novel, life after the prokaryotes, over billions of years, ceaselessly transformed and elaborated itself. Human life emerged over aeons out of this epochal process. Not only are our bodies each a variation on the orchestration of a trillion eukaryotic cells and ten trillion bacteria into an integral, animated organism; but cognitively and behaviourally we require induction into the arts and skills—and common stories—that go to make up a competent, let alone a highly cultivated human being.

120

Culture vs dissipation: Dissipative forces are forever at work, so that there are spontaneous abortions, retarded or malformed bodies, disordered minds, illness, deprivation, miseducation, underdevelopment at every turn. And yet, in the midst of all that, the capacities for articulate speech, symbolic art, mimetic dance, musicality, elaborate architecture, social coordination and visionary scientific enquiry have all emerged. Each intentional, creative act, each graceful or skilled movement, each attempt at beauty and proportion is expressive of this specifically human *autopoiesis*—self-organizing creativity. Even so, we marvel at the myriad beauties of plants, the stunning variety of faunal forms, the flight of birds, the play of seals and dolphins and the song of whales. Or, rather, we do so just to the extent that we are—like Zhivago—actually *alive*.

121

Mind-beggaring complexity: All these capacities have their roots deep, deep within our ancestry, even where they have only come fully into fruition in very recent time—which is to say, within the last 20,000 years. 'One million years back places us at a moment when behaviours and capacities that ultimately would underlie modern musicking do not so much appear for the first time, as become legible,' writes Gary Tomlinson. His attention is on how our capacity for making music and responding to it became possible at all, since the processing of music in the brain is 'a matter of mind-beggaring complexity.' He adds that the differences 'between a Mahlerian orchestra and a lullaby hummed to a nodding child', while superficially enormous, are insignificant 'wrinkles on the surface of the stark immensity of brain resources required for musicking to *happen at all* ... from its most recent parts ... to ancient, deep brain structures..'[104]

---

104.   Gary Tomlinson *A Million Years of Music: The Emergence of Human Modernity* (Zone Books, New York, 2015) pp. 26-27. He remarks further:

> *Humans are symbol-makers ... a feature tightly bound up with language, not so tightly with music. The species Cassirer dubbed Homo symbolicus cannot help but tangle musicking in webs of symbolic thought and expression, habitually making it a component of behavioural complexes that form such expression. But in fundamental features musicking is neither language-like nor symbol-like, and from these differences come many clues to its ancient emergence.*

He goes on:

> *If musicking is a primary, shared trait of modern humans, then to describe its emergence must be to detail the coalescing of that modernity. This took place, archaeologists are clear, over a very long durée: at least 50,000 years or so, more likely something closer to 200,000, depending in part on what that coalescence is taken to comprise. If we look back 20,000 years, a small portion of this long period, we reach the lives of humans whose musical capacities were probably little different from our own. As we look farther back, we reach horizons where this similarity can no longer hold—perhaps 40,000 years ago, perhaps 70,000, perhaps 100,000. But we never cross a line before which all the cognitive capacities recruited in modern musicking abruptly*

122

The pre-conditions for creativity: The same considerations—about the 'mind-beggaring complexity' of the neural resources involved—apply to language, religion, myth-making more generally, mime, dance and complex kinship structures. It cannot be too strongly emphasized that we are only now, only in the past few decades, beginning to piece together a clear understanding of any and all these things. In doing so, we are uncovering a whole new basis for comprehending what we are and how we have *become* what we are. But all that long evolution, all that 'mind-beggaring complexity' is implicit in every act of *poiesis* or mimesis we undertake. It is a given in every conscious attempt to 'rehearse both rhyme and metrical control', whether literally or metaphorically; whether in reason, verse, musicking or dancing. It is what we are.

123

Arguing with Augustine of Hippo: For millennia the 'holy men' of civilization have had deep misgivings about our humanity and its natural longings. They can be found in various cultures around the world, not least in the Axial Age, as Karl Jaspers dubbed it; but there are few more poignant or articulate cases than that of St Augustine of Hippo. Heir to both Plato and the Bible, he thought he could see a conflict between earthly, carnal love and pure, divine love.[105] He regretted the first and longed for the second. In his justly celebrated *Confessions*, he remarks that he should have heeded the advice of St Paul (in the first epistle to the Corinthians) to abstain from all sexual congress with women, since he who is unmarried is concerned with how to please God, whereas he who is married is

---

disappear. Unless we embrace the incredible notion that music sprang forth in full-blown glory, its emergence will have to be tracked in gradualist terms across a long period. (p. 24).

105.   I know of no better or more thought-provoking reflection on this question of sexual renunciation and its imagined link with transcendence and salvation than Peter Brown's *The Body and Society: Men, Women and Sexual Renunciation in Early Christianity* (Columbia University Press, New York, 1998). There is so much in ascetic practices from the 'heroic' centuries of Christianity which cannot but seem to us now gruesome and masochistic. Yet Brown is able to show, with acute sensitivity and fine-grained nuance, how closely such practices were linked to a fierce longing for transcendence. This longing must be counted among the strange and yet in some ways startlingly fertile and impressive convolutions of human culture, both East and West, as our ancestors strove to come to terms with consciousness and possibility in a bewildering cosmos. Like language and music, human sexual psychology is of 'mind-beggaring complexity'. Such complexity is deeply ingrained in the asceticism and poetry of Gerard Manley Hopkins, not least in his poem 'The Habit of Perfection', written in 1866, which begins: 'Elected Silence, sing to me/And beat upon my whorled ear/Pipe me to pastures still and be/The music that I care to hear.'

concerned with how to please his wife. He went so far as to declare, echoing the Gospel of Matthew, 'if I had made myself a eunuch for the love of the Kingdom of Heaven, I should have awaited your embrace with all the greater joy.'[106]

124

The saint surely went astray: He took a mistress and was faithful to her, but felt that involvement with her drew him away from the one thing which alone could satisfy his psyche—the contemplation and love of God.[107] His longing was for a higher form of beauty and he even wrote a book, as he recalled, in two or three volumes, on *Beauty and Proportion*.[108] He longed for a profound and integral understanding of things; to be able to live a life which brought such an understanding together. He is rightly honoured for this. Yet the sexual aversion and renunciation that he seemed to regard as a precondition for it are troubling. Our poem presses back in the other direction, insisting on the possibility of an authentic *human* love, which does *not* disperse the self or soul and though facing challenges, regathers *sound* from each reverse. Can't that be our aspiration—given what we now know about ourselves, which St Augustine did *not* know?[109]

---

106.   St Augustine *Confessions* Book II: 2 (Penguin, 1961) p. 44.

107.   He loved her dearly, he tells us, but gave her up rather than marry her, though she had borne him a son. Book VI: 15. Famously, in Book VIII: 7, he confessed to his God, 'I had prayed to you for chastity and said, 'Give me chastity and continence, but not yet.' For I was afraid that you would answer my prayer at once and cure me too soon of the disease of lust, which I wanted satisfied, not quelled.'

108.   Ibid. Book IV: 13, p. 83.

109.   Brian Stock has written a wonderful tribute to Augustine as a reader and thinker, which is a superb companion piece to Augustine's *Confessions*—*Augustine the Reader: Meditation, Self-Knowledge and the Ethics of Interpretation* (Belknap Press, Harvard University, 1996). It is a luminous book from the beginning, where Stock observes:

> *This is a study of Augustine's attempt to lay the theoretical foundation for a reading culture. Augustine was convinced that words and images play a fundamental role in mediating perceptions of reality. From the spring of 386, when his interest in Christianity was renewed, he attempted to situate his inquiries into such transfers of meaning within a programme of scriptural studies. The subsequent union of philosophical, psychological and literary insights gave birth to the West's first developed theory of reading ... An act of reading is ... a critical step upwards in a mental ascent: it is both an awakening from sensory illusion and a rite of initiation, in which the reader crosses the threshold from the outside to the inside world.*

125

Loving and departing from Heidegger: Hannah Arendt was German, Jewish, an exile for most of her life, brilliantly intelligent and an uninhibitedly emancipated 20th century woman. Yet she was fascinated by the figure and writings of St Augustine all her life. In the late 1920s, she wrote her doctoral thesis on the idea of love in St Augustine's thought. As she did so, she was thinking through her erotic relationship with her teacher, Martin Heidegger. She was thinking through the very idea of love for herself, through a closer reading of Augustine, the classical close reader. Martin Heidegger was later to declare that Hannah Arendt had been the love of his life—though his lover only briefly, when she was a young university student—and the inspiration for his best work. Her own thought developed in many ways as a critical response to his work.

126

A deity or amor mundi? It was not Heidegger, however, but Augustine who might be said to have been the inspiration for *her* best work, from her doctoral dissertation to her great books of the years after the Second World War. Her point of departure was Augustine's definition of love as a kind of craving, prompting both possessiveness and fear. Governed by such fear, human beings are estranged from themselves, Augustine argued, and he called this estrangement 'dispersion'. What he sought was a God—an eternal and immutable Being—who would gather him in from the dispersion which tore him apart.[110] Yet this was not the conclusion at which Arendt arrived from her study of the writings of the Catholic saint. She secularized and amended his thinking to insist on *amor mundi*—love of the world and recollection of the self through that love, amid change and misfortune, rather than through the love of an eternal Deity.

127

The possibility of new beginnings: At the age of sixty, in 1966, Hannah Arendt wrote to Martin Heidegger that their love had somehow endured despite decades of disruption and the profound gulf that had yawned between them on account of Nazism and the Holocaust. As Daniel Maier-Katkin remarks, in a beautiful study of their relationship, both thinkers 'were attentive to beginnings and ends'. Heidegger 'celebrated the power and radiance of beginnings, but experienced them as distant and cooling explosions like creation itself or the Greek invention of philosophy. His thought was drawn to the brevity of each individual's existence and the infinite nothingness that surrounded it.' He knew little archaeology, however, and less science.

---

110.   St Augustine *Confessions* Book II: 1: 'For love of your love I shall retrieve myself from the havoc of [dispersion] which tore me to pieces when I turned away from you, whom alone I should have sought, and lost myself instead on many a different quest.'

128

From the seminar to the Black Forest: Arendt's stance was different. She emphasized the wonder of *natality* and the possibility of new beginnings, even after such a colossal collapse as that in the world of the 1930s and 1940s. She also insisted on the realities of spontaneity and freedom, but within a world which exists before, over and beyond us. She quoted St Augustine himself in this regard—*Initium ut esset homo creatus est* (That a beginning might be made, humanity was created), while allowing that, of course, humanity was by no means created at the beginning. The important point was that, when each of us is born into the world we find it already in being. As her biographer, Daniel Maier-Katkin summarized her thinking: The world is already in motion when we arrive and it is only by joining the dance that we become ourselves.[111] She and Heidegger fell in love in 1924, when she was only eighteen and he a young professor of philosophy at Marburg—where Pasternak had studied just over a decade earlier.[112] Their love was a poetic beginning. It was dispersed and yet regathered, years later, on walks in the Black Forest.

129

America—Russia—America: Sergei Rachmaninoff's 'The Bells' is his musical response to and rendering of a poem originally written by Edgar Allan Poe about the course of life: birth, romance, turbulence and death. One can read Poe's poem in a few minutes, while the choral version by Rachmaninoff runs for seventy three minutes in four parts: Allegro ma

---

111.   Daniel Maier-Katkin *Stranger From Abroad: Hannah Arendt, Martin Heidegger, Friendship and Forgiveness* (W. W. Norton & Co., New York and London, 2010), pp. 13-14.

112.   Maier-Katkin recaptures poignantly the occasion of the first encounter between the self-confident, iconoclastic philosopher and the 'stylish young woman with stunning eyes':

> *For Heidegger nothing was more powerful than questions about the meaning of existence: Not simply why should you or I exist, but why should anything exist, why should there not be just nothing? What is the meaning of the nothingness by which Being is surrounded in the moments of its existence? The air around her brilliant professor seemed to crackle with ideas and questions; and like him, young Hannah was a creature who thrived in such air. She seems to have loved him from the very first day, and he seems to have been drawn to her immediately; twenty-five years later, after the Nazis and the destruction of total war, after his self-serving betrayal and disloyalty, Heidegger wrote a poem that recalls the excitement and dissipation of listlessness he experienced at the moment in November 1924 when he first saw Hannah in the seminar on Plato's Sophist: 'If only she, from withdrawn grace, would fall towards me ...'* (pp. 29-30).

non tanto, Lento, Presto and Lento lugubre.[113] Rachmaninoff, an older contemporary of Pasternak, loved liturgical music and composed a good deal of it. The Russian Orthodox Church took exception to it, as the Catholic Church did to Verdi's *Requiem*, on the grounds that it was too 'secular' in character. Rachmaninoff composed his 'sacred' music out of a love for what lay beneath or beyond it, rather than out of a simple religious belief. We should listen to it also in that spirit.

130

The composer against the revolutionaries: 'The Bells' was composed in 1913, the year Pasternak completed his studies in philosophy and the year before the disaster of the Great War smote Europe—Russia not least. As much as any composition, it embodies the modern *musicking* of humanity in all its masterful, expressive complexity. It is scored for three solo vocalists (soprano, tenor and baritone), a choir, and an idiosyncratic orchestra. The orchestra requires a piccolo, three flutes, three oboes, a *cor anglais*, three soprano clarinets, a bass clarinet, three bassoons, a contrabassoon, six horns, three trumpets, three trombones, tuba, timpani, four tubular bells, glockenspiel[114], triangle, tambourine, snare drum, cymbals, bass drum, tamtam[115], pianino, celesta[116], harp, organ, first and second violins, violas, cellos, and double basses. This Rachmaninoff fled the Presto of the Bolshevik revolution; dying in exile—Lento lugubre.

---

113.   Joyful but not too much, Slow, Rapid and Slow and lugubrious—the moods of the four parts of Poe and of Rachmaninoff's composition. In Poe's original poem and likewise in Rachmaninoff's musical rendition of it, the four parts were aligned to phases of human life, from the naïve joys of childhood to the inevitable trials of maturity and old age.

114.   The glockenspiel is a musical instrument consisting of a series of bells or metal bars or tubes struck by hammers.

115.   The tamtam is a large metal gong. The word derives from the Hindi word for a hand beaten drum and is often translated tom-tom.

116.   The celesta is a small keyboard instrument with hammers striking metal bars, giving off sounds like those made by a glockenspiel.

Ah, that is an isle of cypresses high

9
The Bell and the Choir

There are hymns to be heard
On the Isle of the Dead,
Or such is the word
That is still being spread:

Neither brimstone nor fire,
As threatened of old;
But an angelic choir
With voices of gold.

The singing will start
With a high, ringing bell
And conclude with a chant
That will solemnly tell

Of salvation history,
Wonders made plain,
And of life's inner mystery,
Its glory and pain.

Our labours well done,
Past the portals of night,
We'll rejoice in the One
And repose in His sight.

Oh, if life would end so,
On that Isle in the West,
Under Evenstar's glow,
Then I'd go to my rest;

But we all should beware
Of the Sirens of death
And resist going there,
While still we have breath;

For in truth all the Muses
Of rest and delight
Demand that one chooses
The noon, not the night.

The bell and the choir,
The chanting of story,
To be heard all require
The world's 'passing glory'.

So I'll not dream of songs
On the Isle of the Dead,
But proclaim what belongs
To the living instead.

For I am a being
Of flesh and of bone,
Not a soul that is fleeing
To star and to stone.

It is here, it is here
And not in the West,
That what touches the ear
Can make it feel blest.

It's through metaphors drawn
From our love of the world
That our souls are reborn
And our hopes are unfurled;

And so we conceive,
With extravagant eye,
An eternal reprieve
For all those who die.

Too often this tends
To a fervid belief
That the visionary bends
To delusion and grief;

So, though we must die,
Let us love while we may,
The light in the sky,
The sensations of day.

Let life be renewed
By the joys that we find
In what saints have construed
As 'the world' of our kind.

Our religion should nourish
The flowers and trees;
The creatures that flourish
In the skies and the seas.

Our solemnest vow
Of our purpose and worth
Should centre on how
We have sprung from the Earth;

Nor should we yet long
To flee from this green,
With the thought we belong
In places unseen;

For indeed we do not,
But have gardens to tend,
On our aqueous plot
At the Milky Way's end.

Let's cherish, then, all
Of the gifts of the Muses
No longer in thrall
To the One who refuses

To grant us surcease
From predation and strife
Except through release
From the pleasures of life;

And with Orphic intent,
With sublime orchestration,
Spend all we've been lent
In the brilliant creation

Of a culture profound
With its halls full of song,
In which will resound
The cry, 'We belong!'

Ah, that is an Isle
Of cypresses high
Where I'd live well awhile,
Then peacefully die.

131

The history of fire and brimstone: Rachmaninoff's 'The Isle of the Dead', inspired by the famous Arnold Bocklin painting, is sombre. It is less than a third the length of 'The Bells', but it taps into millennia-old Western ruminations on mortality and the imagined Underworld, in which disembodied souls abide in a diminished state. There is, however, all the world of difference between this diminished state, as we find it in the Hebrew Bible or in Homer or Virgil (and again in Bocklin's painting in the early 20th century) and the afterlife as a place of bliss in Heaven or eternal torment in Hell, as we find it in Christian teachings and celebrated in the writings of Tertullian, Thomas Aquinas and Dante. Bocklin's 'Toteninsel' holds no terrors, but is a place of final rest. That is not the doctrine of Hell as taught by the Christian churches.

132

To see perfectly the punishment of the damned: On the day of Christ's triumph, exulted Tertullian in the 3rd century, before Christianity had been 'corrupted' by becoming the state religion of the declining Roman Empire, all the proud kings, governors, philosophers, poets and actors of the unbelieving pagan world will be *consumed in one great flame* and we, in heaven, will be able to *delight in their suffering* and eternal damnation. Aquinas, that most authoritative of Catholic theologians, stated explicitly, a thousand years later:

> In order that the bliss of the saints may be more delightful for them and that they may render more copious thanks to God for it, it is given to them to see perfectly the punishment of the damned.

Dante's descriptions of Hell are proverbial, though he strangely stated that Hell was created by 'eternal love'. Whatever the *psychology* that created these infernal visions, it deserves a place in our 21st century civilization in the *museum* of religions and anthropology, alongside accounts of head-hunting and human sacrifice. There is no Hell, save in the human imagination (which, to be sure, is extremely fertile) and conjuring it religiously perverts rather than elevates the human mind.

133

The Book with Seven Seals: With the vision of Hell belong all intimations of the Apocalypse, in which the secular order will be cast down in ruin, amidst blood and fire precipitated by the trumpets of seven angels, as we read in the famous Book of Revelation. Its author wrote of a Book with Seven Seals as revealing the vast upheaval and reckoning that was coming upon the world. In the fifth and sixth chapters of the Book of Revelation, it is stated:

I saw a strong angel proclaiming with a loud voice, who is worthy to open the book and to loose the seals thereof? And no man in heaven, nor on Earth or under the Earth was able to open the book or to look thereon.

These are not words of enlightenment, but of religious obscurantism and darkness.

134

The natural world is our Book of Revelation: Only Christ—the Lamb of God—could open the Book with Seven Seals; and when he did so there sprang forth the Four Horsemen of the Apocalypse: white, red, black and pale, whose commission was to go forth and wreak havoc upon the Earth: 'to kill with the sword and with hunger and with death and with the beasts of the Earth.' But the only Book with Seven Seals worthy of the name is not this phantasmagorical conjuration of John of Patmos; it is the natural world. And it has been opened to us all not by the Lamb of God or any religious 'revelation', but by the natural sciences. Giordano Bruno and not the Catholic Inquisition was correct about the path to knowledge. And it is within the natural world, in the light of the sciences of modernity—foreshadowed in the Hellenistic epoch long before the rise of Christianity—that we must both seek our awakening and find ways to *avoid*, if we can, any natural or man-made apocalypse.[117] It is folly to welcome signs that one is coming.

---

117. The Christian Book of Revelation was, of course, by no means the beginning of apocalyptic thinking. It had a long history before that, even if that particular articulation of the vision has had uncommon sway for much of the past two millennia. See Norman Cohn *Cosmos, Chaos and the World to Come: The Ancient Roots of Apocalyptic Faith* (Yale University Pres, New Haven and London, 1995). Cohn begins his book with the remark:

> *This book investigates the deepest roots and first emergence of an expectation which is still flourishing today. That there will shortly be a marvellous consummation, when good will be finally victorious over evil and forever reduce it to nullity; that the human agents of evil will be either physically annihilated or otherwise disposed of; that the elect will thereafter live as a collectivity, unanimous and without conflict, on a transformed and purified earth—this expectation has had a long history in our civilization. In overtly Christian guise it has exercised a powerful fascination down the centuries and continues to do so; and in secularised guise it has been easily recognisable in certain politico-social ideologies ... .*

> *So where and how did the expectation originate? And what kind of world-view preceded it? Those questions have been preoccupying me on and off for almost half a century—in fact ever since I wrote my first study of collective beliefs, The Pursuit of the Millennium, in the years immediately after the Second World War. They had, of course, preoccupied others before me; but the standard answers left me unsatisfied ... The whole matter seemed to call for re-examination. Some twenty years ago I set out to re-examine it. This book summarises the conclusions which bit by bit, over that long span, have forced themselves upon me.*

135

Pleasure in cruelty: Of course, the desire for a great reckoning and for revenge run deep in human beings, especially if stoked and encouraged by demagogues, religious 'reformers' or incandescent mullahs. That acute diagnostician of the place of cruelty in human culture, Friedrich Nietzsche, remarked even of Homer that he well knew the appeal of such cruelty—as well as Tertullian would do a thousand years later:

> The gods conceived of as the friends of cruel spectacles—oh how profoundly this ancient idea still permeates our European humanity! Merely consult Calvin and Luther. It is certain, at any rate, that the Greeks still knew of no tastier spice to offer their gods to season their happiness than the pleasures of cruelty. With what eyes do you think Homer made his gods look down upon the destinies of men? What was at bottom the ultimate meaning of Trojan Wars and other such tragic terrors? There can be no doubt whatever: they were intended as festival plays for the gods; and, insofar as the poet is in these matters of a more 'godlike' disposition than other men, no doubt also as festival plays for the poets.[118]

Yet Homer's depiction of 'the Kingdom of the Dead' in Book XI of *The Odyssey* is far more humane than the vision of Hell in Dante. There the bloodless dead long for life, but they are not tortured for real or imagined sins, or made a spectacle for the delectation of the elect above; though some few Titans are bound in tortures at the instigation of the vengeful gods: Tityus, Tantalus, Sisyphus. But these are a very pale anticipation of what Dante was to depict. Chiefly, Odysseus recounted 'down the shadowed halls' of Queen Arete in Phaeacia, the melancholy wonder of meeting in the Underworld so many solemn, fallen heroes, still of glorious memory.

136

In the footsteps of Aeneas: Virgil's account of the Kingdom of the Dead, in Book VI of *The Aeneid*, is more vivid and moving than Homer's before him, but remains a stark contrast to Dante's nightmare vision twelve centuries later—though in that case Virgil will guide Dante himself through Hell. Aeneas seeks permission to visit the Underworld in order to see again the ghost of his father. The Sibyl tells him:

> Born of the blood of gods, Anchises' son, man of Troy, the descent to the Underworld is easy. Night and day the gates of shadowy Death stand open wide, but to retrace your steps, to climb back to the upper air—there the struggle, there the labour lies.

---

118.   Friedrich Nietzsche *The Genealogy of Morals,* Second Essay 'Guilt, Bad Conscience and the Like' Section 7, in Walter Kaufmann (ed) *The Genealogy of Morals and Ecce Homo* (Vintage Books, Random House, New York, 1969) p. 69.

It is in Virgil that we meet Charon the ferryman who conducts the shades of the dead across the River Styx to the shore of the Underworld—a first intimation of Bocklin's painting. And in his Underworld we find for the most part pity for the lot of all those who died either tragically, prematurely or in suicidal despair. Virgil's Epicurean compassion puts Christian belief to shame.

137

The poet glimpses Tartarus: There is, on the other hand, a first inkling of the harsh world of punishment that will be taken up with such relish by the Christians. Aeneas sees:

> an enormous fortress ringed with triple walls and raging round it all a blazing flood of lava, Tartarus' River of Fire, whirling thunderous boulders. Before it rears a giant gate, its columns solid adamant, so no power of man, not even the gods themselves, can root it out in war.

From within come the groans of those suffering punishments for their offences in life, 'the savage crack of the lash, the grating creak of iron, the clank of dragging chains.' There is retribution in Virgil's Kingdom of the Dead, but it is tucked away in a repugnant corner, behind triple walls. There is no delight in it and certainly no sense of what we will find in Tertullian: that it is visited upon rulers, philosophers and poets merely for being unbelievers in a 'loving' Deity.

138

Hell and the psychology of Christian order: Writing in 1971, George Steiner observed that he found it 'acutely disturbing' that T. S. Eliot had failed, in his *Notes Towards a Definition of Culture*, itself written only three years after the end of the Second World War and the revelation of the Holocaust, 'to allude to it in anything but an oddly condescending footnote.' He asked a searing rhetorical question:

> How was it possible to detail and plead for a Christian order when the holocaust had put in question the very nature of Christianity and of its role in European history?[119]

---

119. George Steiner *In Bluebeard's Castle: Some Notes Towards the Re-Definition of Culture* (Faber & Faber, London, 1971) p. 34. I have discussed this matter of Eliot, Steiner, religion and the Holocaust in my Preface.

Steiner was not the first Jewish scholar to raise this question and it is a profound one, much as it might rankle with those Christians who prefer to believe that it was Christian civilization that saved Europe from the barbarism of a pagan Nazism and an atheistic Communism. Hannah Arendt had written, at the conclusion of her stirring Preface to the first edition of *The Origins of Totalitarianism*, in the northern summer of 1950:

He asked the question because, as he put it, 'It seems to me incontrovertible that the holocaust must be set in the framework of the psychology of religion, and that an understanding of this framework is vital to an argument on culture.' His 1971 concerns are worth pondering still—if only as a thought experiment or an exercise in thinking seriously about our history.

139

Intolerable demands? Steiner's own brilliant essay argued forcefully that the Holocaust was a lashing out from within the heartland of European civilization at the intolerable demands of pure monotheism—Judaic monotheism. At one and the same time, the 'secular, materialist, warlike community of modern Europe sought to extirpate from itself' the haunting embodiment of the ideal; even as radical socialist movements overwhelmingly led by Jews[120], sought to give that ideal a new, modern, secular and materialist embodiment. The genocide of the Jews and the widespread—though by no means (and this is crucial) universal—European participation in it, he saw as rooted not simply in centuries of Christian anti-Semitism, but in revolt against God.

140

The pornography of fear and vengeance: The world of the extermination camps, he argued, had its direct antecedent and analogue in the vision of Hell long since spelled out in Christian teachings. 'The concentration and death camps of the twentieth century, wherever they exist, under whatever regime, are Hell made immanent,' he argued. Here 'the millenary pornography

---

We can no longer afford to take that which was good in the past and simply call it our heritage, to discard the bad and simply think of it as a dead load which by itself time will bury in oblivion. The subterranean stream of Western history has finally come to the surface and usurped the dignity of our tradition. This is the reality in which we live. And this is why all efforts to escape from the grimness of the present into nostalgia for a still intact past, or into the anticipated oblivion of a better future, are vain.

The very expression 'subterranean stream' inevitably evokes images of the River Styx and of Charon the ferryman. One imagines Charon being overwhelmed by the corpses of the Holocaust and the terrible wars and terrors of the thirty six years prior to Arendt's Preface (the Korean War had just begun as she wrote). But even more than the River Styx, the phrase surely calls to mind—and was surely intended to call to mind—the very analogy Steiner used a generation later: the haunting likeness between Hell and the German death camps.

120.   '(Some political scientists put at roughly eighty per cent the proportion of Jews in the ideological development of messianic socialism and communism)'. Ibid. p. 41.

of fear and vengeance cultivated in the Western mind by Christian doctrines of damnation, was realized.'[121] And, he commented:

> I am not sure whether anyone, however scrupulous, who spends time and imaginative resources on these dark places, can, or indeed, ought to leave them personally intact. Yet the dark places are at the centre. Pass them by and there can be no serious discussion of the human potential.[122]

We have to have and must not evade that serious discussion, in order that, like Aeneas in Virgil's classic, pre-Christian epic, we might return to the light in the upper air. We need to breathe freely.

141

The need to rethink religion: Steiner's thesis is as seductive as it is horrifying, though it does insufficient justice to the long and complex history of Western religion. The crucial axis of his case is that religion and its convolutions play a vital role in culture and one which became deeply troubling, in the 20th century, with an unexpected and savage recoil against the Enlightenment. From that point, there could be no going back. There could be no further insistence on the metaphysical reality of Hell. There could be no avoiding the need for a profound rethinking of religion and its relationship to a humane civilization worth striving for. Yet it was far from clear what was to come next. Too many Christians 'did an Eliot', as far as culture was concerned.

---

121.   Ibid. pp. 47-48.

122.   Ibid. p. 32. Steiner's most bracing, radical and thought provoking argument, as I have analysed it in my Preface, is that the Holocaust was a terrible, atavistic reflex; an attempt to erase from the European world the nagging and impossibly utopian demands of pure (Judaic) monotheism. But there are other preconditions for the calamities of the 20th century, as he readily conceded. His most haunting speculation other than the religious one, given the massive increase in human numbers since the early 20th century, is that of a psychological lashing out against crowding:

> *There may be, in the genocidal reflexes of the twentieth century, in the compulsive scale of massacre, a lashing out of the choked psyche, an attempt to 'get air', to break the live prison-walls of an intolerably thronged condition. Even at the price of ruin. The void quiet of the city after the fire-storm, the emptiness of the field after the mass murder, may speak to some obscure but primal need for free space, for the silence in which the ego can cry out its mastery'.* (p. 46)

Read against the evolutionary history of the species and not merely the modern history or that of the past few millennia, these lines raise disturbing questions. Yet, if his hypothesis was correct, one would expect far greater mayhem, surely, in the world's vast cities in our time. What is striking, actually, is the degree of order and cooperation they exhibit.

142

Our return to the upper air: Steiner himself was not at all sure what would come next. He certainly did not urge a universal conversion to Rabbinic Judaism; much less a barren surge to dialectical materialism and atheistic 'revolution'. But as the Sibyl long ago warned Aeneas: to retrace our steps, to climb back to the upper air—there the struggle, there the labour lies. We, collectively, were left with the need for rethinking and renewal. Alas, far too many still seek it in varieties of religious dogmatism and even fanaticism. Some point to the manifest failings of secular utopias, whether of communism or materialist capitalism and declare that *only* in religion—Biblical or Qur'anic—can humanity find a sure refuge. We can and must do *better* than that. Our sciences have opened up to us as never before the horizons of the real and the criteria of truth.[123] Within those horizons, we *must* now seek to lay anew the foundations for a humane civilization.

143

What will be our songs? Within any such order, it should be clear, a prime place will need to be assigned to music and song.[124] 'Linguists may rightly tell us of sovereign mysteries of language

---

123.   On the limits and the criteria of truth, see Noson S. Yanofsky *The Outer Limits of Reason: What Science, Mathematics and Logic Cannot Tell Us* (MIT Press, Cambridge Massachusetts and London, 2013). It was the faith of Ludwig Wittgenstein a hundred years ago, as expressed in his *Tractatus Logico-Philosophicus* (1916) that 'Everything that can be thought at all can be thought clearly. Everything that can be put into words can be put clearly.' Yanofsky concluded his book with the cautionary observation that 'reason is the only methodology that improves our well-being' (p. 349). Consistent with the conclusions of Kant and Wittgenstein before him, he remarks:

> *Although it is nice to speculate, unfortunately I do not think it is possible to say anything intelligent on [the topic of what lies beyond the bounds of reason and science]. Our definition of reason is an approach that avoids contradictions or false facts. Anything intelligible about the information beyond such boundaries must be a guess and hence there is nothing intelligent we can really say.* (p. 351).

Yet reaching such a point is salutary in two respects: it teaches us severe disciplines in reasoning and it requires a certain modesty or humility as regards going beyond the bounds of reason. If our new civilization could make such standards and such virtues universal, it would transform humanity and raise our dealings with one another and our understanding of the world around us to an unprecedented level of sophistication and an all but perfect level of intellectual integrity.

124.   Inevitably, in making such a statement, one is reminded—as if by a conscience—of the reflections on music and its role in society put down by that first great Western theoretician of human social order, Plato. He was attuned, as it were, to the importance of music, but argued in several of his dialogues and especially in the late and severe *Laws*, that music had been corrupted by the

structure and process,' writes Gary Tomlinson, 'but only *lift a voice in song* and all humans are struck—enthralled, seduced, threatened, made or unmade—by these powers.'[125] Music, song and dance are not, as Steven Pinker asserted a few years ago, evolutionary 'cheesecake'; a kind of frivolous accidental by-product of human cognitive evolution. They are, rather, primeval and fundamental aspects of our humanity. They have, from primordial times, been a means, transcending language, for weaving communities together through ritual, rhythm, emotional elevation or catharsis. They have from the beginning been deeply implicated in religion. Whatever the extent of our irony or apprehension, we cannot do without them now.

144

A religion for the Anthropocene: Our problem now, in the so-called Anthropocene—the very recent era in which our species has completely overrun the planet and is stretching the ecological limits of the biosphere—is that music and dance have, to too great an extent, become detached from shared social meaning. Millions of human beings are turning—or perhaps one should say 'tuning'—inwards, away from social engagement and the challenges of the era. If we are to surmount the challenges that are now arising, we will need to reinvent our religions and, in the process, rediscover the ancient and profound significance of music, dance and song. The key, as it were, will be the strenuous work required, the hermeneutical and dialogical work entailed, in overhauling those religions in the light of our new knowledge—not merely seeking to attack or demolish them, as certain sectarian and atheistic enthusiasts urge.

---

poets, should be used to impart wholesome discipline to the members of society rather than used merely for pleasure; and should be a key subject of study for the Guardians of the state, since it is both understanding it is important and difficult. Music was, he argues, strictly regulated in Crete and Sparta and unchangeable in Egypt. As with so many aspects of his utopia, Plato's strictures on music make him sound puritanical; but the more we learn about the origins and neurological roots of music, the more interesting Plato's thinking on the subject long ago becomes.

125. Tomlinson op. cit. p. 288. This lifting of voice in song, alas, cuts both ways. There is a scene in Bob Fosse's brilliant 1972 film *Cabaret,* set in the beer garden of a country hotel, in which young Nazis sing a beautiful, stirring and seductive song called 'Tomorrow belongs to me'; which magnificently illustrates the power of a voice raised in song, but in disturbing ways given the context. It throws into high relief both Tomlinson's argument and Plato's concerns, but leaves us a great deal of thinking to do about our approach to music and song in the remaking of civilization—if that is, indeed, what we are prepared to embark upon.

You see, my dandled darling one

10
Lullaby for Junius

Little Lumpkin Junius,
Sit lala on my knee
And I will sing a song to you
Of how to human be.

Little Lumpkin Junius,
Oh apple of my eye,
You'll need to transform everything,
Then bid it all bye-bye.

You see, my dandled darling one,
To sing the thing quite plain,
The loving world I've placed you in's
Completely in the brain.

Your Papa's conjured up a world
Of memories, hopes and dreams
To play with Little Lumpkin in,
But little's what it seems.

You'll find, as you reach out for it,
That much of it recedes;
You'll have to make it all again
Consistent with your needs;

But sing lala with Papa now
And grin and clap your hands;
There's time enough, when you grow big,
For making future plans.

Little Lumpkin Junius,
Sit lala on my knee
And I will sing a song to you
Of how to human be.

Little Lumpkin Junius,
Oh apple of my eye,
You'll need to transform everything,
Then bid it all bye-bye.

145

The archives of civilization: Whether in language or music, in ritual or the metaphysical imaginary, we have, over the past 20,000 years, become creatures of the most fantastic cognitive and cultural complexity. Overwhelmingly, this complexity—and all the accelerating and generally liberating innovation it has made possible—is stored *externally* to the brain or memory of any given individual.[126] In oral cultures it was stored in myths and rituals and social practices. In literate cultures it has increasingly been stored, as it grew, in archives, libraries and databases. But for any given individual to access these archives and make creative use of them requires quite lengthy education. In the process, the *individuation* involved becomes, to varying degrees *unique*.

146

The child must start again: Just to the extent that a person becomes highly creative, they stand *apart* from the archives as such and from other individuals in ways that they *cannot directly pass on* to others. To get to where they stood, anyone else has either to very closely study their methods and work or approach a similar height via a different route. This is especially true of parents and children, mentors and students, masters and apprentices. The less creative a person is, of course, the easier it is to replicate what they do. But how do you pass on to a child or a pupil the creative use you have made of a personal library or the appreciation you have developed over a lifetime of the musical tradition or the art of the ages? In irreducible respects, it *cannot* be done. They have to start from the beginning and discover most things for themselves—in the archives.[127]

---

126.   Merlin Donald argued, in 1991, that human cognitive evolution had taken three successive steps beyond what he dubbed the 'episodic culture' of pre-human primates: mimetic, mythic and theoretic culture. The third pivoted on the invention of what he called external memory storage, beginning with visuographic symbol systems and the myriad developments of thinking that they (writing, mathematics, mapping, charts, musical notation) made possible and coming to an unprecedented intensity of storage and connectivity with the invention of computers and the internet in the last half century or so. *Origins of the Modern Mind: Three Stages in the Evolution of Culture and Cognition* (Harvard University Press, 1991).

127.   Such considerations inevitably connect us with the work of Lev Semenovich Vygotsky, the great Russian theoretician of language, thought and pedagogy. His classic book *Thought and Language*, first published in 1934, as Stalin's grip on the Soviet Union tightened remorselessly, was banned in 1936 and not allowed publication again until 1956, three years after the tyrant's demise. Vygotsky would not bow to the epistemological crudeness of dialectical materialism, nor would he accept other forms of materialist reductionism or Cartesian dualism. He rejected

147

Ritual and theory: From the most remote epochs of human evolution, shared knowledge and tradition have been embodied in social practices and rituals more than in theoretical ideas. To a large extent, this is still the case, but more in terms of meaning and custom than technical skills, which are learned explicitly and modified consciously. Ritual, argued Roy Rappaport, is 'the performance of more or less invariant sequences of formal acts and utterances not entirely encoded by the performers'.[128] Religion evolved out of ritual practices, not the other way around. Religious practices had to do with the 'holy' and that word—in the case of English—derives from the Old English word *halig* and is cognate with the words for 'whole', 'healthy' and 'healing'.

148

The whole is so vast: The rise of religions constitutes the human *attempt* to grasp the whole in such a way as to make possible a 'healthy' and 'healing' sense of meaning for ever larger and more complex social orders—nomadic hunter gatherer, sedentary hunter gatherer, agrarian, urban, imperial, cosmopolitan. The rise of monotheism in the 'ancient' world—a mere two to three millennia ago—has to be seen in this context. Our problem in the very recent past has been that the 'whole', opened up by the sciences, has become so *vast* as to defy ritual integration. Meanwhile, many old religious practices have come to seem archaic and unbelievable, even where still appreciated as parts of ancient traditions. Our humanity is challenged by this set of circumstances. We need to be able to regenerate or reinvent a great many of the things that lay at the foundation of our cultures for centuries and even millennia.

149

Holism, healing and 'holy' fanaticism: Since keeping meaning whole is exceptionally difficult within an expanding universe of truth and experience, religious dogmatism and what might be called 'institutional solipsism' (the belief by the adherents of a given creed

---

both dualism and spiritualism in the quest for an integrated scientific understanding of human consciousness and behaviour. He was interested in the internalization of dialogue into inner speech and reflective thought—as we find it articulated in the character of Hamlet—and in the processes of individuation, whereby each human person comes to terms with a complex external environment in his or her own manner. He was a true compatriot of Boris Pasternak.

128. Roy A. Rappaport *Ritual and Religion in the Making of Humanity* (Cambridge University Press, 1999), p. 24.

or sect that *their* story about the world is uniquely true) have often occurred, with grim consequences. The chaotic adaptation of the Muslim world to modernity is simply another instance of this; but the very attempt, from the 7th century, to impose Islam across the Arabian, Greco-Roman, Persian and Central Asian worlds, was a prime instance of it.[129] The modern 'disenchantment of the world' confronts all such institutional solipsisms and dogmas with unprecedented secular challenges. It has done so in an ever more radical manner since the 17th century. It is still our challenge.

150

Disenchantment and the common good: Yet, as has slowly been realized, this very disenchantment has struck at the root of our humanity in ways both direct and more subtle. To recreate a sense of wholeness and meaning in this context is an authentic challenge, not one disingenuously

---

129.   Needless to say, the Spanish conquest of vast tracts of the Americas ostensibly in the name of the Catholic God and with the aim of converting the heathen was another such prime instance. The conquistadors, of course, seized the opportunity along the way to violently dispossess the native inhabitants, destroy their cities and cultures, enslave them in vast numbers and export their treasures wholesale back to Spain for several centuries. The relationship between cross and sword here has been much debated and defenders of the conquest denounce as a 'black legend' the idea that it was motivated by greed or genocidal killing. For a luminous and scrupulous account of the matter of the conquest and its consequences, see Charles C. Mann *1491: New Revelations of the Americas Before Columbus* (Alfred A. Knopf, New York, 2005).

For a more Madrid-centric appreciation of the sixteenth century in the 'New World'—during which, by common scholarly consensus, the native population of the Americas collapsed by a colossal 90 to 95%—see Hugh Thomas *The Golden Age: The Spanish Empire of Charles V* (Allen Lane, Penguin 2010), especially the Prologue sections 3 and 4 'Cortes and the rebuilding of Mexico/Tenochtitlan' and 'Christianity and the New World', Book I section 11 'Three giants of their time: Charles, Cortes, Pizarro' and Book V passim 'The Indian Soul'.

Nor, of course, was it only the Spaniards who undertook such conquest. The tale of commodities in the Americas is one soaked in the blood and sweat of slaves, first the natives and then imported Africans. The growing of cotton and tobacco in the southern colonies and later states of the British colonies in North America is relatively well known. Somewhat less well known is that of sugar in the Caribbean or coffee, later, in the American isthmus and Brazil. On sugar, see Matthew Parker's *The Sugar Barons: Family, Corruption, Empire and War* (Hutchinson, London, 2011). Sugar was not, of course, grown in the name of God, nor were the Caribbean islands fought over in the 18th century for religious reasons. On the history of coffee, see Mark Pendergrast *Uncommon Grounds: The History of Coffee and How It Transformed Our World* (Basic Books, New York, 1999) and Antony Wild *Black Gold: A Dark History of Coffee* (Harper Perennial, 2005).

manufactured by those conducting a rear-guard defence of 'good, old time religion'. The scale of the challenge and the momentum of scientific advance, however, may render it impossible—at least in any near time frame—to succeed in such re-creation. The sheer complexity of the information involved is simply overwhelming. This needs to be the subject of the most earnest and open-ended dialogue between religious believers and the 'children of the Enlightenment'—for the common good. That dialogue is not going well in the early 21st century.

151

Children's stories and lullabies: Around or outside of institutional practices, dogmas and rituals, human beings live inside stories. But what holistic story are bewildered citizens of our current world to pass down to their offspring in the 21st century? Assume that the parent in question is *wonderfully well* educated and not altogether bewildered. What story will he or she tell their children or any other little people in their care about how the world works, what its 'purpose' is and how to find a meaningful place within it? This is where our lullaby kicks in. Any story that we might tell to the young is necessarily foreshortened and has something about it of the nature of a 'fairy tale'—or a lullaby. Above all, it can only ever be an invitation to imagine the vastness of the world and start to dream vaguely about finding a place in it one day.

152

Our stories are being swamped by innovations: Yet when traditions have so widely been swamped by innovations and the scale of reality has grown so immense, even this is a challenge. How can it be compressed into tales or songs for children? If we cannot or do not offer them something authentic, we should expect them to spurn our *telling*, as they become aware of things. But if we do our best to capture and communicate the actual, we can at most hope to impart hints, whether enticing or cautionary. And as they grow they will have to discover almost everything 'for themselves'—which is to say in the archives, rather than through us. Having done so, with great exertion, they will then—like us—confront the brevity of their own lives and have to learn how to let it all go. Such is the perennial human condition. Nor will that change.[130]

---

130. Ray Kurzweil would appear to disagree with this claim. He predicts an exponential increase in the computational capacity of our technologies and the merging of our biology with our machines that will utterly transform humanity. I am frankly sceptical; but for an informed discussion see John E. Mayfield *The Engine of Complexity: Evolution as Computation* (Columbia University Press, New York, 2013).

153

Care and beloved heedlessness: In a lovely book published about a decade ago, William Waters reflected that:

> *by its nature, a lullaby targets someone who is meant to hear but not entirely to heed what is said. It's not that anyone else is meant, nor that one is singing to oneself; and yet a real lullaby is sung in the hope that its listener will turn her back on the utterance and leave the speaker and his words, at the last, unheard and alone.*[131]

In the present case, it is implicit that 'Little Lumpkin Junius' fulfils these conditions of hearing but not entirely heeding, of being soothed insensibly—and, inevitably, turning his little back on the speaker and his words. The stanzas are, in part, the speaker reflecting in the presence of the child on the sheer complexity of the world of meaning he has assembled and the sheer difficulty of imparting it to the little fellow. He has misgivings, but cocoons the child from them in his lullaby.

154

A certain unease: The very idea that Junius will comprehend is gently dismissed, with the asseveration that there will be time enough 'when he grows big' to come to terms with the disenchanted world and make something of it in the normal human way. Yet orientation

---

131. William Waters *Poetry's Touch: On Lyric Address* (Cornell University Press, Ithaca and London, 2003), p. 37. The italics are mine. The book as a whole is exquisite. I have learned more from it about poetry than from any other book. His opening lines set the tone as well as the theme of his book:

> *To whom does a poem speak? Do poems really communicate with those they address? Is reading poems like overhearing? Like intimate conversation? Like performing a script? In this book I pursue these questions by reading closely a selection of poems that say you to a human being and by trying to describe the reading process as it encounters these instances of address.*

He goes on to point out:

> *... poetry's freedom to move between communicative frameworks with a suddenness, or disregard, rare in any other use of language. The awkward fact is that poetry, from the brash parlando of Archilochus to the pronominal lability of John Ashbery, enacts—for us, as readers, now—not so much a stable communicative situation as a chronic hesitation, a faltering, between monologue and dialogue, between 'talking about' and 'talking to', third and second person, indifference to interlocutors and the yearning to have one.* (pp. 7-8)

How is such thinking and awareness to be imparted to young readers, new to verse and to the archives of civilization, in our schools and universities—not as an academic conceit, but as an enrichment of felt life?

to that world cannot, in fact, be postponed in quite this manner. From the cradle up, the emotional and cognitive formation of children alerts them, sometimes traumatically, to the realities into which they have been born. There is, in other words, not only gentleness, but a certain unease and evasion in the dismissal or postponement of instructive induction; just as there is an inevitable element of shielded naïveté in the presumed heedlessness and turning away of the infant being.

155

Fairy tales, hope and illusion in a Grimm world: We induct children, with more or less conscious intent, into the world as it is with 'children's stories', perhaps a little after our lullabies. 'Fairy tales' belong in this category. But they raise two questions: at what point in the raising of children do we disabuse them of the *belief* in fairy tales; and in what way do we conceive of the formative or *conative* value of such tales for little human beings? When the brothers Grimm began collecting folk tales in the early nineteenth century, Jack Zipes tells us, they did *not* think of these tales as 'fairy tales' or as stories for children. They saw them as a body of stories 'preserving an ancient tradition of [oral] story-telling', which they wished to see 'archived' as part of the German cultural heritage. What does not seem to have occurred to them was that their books would be translated into 150 languages and appreciated all around the modern world.[132]

156

Hope and utopian thinking: It was this more universal appeal that fascinated Ernst Bloch, the philosopher of hope and utopian thinking, in the mid-20th century. 'Not only does the fairy tale remain as fresh as longing and love,' wrote Bloch in a 1930 essay—even as the world was on the brink of plunging into a dark era of totalitarianism, genocide, terror and global war—'but the demonically evil, which is abundant in the fairy tale, is still seen at work here in the present, and the happiness of 'once upon a time', which is even more abundant, still affects our visions of the future.'[133] There is an argument for

---

132. Jack Zipes *Grimm Legacies: The Magic Spell of the Grimms' Folk and Fairy Tales* (Princeton University Press, Princeton and Oxford, 2015), p. xii.

133. Quoted in Zipes, ibid. p. 190. His discussion of Bloch's reflections on fairy tales from this point of view is rich and pivots on a conversation on the subject between Bloch and Theodor Adorno in Frankfurt, in 1964. Adorno, gloomy about what he saw as the commodification and banalization of culture in the capitalist West, was inclined to think that the deeper values of art and literature were being eroded. Bloch was less certain of this and held that even in circumstances of real

the value of such tales. But in our specific time, what tales should we most seek to tell to our children? Who can now tell fairy tales with a good conscience?

157

Songs and the stars: The key to what we might seek to impart or preserve, both on the micro-personal scale and on the largest scale in an emerging global culture, is surely the link between what is *so*, as discovered by the sciences, and those germs of hope and imagination, emancipation and justice, which Bloch found again and again in popular literature. We see this in the most popular science fiction and fantasy of the past generation, such as *Star Wars*. However much most of it seems rather trite and merely cinematic, it is worth pausing to reflect on the implicit meanings and morals it imparts—generally hopeful ones; just as one might have done in the past with Westerns or other Hollywood tales of heroic derring-do, drawn from historical legends.

158

Stories at the oasis: The strongest such tales will not merely provide illusory or fatuous hopes to individuals, but will tap into the very deepest of human needs on a collective scale and help great numbers of people to find their bearings and some meaningful purpose in a crowded, fast-moving, technologized world that is now known to be a tiny, aqueous oasis in the midst of an almost inconceivably large and inhuman Cosmos.[134] Such stories are hard

---

darkness and moral evil, simple folk tales of heroism and hope had an enduring appeal and value. Indeed, even short of radical evil, he believed, as Zipes expresses it, that 'the fairy tale in all its forms, ancient and modern, remains vibrant and touches the dreams and wishes of common people who want to overcome the dreariness of their daily lives.'

This, of course, simply pushes to surface the question: what ought to or can constitute real relief from such 'dreariness' in our time? By what criteria are we to judge, if there are not agreed transcendent ones? My own path forward in life was powerfully influenced by children's stories, read to me and then by me when still at primary school. I have delighted, when it was possible, in reading some of those stories to the young children in my own family, helping to bring alive the hopeful imaginations of the next generation.

134.   It is always worth reminding ourselves that we have only been able to see our world from space since 1969 and that the Hubble Telescope has only been in orbit since 1990. It has only been in the last year or two that we have been able to see images of the remote and tiny Earth taken from Mars, underscoring yet again its smallness and evident 'fragility' in the cosmic context. Our graphically explicit self-awareness, as a species marooned on a tiny and rare planet, in the midst of a vast and largely alien universe, is very, very new and appears not to have registered yet with more than a tiny proportion of the global human population. But it needs to become an integral part of

to generate, with so much changing and so many traditions and even languages being swept away like rainforest landscapes and ocean fauna by the prodigious appetites of our species in the Anthropocene. But we need them, almost in the form of rituals, all the way down to new lullabies, if we are to cope psychologically and practically with the looming challenges and dizzying possibilities ahead of us.

---

any and all global education worth the name in the generation or two ahead of us. In many parts of the world, that will be a serious challenge; yet it is foundational.

Your wings are our secret

11
Your Architect

Your love is enough for my heart
And your wings for my freedom

Your love has called to me
From the Parthenon and Mount Athos
It has had me hail tyrants
With visions of clearance
It has built Ronchamp for the Sun
It has drawn me through darkness

Your wings have flown me to La Plata
They have created a spectacular residence
A jungle of courtyards and gardens
Cantilevered roofs to shelter my longings
Inspiring me to pitch my freedom
Outside the given ground

Your love is enough for my heart
And your wings for my freedom

I yearned to rebuild Paris,
But your love took me elsewhere:
It had me hurl myself into New York;
It had me scorn the Ossete in his lair;
It had me leapfrog every setback
And take my exuberance to Chandigarh

Your wings are our secret
They free me to swim towards
The star we steer by
Each stroke an act of worship
Of light, of air, of sea -
And the hope of a right ending

Your love is enough for my heart
And your wings for my freedom.

159

A program to change the world: Charles-Edouard Jeanneret (1887-1965), the exuberant architectural modernist, who adopted the pseudonym or artistic name 'Le Corbusier', believed that his visions of designs for living and urban renewal could overcome both the burdens of the past and the confusions of the industrial age.[135] His life is taken over and used as an extended metaphor in 'Your Architect'. Biographical episodes and flights of soaring imagination are taken and used to point to the general possibility of a new architecture for civilization in the 21st century. This is meant both figuratively, in the mental, social and cultural life of individuals; and physically in the rebuilding of global infrastructure and the teeming cities of the 21st century.

160

Imperial visions and the artist: Are architects, any more than commissioned artists, truly able to refashion the world and open it up to new possibilities? Or are they, in general, merely the servants of those with the wealth and power to determine what extravagances and even monstrosities will be erected here and there? From the Hanging Gardens of Babylon, whose unknown architects must certainly have been the servants of an imperial vision[136], or Apollodorus of Damascus, who master-minded the design and building of some of the greatest palaces and forums of Imperial Rome[137], via the (again often unknown) architects

---

135.   Even at the very end of his life, according to his biographer, Le Corbusier 'fervently believed that a few brave individuals had the power to change all of human history' and that he was among them. In India, he was 'certain that he had touched Nehru'; he 'believed himself completely understood and welcome in the halls of power', which had not, to his disappointment, happened in his encounters with Petain, Mussolini or Stalin. Nicholas Fox Weber *Le Corbusier: A Life* (Alfred A. Knopf, New York, 2008), pp. 717 and 563.

136.   Stephanie Dalley *The Mystery of the Hanging Garden of Babylon* (Oxford University Press, 2013), argues that the so-called Hanging Gardens of Babylon never existed at Babylon, but were a magnificent piece of work at Nineveh, built for the Assyrian monarch Sennacherib (705-681 BCE). This was the very King who, in Byron's famous line, was the Assyrian who came down upon Judah 'like the wolf on the fold', only to have the army he sent to besiege Jerusalem smitten by disease and decimated; something inevitably interpreted by the Hebrews as evidence that God was on their side.

137.   Apollodorus of Damascus is said to have supervised the building of the great Palatine palaces of the Roman emperors during the reign of the last Flavian emperor, Domitian; the superb Forum of Trajan and even the fabulous villa of Hadrian at Tivoli, in the course of a long career. See Anthony Everitt *Hadrian and the Triumph of Rome* (Random House, New York, 2009), pp. 109, 118-19, 177, 302-04, 308.

behind the great abbeys of Catholic Europe[138], to those who have won contracts for design in the burgeoning overhaul of China's cities since the 1990s[139], isn't there a constant theme

138.   See Wolfgang Braunfels *Monasteries of Western Europe: The Architecture of the Orders* (Thames and Hudson, London, 1972) for an account of this grand architectural tradition and especially the renewed emphasis on integral design that came very late, after the Reformation and especially in 'faith-torn' Germanic countries.

139.   Arthur Cotterell *The Imperial Capitals of China* (Pimlico, Random House, London, 2007) and Jasper Becker *City of Heavenly Tranquillity: Beijing in the History of China* (Allen Land, Penguin, London, 2008) both provide fine introductions to the history of Chinese imperial architecture. The latter concentrates on Beijing and concludes with critical reflections on the massive destruction of historic Beijing by the Communist Party, first under Mao Zedong and then under the post-Mao modernizers of an increasingly wealthy China. Especially poignant is his account of the career of Liang Sicheng, son of the great late-Imperial reformer Liang Qichao. The younger Liang trained in architecture in the United States during the 1930s and 1940s, but returned to China after 1949, hoping to contribute to the renovation of the country under the supposedly visionary and idealistic Communist Party.

The architect as visionary overridden and in the end destroyed by the masters is embodied in the fate of Liang Sicheng. As Becker remarks:

> *Liang considered it was vital to preserve Beijing as an integral whole ... officials across China would take their cue from what happened to the capital. The protection of China's entire architectural heritage, therefore, hung on the fate of Beijing ... He prepared, printed and distributed at his own expense a plan for the new administrative centre which would allow the new construction to take place without disturbing the traditional central axis of the city. He wrote articles like 'Peking—a Masterpiece of Urban Planning', which he hoped would win his cause public support. Liang suggested that Beijing should become like Washington DC, largely a tourist city, and reminded the new leadership that architecture is 'history made of stone'.*
>
> *We may deny history, he warned, but we cannot cut ourselves off from it. In the illustrations that he drew, Beijing is shown as a gigantic museum. The flat wide tops of the battlements became a continuous public park with flower beds and garden seats. The gate towers and corner towers with their up-swept double roofs were turned into museums, exhibition halls, refreshment kiosks and tea-shops. The moat around the city was turned into a beautiful green-belt where 'the great masses of the working people' could go fishing, boating or ice-skating. The walls of Beijing, he said, are not only China's national treasure but also the cultural relic of the peoples of all nations. 'We have inherited this priceless and unique historical property; how can we now destroy it', he pleaded.* (pp. 190-91)

The Party was not listening. The walls were totally destroyed. None of Liang's vision was realized. He himself died, after suffering persecution, in both the 1950s and the 1960s, in 1972. What he would have made of the Communist Party's radical overhaul of Maoist Beijing since the 1990s is a matter for conjecture.

of serving the visions of the masters, rather than opening the space of possibility for the mass of humanity?

161

Courting dictators while living freely: Le Corbusier was more radical and free-spirited than most. Like many a Futurist and revolutionist, he wanted to erase large parts of what already existed and replace it with his vision of how humanity ought to live. This began with Paris itself, which he wanted to radically rebuild. He sought work in Mussolini's Italy and in Stalin's Moscow. He collaborated with the Vichy regime during the Nazi occupation of France, believing it might prove to be an agent of change in France. He built churches and had a religious vision of light and peace; yet he lived a hedonistic and expressive life wholly liberated from Christian moral prescriptions. He was far from uncontroversial. His aim was architectural renewal, he insisted; and orthodoxies or the objections of the conservatives be damned. For this, he was condemned by critics as the Lenin of architecture and yet praised at his 1965 funeral by Andre Malraux.[140]

162

A temple to the Holy Mother and the Sun: The Catholic chapel at Ronchamp, in south-eastern France, completed in 1955, is one of Le Corbusier's acknowledged masterpieces. As with so much of his work, it was at once devoted to central themes in the religious tradition that commissioned it and yet designed to evoke a wider sense of the human place in the cosmos and the ancient, pre-Christian roots of European religious feeling. It was dedicated to the 'Holy Mother', at once the Virgin Mary, Queen of Heaven and Star of the Sea of the Catholic Church and the eternal feminine as giver and nourisher of human life. 'At Ronchamp', his biographer claims, ' ... Le Corbusier burst the boundaries of architecture by composing with light and colour and by animating a small space so that it is both a vessel of ceaseless motion and ineffable calm ... '[141]

163

The greatest of architects: Le Corbusier's original sketch for Ronchamp, we are told,[142] 'resembles an ancient megalith, an imaginary mix of dolmen and stone from the Bronze Age, where so-called primitive people assembled and worshipped the forces of the universe.'

---

140.   Nicholas Fox Weber *Le Corbusier: A Life* (Alfred A. Knopf, New York, 2008), pp. 13-14.

141.   Ibid. p. xix.

142.   Ibid. p. 654.

It evolved into a finished structure of striking originality which placed it across a vast arc of the religious imagination from the era of the European henges five thousand years ago or more to the cusp of an open future. When the architect died, he was hailed in the Parisian press, despite his often disconcerting proclamations while he lived, as 'the greatest architect in the world' and one who had 'liberated us from a tyrannical past.' Let him be *your* architect in that respect: laying open a capacity to rethink the very walls, conceptual and physical, within which you live and the possibilities for reconstructing them, to access more natural light, air and grace of lifestyle.

164

New temples founded on ancient perceptions: The name 'Ronchamp' derives, like so much in France, from the classical past, being rooted in the words *Romanorum campus* (field of the Romans). It was built on a site overlooking an ancient Roman road, on a hilltop which, like many a Catholic church or monastery, had long ago been the site of a pagan temple; in this case a temple to the Sun. Monte Cassino, the great Benedictine monastery, built south of Rome half a century after the overthrow of the last Roman emperor in the West, when the Goths ruled Italy, was also built on the site of an ancient temple of Apollo, the Sun god. Le Corbusier turned the tables adroitly. Inspired, says his biographer, by his 'faith in a higher being that went beyond any traditional notions of organized religion', he undertook to design a chapel in 'a place that had been used for worship of the Sun, the deity he revered above all others...'[143] Shouldn't we build such precincts in which to listen, after the death of God, to the sublimities of Palestrina's *Canticum Canticorum*?

165

The secret and beloved Muse: For the last thirty years of his life, Le Corbusier conducted a wholly private love affair with an American heiress and writer, while remaining married to Yvonne Gallis. He also had various other affairs, including one with the famous erotic dancer Josephine Baker.[144] The heiress was one Marguerite Tjader Harris, a stylish red-head

---

143.   Nicholas Fox Weber *Le Corbusier: A Life* (Alfred A. Knopf, New York, 2008),pp. 656-57.

144.   The two met in Rio Janeiro in 1929. Each had a marital partner by then—Le Corbusier Yvonne, Baker her Pepito—and, remarks Weber, both of them 'required such partners. But they also craved their equals in imagination and intensity.' The architect saw in the performer someone at once 'ravishing to the eyes' and 'unfettered by tradition'. He thought her performances had the same 'bravery and effrontery' of his architectural creations, combining physical beauty with impeccable mechanics in a sublime blend of heart and intellect. Ibid. pp. 308-09.

from New York; a woman with a very free spirit. In so many ways, from 1935, he became her architect; she his muse. Remarks Le Corbusier's biographer, Nicholas Fox Weber:

> a lot of what he wrote to Marguerite Tjader Harris—the woman he discussed with no-one and who in turn kept their relationship secret until well after his death, and whose name never appeared in any account by or about Le Corbusier during his lifetime—reflected a degree of admiration and love he showed to nobody else.[145]

This is the trope upon which the poem is constructed. It is embedded in the refrain. Yet the poem is not intended simply as a poetic rendition of the affair between Le Corbusier and Tjader Harris; but as an appropriation of their freedom in a new voice, where all their realities have become metaphors and enticements to psychological and erotic liberty—for all free spirits.[146]

166

Places and moments of recovery: Changing the world is strenuous work. It breaks human beings in the attempt and has done so for millennia, not least since the Axial Age, when such concerns largely first arose. It is something which inspires people to see before them Everests they must scale and impels them—individuals, parties, sects, networks of activists—to set about clambering up the formidable col of the mountain, all but unprepared for its icy dangers and heedless of the risk that they will—as many do—slip and fall to their demise on the ascent. Often enough, of course, it is a psychological, not a political ascent and the fall can be broken by retreat and recovery in some base camp or other of the mind. Weber beautifully captures moments of retreat in Le Corbusier's life. We need to prepare them for ourselves and others.

167

Retreating to the intimate scale: The architect went first to the Soviet Union, in the early 1930s, and then to the United States, in each case expecting to be acclaimed as the architect of the new; and ordained the high priest of architectural renovation. He met with disappointment in both cases and retreated to Paris in disillusionment:

---

145.   Ibid. p. 381. 'To no other lover,' writes Weber (p. 382), 'did Le Corbusier express himself with such respect. He had let go of his usual sense of distance; there was none of the condescension of his communication with Yvonne. For the first time, he had met a woman on his own level.' He goes on to quote her, from a late life memoir, as recalling of her affair with the architect 'We had found a free companionship without obligations or demands'. He comments: 'She was as remarkable as he was.' (p. 383)

146.   Their relationship is the primary model for that between Fenimore Moneghan and Margarita Henderson y Mendoza in the novel I am writing, under the title *Darkness Over Love: A Complete Fiction*; for which the present book, along with several others, is a kind of preparatory or ancillary exercise.

After returning from America, Le Corbusier retreated to the privacy and comfort of his studio; it was his usual formula of immersing himself in the luxury of creativity on the most intimate scale whenever he despaired of his ability to change the entire world. Paintbrush in hand, a canvas in front of him, his wife just a room away, the aromas of garlic and tomatoes simmering in olive oil wafting from the kitchen, their dog scurrying around the apartment, he was content. Would that such creative retreats were always available to those who seek to change the world. Too often, it is not an artist's studio but an impoverished garret, a dictator's prison cell, or even a torture chamber in which the fallen find themselves and have done so throughout 'history'.[147]

168

We brave, Nietzschean birds: There can be, however, in any and all of these circumstances, a deep consolation to be had from the love of another whose spirit, whose freedom, whose wings one admires and affirms profoundly. There is a haunting passage in Nietzsche in which he acclaims the spirit of 'all those brave birds which fly out into the distance, into the farthest distance' across the Western seas of existential metaphor, up and away, until they break themselves against infinity and are unable to go on:

> All our great teachers and predecessors have at last come to a stop ... But what does that matter to you and me!? Other birds will fly farther! This insight and faith of ours vies with them ... it rises above our heads and above our impotence into the heights and from there surveys the distance and sees before it the flocks of birds which, far stronger than we, still strive whither we have striven and where everything is sea, sea, sea ... [148]

We have to see ourselves, if we are serious about innovation and renovation, in that kind of context; and not just in regard to discovering 'new worlds', but with regard to placing the real

---

147.   A beautiful recent book explores how writers from Boethius (in the sixth century CE) to Primo Levi (in the wake of the Holocaust) have responded to incarceration and oppression by writing— letters, memoirs, philosophical reflections, theological reflections, poetry and political treatises: Rivkah Zim *Consolations of Writing: Literary Strategies of Resistance from Boethius to Primo Levi* (Princeton University Press, 2014). As Zim writes, in her Introduction:

> *For centuries the experiences of European intellectuals in prisons of various kinds stimulated them to reconsider aspects of the human condition in their responses to personal crises, and Europe's turbulent history of wars, persecution and revolution. While these writers' circumstances and contemporary attitudes to prisoners have varied greatly, similar forms, themes and functions tend to recur in their prison writing ... Prisoners of state or political dissidents, prisoners of conscience, and confined victims of intolerance and hatred often feel a special need to maintain and defend their integrity and that core of convictions for which they have been imprisoned.*

148.   Friedrich Nietzsche *Daybreak: Thoughts on the Prejudices of Morality* (Translated by R. J. Hollingdale with an Introduction by Michael Tanner, Cambridge University Press, 1982), #575, pp. 228-29.

and current world in the cosmological and temporal perspective that will induce the most profound and creative transformation of humanity and it's stewardship of the ecosphere.

169

The Charterhouse of Florence: Le Corbusier was deeply affected, when a young man, by both the monastic architecture of the European past and the classical architecture of the ancient world. This is the way we should all respond to the wonders created by our forebears, as well as to the wonders of the natural world. 'Ah! The monasteries!', he wrote to a friend. 'I'd like to spend my whole life inhabiting what are called their cells.' He had specific monasteries in mind when he wrote this: certain frescoes by Fra Angelico and, above all, the great Carthusian monastery outside Florence, founded in 1341, which endures to this day as a Cistercian establishment. He was profoundly affected by this monastic structure. Four years later he was to be overwhelmed by the Parthenon, but even it did not rival the impression left on his imagination by the six hundred year old Charterhouse at the confluence of the Ema and Greve rivers, in Tuscany.

170

Solitude and tranquillity: His biographer, Weber, writes:

> The intelligence of the plan that gracefully combined community living and the
> sanctity of the individual's private existence made the monastery a perfect small city.

He saw it as a model for future urban designs for *working* class living and as a kind of 'earthly paradise'. He wrote to his parents that he believed that 'all human housing should provide some of the solitude and tranquillity enjoyed by monks.' Years later, in one of his own books, he was to write with reference to this monastic establishment—which had also been praised by John Ruskin—that he had 'never encountered such a joyous version of habitation.' Yet his interest in all this was secular, not traditionally religious. He was looking at designs for human living and had relatively little interest in the religious beliefs that underpinned the building of cloisters.[149]

171

Simplicity and austerity: On a journey through Austria and the Balkans to Greece, in 1911, Le Corbusier visited the thousand year old Greek Orthodox state of Mount Athos on the ancient peninsula of Acte, the easternmost of the three finger-like peninsulas of the Chalcidice on the northern coast of the Aegean. It is inhabited, as it was then, exclusively by

---

149.   Nicholas Fox Weber *Le Corbusier: A Life* (Alfred A. Knopf, New York, 2008) pp. 47-48.

monks, living in some twenty monasteries; and is an autonomous republic within the Hellenic federation. He stayed for two weeks within Acte, exploring this all male domain, from which not only women but female animals had been excluded for a thousand years. It affected him, if anything, even more profoundly than the Charterhouse of Florence. He revelled in the Aegean sun, the simplicity and austerity of the monastic establishments and the horizon of sea and sky viewed from sublime elevations. All this infused his designs for villas, apartments and chapels for decades to come.[150]

172

Sublime proportions and settings: This kind of profound aesthetic reaction can be seen even more clearly in his response to the Parthenon, which he visited in September 1911, in those halcyon European days before the Great War. He anticipated that climbing the Acropolis would be overwhelming, writes Weber, but nothing prepared him for the scale, sublime proportions and landscaping of the Parthenon, which 'stupefied him', so that 'he was exhilarated beyond all expectations.' All manner of artists and poets have extolled the Parthenon for centuries as the very epitome of classical perfection and good taste in design. Le Corbusier came away from the site wanting, for the rest of his life, to 'create such thrills for others'—above all the integration of the built environment into its natural setting; an equipoise between air, water, light and stone. He loved the Parthenon's elevation and its vistas. He saw in it the temple as part of the world.[151]

---

150.   Ibid. pp. 86-91. Le Corbusier and his (male) travelling companion arrived by boat at Daphne, the port of entry to the Republic of Mount Athos, half way down the western coast of Acte on 24 August 1911. Weber records that:

> *The grandeur and majesty of the mountain in front of him was more impressive than any man-made construction he had ever seen. And he exulted in the myth of this bold pyramid form shooting up from the sea—said to have been the rock that Athos, the leader of the Giants, had cast at his foe Poseidon, the leader of the Olympians, but that had missed him and fallen into the ocean. (p. 87)*

Millennia later, as Grecian mythology dating back to the Neolithic gave way to Christian mythology, it was claimed that the Virgin Mary had actually visited the peninsula of Acte (perhaps at some point subsequent to her assumption into heaven). The mountain at Daphne was therefore dedicated to the 'Mother of God', the proverbial 'Holy Mother', purified heiress to all the goddesses of antiquity. This was one of many influences acting upon Le Corbusier that led him, some forty years later and more, to dedicate the chapel at Ronchamp to the Holy Mother—as well as to his primary deity, the Sun.

151.   Ibid. pp. 94-95.

173

The enigma of the Parthenon: Yet Le Corbusier knew very little about the Parthenon. Over the past three decades, long after his death, we have learned more about the construction and meaning of the Parthenon than anyone seems to have known or remembered since the era in which it was built (447-432 BCE)—perhaps not even then. Through much of the modern era, the Parthenon has been extolled as the supreme artistic and architectural product of classical Athenian democracy. Yet, as a contemporary specialist on the subject remarks:

> There is much more to Athenian culture than democracy and more to its conception of democracy than what can be perceived by viewing it through a modern lens ... At the very core of Athenian *politeia* lies the culture's fundamental understanding of itself and its origins, its cosmology and prehistory—a nexus of ideas that defined the values of the community and gave rise to a complex array of ritual observances of which the Parthenon was the focal point for nearly a thousand years. Until now the Parthenon has received relatively little consideration in this light.[152]

This has implications not only for rethinking Le Corbusier's enthusiasm for the Parthenon, but for our own, more general coming to terms with our cosmology, our prehistory and our religious heritage. For in truth, all our current cultures, all of human civilization, now stands as a kind of Parthenon looked at through modern eyes in substantial ignorance of the cosmology and prehistory that lie behind and beneath it. This is the case not only with folkloric or traditional cosmology, but with the relationship between where we stand—on the 'Acropolis' of the 21st century world—and the *actual* cosmology and prehistory of our world and our species. From this high place, everything needs to be thought through again—from the mental foundations up.[153]

---

152.   Joan Breton Connelly *The Parthenon Enigma: A Journey Into Legend* (Zeus Head, London, 2014) pp. xvii-xviii.

153.   'The study of Greek ritual and religion has burgeoned over the past thirty years,' writes Connelly. ' ... The more we have discovered, the more enigmatic the Parthenon has come to seem, and the more inadequate appear the simplistic meanings ascribed to it by later cultures. As a vastly complex world of cult ritual and spiritual intensity reveals itself, it still remains to be asked of the structure at the very heart of so much strange, dark practice, 'What exactly is the Parthenon?' p. xix.

The Acropolis had been the site of strongholds at Athens long before the classical era. There are remains dating back to the 4th millennium BCE and a major Bronze Age fortress and palace, dating back almost a thousand years before the Parthenon as we know it, was constructed in the 5th century BCE. It was these massive walls, which stood some 33 feet

174

His fingers are fat as grubs: Back in the 1930s, in the wake of forced collectivization and the beginnings of the Great Terror, a poet with a bold enough spirit to indulge a kind of death wish, Osip Mandelstam, wrote a poem aimed squarely at Stalin, the murderous and unforgiving dictator. He must have known it would get him into trouble, but unlike so many of his countrymen, he dared the brutal Ossetian (Stalin being of Ossetian or Georgian extraction) with his barbed words—and paid the price. He perished in the GULAG in 1938. The poem does justice to dictators and gang bosses of all stripes, but Stalin was as bad as they come. The poem reads:

> We live deaf to the land beneath us
> Ten steps away no one hears our speeches
> All we hear is the Kremlin mountaineer
> The murderer and peasant slayer
> His fingers are fat as grubs
> And the words, final as lead weights, fall from his lips
> His cockroach whiskers leer
> And his boot tops gleam
> Around him a rabble of thin-necked leaders –
> Fawning half-men for him to play with
> They whinny, purr or whine
> As he prates and points a finger
> One by one, forging his laws, to be flung
> Like horseshoes at the head, the eye or the groin
> And every killing is a treat
> For the broad-chested Ossete.

With that piece of verse, Mandelstam outdid and outbraved generations of 'revolutionaries', fellow-travellers and Western statesmen. He got it right—and he died for his poetic candour.[154]

---

high and up to 16 feet thick, that were stormed by the Persian armies of the Great King in 480 BCE, after the huge Persian force had overwhelmed the Spartans at Thermopylae and broken into Attica. Some remnants of them can still be seen to this day.

154. By far the best introduction to the life and fate of Osip Mandelstam is the two volume memoir by his widow Nadezhda Mandelstam *Hope Against Hope* (Penguin, 1975) and *Hope Abandoned* (Penguin, 1976); but Clare Cavanagh's *Osip Mandelstam and the Modernist Creation of Tradition* (Princeton University Press, 1995) is a fine introduction to his poetics and the cultural climate

175

Oblivious to famine: Le Corbusier, in his prime, and to be sure, a few years before Mandelstam met his end, saw Stalin as a tyrant bent on innovation and he hoped to win contracts to help design the new Moscow and the landscape of the industrializing Soviet Union. For this he was excoriated in the conservative press. In Nazi Germany he was even denounced as 'the Lenin of architecture' and his books were banned. He was heartened when invited—along with eleven other international architects—to submit a design for the proposed Palace of the Soviets. It was 1931 and Stalin's forced collectivization had been undertaken two years before. The rural areas were wracked by famine and terror. What did Le Corbusier know of all this? He seems chiefly to have been filled with a sense of what modernist vision he could bring to the rebuilding of Moscow—never mind Stalin's monstrous impositions on the peoples of the 'socialist paradise.'

176

An act of criminal thoughtlessness: Weber tells us that the design, as the visionary young architect conceived it:

> evoked soaring confidence and imagination. It called for an enormous and sweeping concrete arch, with the roof of a fifteen thousand seat auditorium suspended from it. Perpendicular to the arch at the other end of the building complex, were five right-angled buttresses resembling oversized angle brackets. A flurry of cylinders and rectangles, vastly different in scale from one another, contained, among other spaces, a second auditorium—for nearly six thousand people—and two theatres. Some of the surfaces were opaque and solid, others translucent. Graceful curves, rigid verticals, gentle horizontals and long, sloping angles, each the by-product of the demands of the interior circulation, combined to give a fantastic energy to the overall result.[155]

He overestimated, however, the creative *élan* of the 'radical progressives' in the Kremlin. When the short list of three designs was announced on 28 February 1932, his was not among them.[156] His design was ridiculed in *Izvestia*, even as his Western critics were denouncing him as a Communist. Le Corbusier was incensed at his rejection, not least because the winning design was a highly conventional neo-classical one. He drafted a telegram to Stalin

in which he became first a poet and then a fatalistic and unrepentant dissident. Robert Littell's historical novel *The Stalin Epigram* (Simon & Schuster, New York, 2009) is an engaging dramatization of the poet's last years. The translation of the poem cited above is from Littell's novel, pp. 94-95.

155.   Weber op. cit. p. 332.
156.   Ibid. p. 342.

describing the jury's decision as 'an act of criminal thoughtlessness' that robbed the Soviet Union of the mantle to which it aspired—that of leading the 'enormous cultural effort of Modern Times.'[157] He turned his back on Stalin in disdain—not as a despot, but as a man without architectural vision.

177

Taking exuberance to Chandigarh: Almost twenty years later, Le Corbusier was approached about plans for building a completely new capital for the Indian province of Punjab. India had only been independent of the British Empire for three years and a large chunk of Punjab had been hived off at independence to become West Pakistan, the larger part of a new Muslim state. He leapt at the opportunity. The site alone could have been enough to entice him: a vast plateau within sight of the majestic Himalayas. But the proposed name of the new city—Chandigarh—would have awoken deep responses in Le Corbusier. It was taken from the name of the goddess of power, Chandi, a manifestation of the Hindu goddess of vitality and transformation. As Weber remarks, she was 'the perfect avatar for Le Corbusier'. He conceived something that would not be European in inspiration, but Indian and modernist at the same time. Far away in New Delhi, Pandit Nehru was delighted. The man who yearned to remake the world at last had a great urban project on a large scale and the political support for doing it as he imagined it.[158]

---

157.   Ibid. p. 344.

158.   Ibid. pp. 534-539. Weber's summation of the case is eloquent:

> *Chandigarh was the summons of a lifetime. All of Le Corbusier's ideals might at last become the everyday reality of a city built for five hundred thousand people—and that in less than half a century would house well over a million. Through design, he could give daily existence the qualities of rightness and morality he held sacred. He could apply the ideas of urbanism he had developed but not been given the chance to execute in Paris, Algiers, Bogota, Stockholm and a range of other cities. Here Le Corbusier would fulfil his dream of subdividing a city into regions for business, administration and housing. He could lay out a transportation network, erect individual buildings of monumental value and redesign the life of everyone from the highest government official to the poorest worker.*

> Everyone, it might be said, who hopes to see the making of a new foundation for human civilization dreams, at their most euphoric, of being able to do it in this manner. Rarely is anything like that possible—except in visionary schemes and perhaps manifestos. Human reality is far too complex to be made over in any such sweeping fashion. Yet the dreams and designs, like free oxygen, it is to be hoped, enter into the atmosphere that all human civilization breathes and, little by little, open up new possibilities for renewal and even for transformation.

178

Swimming towards the star we steer by: 'How nice it would be to die swimming toward the Sun,' Le Corbusier is said to have remarked on at least two occasions. His doctor once asked him what he, Le Corbusier, would do if he was a doctor himself; to which the architect replied: I wouldn't do anything. I would just let people die peacefully.

According to Weber, Le Corbusier believed that:

> death, like architecture, is ideally in accord with the inescapable cycles of the universe and should have grace and proportion. Like the terraces and roof gardens of Le Corbusier's houses, one's way of dying should provide a direct connection to the cosmos.[159]

Is that a civilized idea, a 'pagan' one with ominous implications, or one open to creative acts?

179

What, then, is a way of dying? The 'inescapable cycles of the universe' include all manner of explosive, random and destructive occurrences. The Earth has been subject to many of these, punctuating the relative equilibrium of the epochs of life with grand calamities. We, also, both collectively and as individuals, are subject to such disruptive intrusions into the 'natural cycles' of our social affairs and personal lives. What, therefore, is a 'way of dying that provides a direct connection to the cosmos'? It must be a ritualized and deliberate approach to the conscious awareness of mortality. Collectively, we need to reinvent the funeral rites of our religions. Individually, we need to exercise imagination and choice, as contributions to this.

180

From a private retreat on the Cote d'Azur: On 27 August 1965, Le Corbusier, an individual with wide artistic knowledge and considerable personal liberty, chose the manner of his own death. He had long felt that 'moving weightlessly through water under the open sky was his salvation'. When he discovered, in the northern summer of 1965, that he had an incurable heart condition, he took himself to his long established coastal retreat on the Cote d'Azur overlooking the Mediterranean and swam out to sea until his heart gave out. He chose the manner of his death and died 'swimming toward the Sun'. Insofar as we can choose, should we not all seek to do likewise, rather than clinging fearfully to existence at the last, without autonomy or dignity?

---

159.   Ibid. p. 8.

Where flamencos and tangos are played

12
Dance me on down from Toledo

Come and dance with me down from Toledo,
By the light on the bridge we have made;
To a land with a non-Christian credo,
Where flamencos and tangos are played.

Dance me speechless to high, snow-capped mountains,
From which orchards and pastures are fed,
Then the cypresses, arches and fountains
Of Alhambra, the Isle of the Dead.

There the rich Andalusian muses
Sing softly to all who can hear,
Though a pallid, blue past still confuses
The mind and the heart and the ear;

For vengeful and dark Catholic violence
Five centuries since overthrew
And condemned to the grave or to silence
The voice of the Moor and the Jew.

But dance with me down from Toledo,
By the light on the bridge we have made;
To a land with a non-Christian credo,
Where flamencos and tangos are played.

Though golden Al-Andalus perished,
Suppressed by the sceptre and cross;
The ballads and songs Gypsies cherished
Plucked songlines from ruinous loss.

The spirit of Araby lingers
In the genius of Spanish guitar;
In flamencos for feet and for fingers;
In Tarrega and in Falla.

Those flamencos and songlines in flower,
The soul of Granada reborn,
So offended the fascists in power
That they murdered poor Lorca at dawn.

Still, dance with me, down from Toledo,
By the light on the bridge we have made;
To a land with a non-Christian credo,
Where flamencos and tangos are played.

From there, let's dance on out of reason,
With our hearts full of Lorca's deep song;
Until beauty has come into season,
And we know that that's where we belong.

While we dance, let's sustain that illusion,
With whatever good faith we can find.
May our steps take us wide of confusion;
May our love keep us blissfully blind.

For to sing and to dance in our yearning,
To share our deep song face to face;
To glide into each twist and turning
Is to live with both freedom and grace.

And so dance me on down from Toledo,
By the light on the bridge we have made;
To a land with a non-Christian credo,
Where flamencos and tangos are played.

181

Toledo as a point of departure: Why choose Toledo as a point of departure for dancing on down to Granada, to the Alhambra, 'the Isle of the Dead'—the land of a non-Christian credo? The 'non-Christian credo' referred to is not another of the monotheistic religions: Judaism or Islam.[160] Toledo serves as a convenient port of embarkation for the journey my *own* credo

---

160.   The admirable and courageous Ayaan Hirsi Ali, in her most recent book, *Heretic: Why Islam Needs a Reformation Now* (Fourth Estate, Harper/Collins, 2015) has called for Muslims to radically rethink their commitment to five core doctrinal positions:

   1.   *Muhammed's semi-divine and infallible status along with the literalist reading of the Qur'an, particularly those parts that were revealed in Medina;*

   2.   *The investment in life after death instead of life before death;*

   3.   *Sharia, the body of legislation derived from the Qur'an, the hadith and the rest of Islamic jurisprudence;*

   4.   *The practice of empowering individuals to enforce Islamic law by commanding right and forbidding wrong; and*

   5.   *The imperative to wage jihad or holy war.* (op. cit. p. 27)

   This would, indeed, constitute a radical upheaval within Islam; but it is not clear that we should call such a change a 'Reformation'. It would be far more like the Enlightenment of the 18th century.

   The great Christian figures of the Reformation, Luther, Calvin and others, in the early 16th century and the Puritans well into the 17th century demanded a purification of Christianity and a return precisely to scriptural rigour, belief in the afterlife and enforcement of God's law against Catholics, infidels and heretics. This led to a deep schism within Christendom and a convulsive series of religious wars, culminating in the immensely destructive Thirty Years War (1618-1648), which put an end to the real or imagined unity of Western Christendom and opened the way to an era of religious pluralism and finally secular Enlightenment. Mark Greengrass has provided a new account of all this, in *Christendom Destroyed: Europe 1517-1648* (Allen Lane, Penguin, 2014). It is to be imagined, therefore, that a Muslim 'Reformation', if modelled on the Christian one, would lead to a widespread insistence on exactly what the radical Muslims are calling for—a return to the Qur'an, the hadith, and sharia law and a denunciation of the compromised and 'corrupt' Islam of quasi-modern Muslim countries.

   Ayaan Hirsi Ali is, in fact, calling for secular Enlightenment in the Islamic world, *not* a Reformation and this will take a lot of achieving. She distinguishes between what she calls Medina Muslims, Mecca Muslims and Modifying Muslims. The first are those who take their cue from Mohammed's determination after his *hegira* or *hijra* —his move from Mecca, where he had been rejected, to Medina to try again—in June/July 622 CE to *enforce* his religious vision on unbelievers, whether pagan polytheists or Jews and Christians. The Mecca Muslims, she defines as those with the inclinations of the early Mohammed, to seek to *persuade* unbelievers to accept

proposes, because there, long ago, for a short while, the three monotheistic religions rooted in the Bible and the Qur'an, co-existed in a civilized, learned and cosmopolitan way. Their co-existence was possible because each recognized a transcendent good beyond sectarian dogmas; each of them recognized the communal and existential integrity of the others. My own credo, which consists of beliefs, but not of dogmas, seeks to articulate such a vision. It points to a global future in which a transcendent good will set the benchmark for relations between sects, cultures and states.

182

The rise of El-Andalus and the fall of the Caliphate: There is a broader background to Toledo, which is too little remembered, whether in the secular world or by monotheists across the board.[161] It goes back to the 8th century conquest of Spain by the Muslims and especially the epic life of Abd el-Rahman, last of the Umayyads, who fled from Abbasid usurpers and assassins in Damascus across the breadth of North Africa and established a revived and autonomous Umayyad caliphate in Spain, in the 750s CE. The Abbasids slaughtered all of Abd el-Rahman's family, seized power over the House of Islam and moved its capital from Damascus to Baghdad, where it was to remain until Baghdad was sacked by the Mongols in 1258. The caliphate was then incorporated into the gigantic Mongol Empire, extending from the East China Sea to Poland and from Lake Baikal to the Himalayas. During those centuries, the brightest and most tolerant part of the Muslim world was al-Andalus—the domain of Abd el-Rahman and his heirs.

---

that he was the Prophet of the Deity and that they should follow his teachings. The third group, Modifying Muslims, she describes as those few who grasp that even Mecca Muslims live with an *intractable cognitive dissonance* and that a major doctrinal shift is necessary if Islamic culture is to be adapted to the modern world without a terrible catastrophe—of the kind we are already beginning to see in North Africa and the Middle East. She identifies with the third, appeals to the second and condemns the first. The Enlightenment, if it comes to the Muslim world at all, may be very long in coming. What we are currently seeing in Africa and the Middle East bears far more resemblance to the religious wars of the 16th and 17th centuries than to the scientific and sceptical Enlightenment of the 17th and 18th centuries in Europe.

161.   'Even the histories traditionally told within the Muslim world,' writes Maria Rosa Menocal, 'rarely take the Umayyad path, and they spend relatively little time in al-Andalus, despite the fact that al-Andalus represents, in one form or another, the presence of Islam in Europe for the subsequent seven hundred odd years, some three times the present duration of the American Republic.' *The Ornament of the World: How Muslims, Jews and Christians Created a Culture of Tolerance in Medieval Spain* (Little, Brown & Co, New York, 2002) p. 9.

183

El-Dakhil and Toledo: Abd el-Rahman was called El-Dakhil—the Emigrant—by those back in Syria and Mesopotamia. He was also called the Falcon of the Quresh, the greatest of the tribe that had been enmeshed with the Prophet from the beginning. He took Cordoba and made it into a shining city, with vast gardens and a great library. It became, for two hundred years, the most civilized city in Europe. When it was sacked by Islamic fundamentalists from North Africa, in the 10th century, a smaller version of it was created at Toledo—the old Roman and Visigothic capital. There the cultural memory of the Umayyad caliphate at its best was kept alive for another century and more. For a time it was honoured even by the Catholic conquerors who took the city from the Muslims in 1085. In Toledo, many of the works of Greek learning, including Aristotle's treatises on reasoning, were translated from Arabic into Latin and thus found their way into renewed circulation in the Latin West. It is from there, consequently, that we begin our journey not *back* to antiquated creeds, but *forward* to a cosmopolitan humanistic renaissance.

184

Federico Garcia Lorca: The name of Lorca is one to conjure with. He was born and raised in Granada, the last of the outposts of El-Andalus to fall (in 1492) and was enchanted, even as a child, by the haunting site of the Alhambra. He looked back nostalgically to the gardens of Cordoba as the authentic civilization of Andalusia. He was profoundly poetic and musical. Although he suffered all his short life from sexual ambivalence and romantic confusion, he was full of tenderness and vitality. He looked to Gypsy song, *cante hondo*, as an inspiration, but longed to make things new. He was shot by a fascist death squad at the age of 38, on the outskirts of Granada, within sight of the Alhambra—before dawn, on the morning of 18 August 1936. That was at the very beginning of the Spanish Civil War, during which, it is estimated, the fascists were to execute some 114,000 people, while Stalinist hit squads killed many, also.[162] But it is Lorca's passion and sensitivity that this

---

162. On the killings in Spain in the 1930s, see Paul Preston *The Spanish Holocaust: Inquisition and Extermination in Twentieth Century Spain* (W. W. Norton & Co., New York and London, 2012). Preston relates (pp. 173-74) that some 5,000 citizens of Granada, including numerous 'doctors, lawyers, writers, artists, school teachers and, above all, workers' were murdered by the fascists. Lorca was among the more celebrated of the victims. Granada was an 'ultra-reactionary' constituency and Lorca had been notorious among the Right for his support for the downtrodden and, even worse, a kind of treason in their eyes, for his belief that 'the Catholic conquest of Moorish Granada in 1492 had been a disaster', because it had 'destroyed

poem celebrates and seeks to resurrect. It is into the world of his imaginings that the poem bids one dance from Toledo down to old Granada.

185

Growing up in sight of the Alhambra: Lorca's father and his aunt Isabel were both spirited guitarists; his uncle Luis a fine pianist. He himself was given a piano when very young and grew to adore the works of Beethoven, which he acclaimed later as the most sublime expression of the longing after 'impossible love'.[163] Within his own family, he imbibed from his earliest years, a feeling for and knowledge of all manner of Gypsy flamenco songs and ballads. Although Spain in his youth was dominated by a severely conservative Catholicism, the landscape around him in Granada physically evoked a vastly more cosmopolitan and hauntingly romantic past—Celtic, Carthaginian, Greek, Roman, Visigothic, Arabic—and the rural areas were alive with the restless Gypsy spirit. He saw the Alhambra as the ruined temple of a higher civilization and lamented the centuries long war between Moorish and Latin cultures. Such sentiments as his were expressed in Francisco Tarrega's 'Capricho *Arabe*' and the gentle tremolo guitar chords of his 'Recuerdos de la Alhambra' (Memories of the Alhambra), composed in Granada itself in 1896. This is the poem's land of a non-Christian credo, where flamencos for feet and for fingers are played.[164]

186

A festival of deep song: From 1921, Lorca befriended and collaborated with the composer Manuel de Falla in a deliberate effort to recover and revitalize the rich traditions of Andalusian song and, above all, the so-called *cante hondo* (deep song) associated with the Gypsies. Falla lived in a tiny white house on the very slopes of the Alhambra. Lorca and a small circle of like-minded friends 'talked of founding a musical cafe', but Falla 'proposed a more ambitious idea. Why not stage a *cante hondo* festival in Granada, a festival of national scope and importance', taking customary flamenco and infusing it with the haunting depths of deep song?[165] Here is Lorca's biographer on what deep song meant to him:

---

a unique civilization' and that its contemporary bourgeois masters had made of it a philistine wasteland.

163.   Beethoven did, in fact, compose a great deal of music while longing for an apparently impossible love. See Maynard Solomon *Beethoven* (Second Revised Edition, Schirmer Books, New York, 1998), especially chapter 15 'The Immortal Beloved', pp. 207-46.

164.   On the life of Lorca see Leslie Stainton *Lorca: A Dream of Life* (Bloomsbury, London, 1998).

165.   Ibid. p. 90.

Struck by the 'naked' emotion of deep song, Lorca later said that 'all the passions of life' could be found in its abbreviated form, that it 'comes from the first sob and the first kiss'. He understood *cante hondo* intuitively and interpreted it romantically, both as a poet and as an Andalusian whose great-grandmother had been part Gypsy—or so he claimed. Deep song contained the well-springs of his own writing: love, pain and death. It embodied the essence of the Andalusian temperament. He admired the pagan tones of the form, the candour of its language, its pantheism and the fusion of cultures—Indian, Jewish, Byzantine, Islamic—implicit in its sounds.[166]

It is for the sake of all this that one would dance on down from Toledo, by the light on the bridge made in the poem and in this book. Yet, again, Lorca's example is a metaphor. The challenge before us is not literally to re-enact his work in Granada in the 1920s, but to conceive of a culture attuned to 'deep song' across the 21st century world; informed not only by centuries of Andalusian history, but by Deep Time and the newly unveiled human past more generally.

187

Capturing music: How is it possible to do on a global scale what Lorca and Falla did on a local or national scale? Isn't the whole idea of a global 'festival of deep song' a contradiction in terms? Wouldn't that empty all folk traditions of their character, since they are, in region after region, as in Andalusia, rooted in and nourished by very particular ethnic, cultural and musical histories? To believe that is to be a mere antiquarian. We are on the cusp of an era of informed and open humanism, in which a great in-gathering of human musical accomplishment— informed by a comprehension at last of the very roots of the human addiction to music—has become possible. The horizon for appreciation, learning and creativity has never in history been more open. The technical means for bringing music alive in all its rich variation and across all borders have never been more extraordinary. The task before us is not to retreat into any kind of insularity, but to inhale freely the musical oxygen that diverse human cultures have been giving off for millennia.

---

166.   Ibid. p. 93. Lorca was, by the early 1920s, deeply immersed in Spanish folk songs. He knew dozens by heart and, according to Stainton:

> *Seated at a piano, his head thrown back, hands stretched wide on the keyboard, he was capable of spending a whole evening playing and singing songs from each region of the country without repeating a single example. He owned several ballad books and, like many of his contemporaries, including Falla, he was an aficionado of composer Felipe Pedrell's* Cancionero Musical Popular Español, *a massive compendium of traditional Spanish song published in four volumes between 1918 and 1922. For many in Lorca's generation, Pedrell's* Cancionero *served as a secular 'book of hours.'*(p. 95).

188

Notation and the singing voice: We commonly think of 'history'—which is to say recorded history—as beginning with the invention of writing in Sumer, five to six thousand years ago. Such writing was for recording first commerce and then spoken language. Notation for recording *music* did not come until much later. This is interesting, surely, given that music as a human proclivity seems to be at least as old as language. Notation for denoting *musical* sounds did not begin until about one thousand years ago: in European monasteries at the height of what used to be called 'the Dark Ages'.[167] And it was invented to go with words—to show how to intone the chants that were the central feature of liturgical and monastic music. In short, it was not music as such that was the basis for creating musical notation, but the singing voice.

189

Truth and beauty: Some years ago, the American Catholic theologian George Weigel wrote a book called *The Truth of Catholicism*.[168] He would have done better to have written a book

---

167.   Thomas Forrest Kelly *Capturing Music: The Story of Nota*tion (W. W. Norton & Co., New York and London, 2015). As he points out (pp. 5-10), there was plenty of music long before notation, but we have no record of it in any form—except for occasional verbal accounts of what it was like. In a notable passage with considerable implications, he remarks on a contemporary account of the Easter Sunday mass at Santa Maria Maggiore in Rome, celebrated by the Pope, in 720 CE, which was 'enriched with candles, incense, elaborate ritual, rich vestments'. According to the individual who described the mass, much of the ceremony was, in Kelly's words, 'coordinated by music', with a choir and soloists. The Basilica of Santa Maria Maggiore is still there. We have art and architecture from that era, but the music we do not have, because it could not be recorded.

168.   *The Truth of Catholicism: Ten Controversies Explored* (Harper Collins, 2001) was the ninth of Weigel's seventeen books. He is a formidable Catholic scholar and would, of course, strongly disagree with my claims here. He has staunchly championed the idea that Catholicism has a vital and invigorating role to play in Western society and in the world at large. His most recent book, *Evangelical Catholicism: Deep Reform in the 21st Century Catholic Church* (Basic Books, 2013) continues and extends this argument. Unlike some of those who are openly hostile to the Catholic Church, I do not disagree with him about this central proposition, though we would differ on many points of detail. The difference is that he believes everything depends on the claim that Catholicism is 'true', while I see it as a highly complex and evolved cultural inheritance which cannot, in all truth and honesty, be epistemologically reconciled with what we now know about the cosmos and biological evolution and which does its role in the world little good with dogmatism—only by what consistency and integrity it can occasionally muster.

called *The Beauty of Catholicism*.[169] He might then have placed his emphasis on Gregorian chant, the abundant music that has been composed around the liturgy of the Mass, including the many magnificent requiem masses, climaxing with Verdi's requiem for Alessandro Manzoni, in 1873.[170] Naturally, he would have included extended sections on the beauties of monastic and cathedral architecture, the pageantry and ceremonial that have for so long accompanied the sacred festivals and high rituals of the Catholic Church[171]; the greatest writings of the Church Fathers; the metaphysical poetry and literary reflections of numerous Catholic writers. But the music, the chant from a millennium ago, might have pride of place. If anything expresses the solemnity and allure of 'good religion' it is, surely, this music and singing; perhaps reaching its apotheosis in the Counter-Reformation compositions of Palestrina. Any 'religion' for the 21ˢᵗ century will have great difficulty in transcending this *beauty*; whereas we have no difficulty in repudiating the *truth* claims of Catholicism. How do

---

169.   Not, of course, that everyone would readily agree that Catholicism has been altogether beautiful. Yet it has been, at the very least, severely majestic. Its metaphysics and spiritual aspirations go back not only to the Hebrew Bible, but to Plato, Pythagoras and even the religion of ancient Egypt. It should on no account be treated lightly or destructively—only freely!

170.   Verdi was not himself particularly pious or 'religious', but was a very fine and free human being. His operas are, surely, the greatest body of operatic work created by any composer. When his requiem for Manzoni, the great Italian patriot and humanist, was performed in 1873, there were Catholics who regarded it as almost grotesquely operatic and bordering on the sacrilegious. Similar reactions by Greek Orthodox conservatives to 'sacred' music by Tchaikovsky and Rachmaninoff point to a central question in the transition from historical Christianity to a possible, more transcendent religion for the third millennium. Clearly, none of those three magnificent composers intended their works to be travesties or caricatures; nor are they. The Verdi requiem is tremendously moving and powerful. It might best be seen—or more precisely heard—as an attempt to respond in the modern world, the Enlightenment world, to what is most beautiful and profound in the ancient liturgies.

171.   Even David Hume, no apologist for the Catholic Church or the Papacy, observed regarding it, in his path-breaking history of Great Britain:

> *The splendour too and pomp of worship, which that religion carefully supports, are agreeable to the taste of magnificence that prevails in courts and form a species of devotion which, while it flatters the pampered senses, gives little perplexity to the indolent understandings of the great. That delicious country wherein the Roman Pontiff resides was the source of all modern art and refinement and diffused on its superstition an air of politeness which distinguishes it from the gross rusticity of other sects.*

Quoted in J. G. A. Pocock *Barbarism and Religion* Volume 2 *Narratives of Civil Government* (Cambridge University Press, 1999), p. 210.

we capture the beauty—the music, the 'soul' of the old religion, while remaining free of its dogmatic claims? That is a central cultural challenge for our time.

190

Dancing beyond all dogmas: The life of Lorca, as much as any life, embodied the quest for musical transcendence, free from the severity and dogmatism of conservative Catholicism. Much as champions of the Church like George Weigel would have it otherwise, we need to do with all the old religions, including Catholicism, what Lorca and Falla did with Spanish folk song: gather in the riches freely and create a new festival for the human spirit that will reanimate and regenerate the greatest 'spiritual' and existential insights and the greatest creative beauties of those religions for the scientific era, the new Axial Age, in which we now live. That will not be easy; it will not be simple. It is a gigantic task. But we face *many* gigantic tasks in the 21st century. Why baulk at this one? It is actually a pressing necessity. Let us extend ourselves, not contract into an ossified past or a sectarian haven. To withdraw behind walls of dogma is to invite the barbarians to lay siege. To go forth as barbarians is to compel others to raise walls. The civilizing process demands the creation of beauties, led by songs, which will exert Orphic charm over both the fearful and the aggressive. Orpheus is older than the religions and also, forever, newer.[172]

191

A mystical idea: The poem sings of *dancing* on down from Toledo, not marching or strolling or flying or driving. Dour Puritans and violent Islamists denounce music and dancing as diabolical seductions of the soul. That is in itself a damning objection to their beliefs. Yet who is to compose, orchestrate or lead the dance in question? Lorca and Falla had an almost mystical belief in the revival of deep song and would say that the common flamenco was rather debased and vulgar compared with what they sought to retrieve from *cante hondo*. We should take a lesson from this. The dance down from Toledo is a mystical idea; it is not some debased or vulgar parade. It cannot be what it needs to be if taken over by some grotesquely domineering ideology, in the way, for example, that the utopian socialist idea was taken over and debased by Stalinists and Maoists. It will of necessity be an *emergent* phenomenon and a beacon—like the old, much squabbled over and now jaded idea of the 'New Jerusalem'. There is scope for endless creativity.

---

172.   The tenth book of Ovid's great Latin poem *Metamorphoses* is the richest evocation of Orpheus as the original and greatest lyrical bard, in the springtime of the world, charming the very stones and all wild creatures with his song.

192

Show us how you can dance: Only to the extent that we come to *embody* our freedom in relation to our humanity and our relations with others will we be able to dance, rather than assert control or squabble. To dance well requires being at ease with one's body, with the rhythms of music, with the presence of one's dance partner or partners, with the gaze of onlookers. Do you want to persuade us that you are 'saved'? Then show us how you can dance! Do you want to inspire us to welcome a new 'caliphate'? Then show us what glorious dancing it will make possible! Do you want to demonstrate that material abundance and technological revolutions are worthwhile? Then show us the joy, art and beauty of the *dancing* that they make possible.[173] All else is delusion, oppression, vulgarity and waste. To share our deep song face to face is to live with both freedom and grace—to live inside and for the sake of the dance. There is a creed.

193

The loss of echo: But how can all this relate to the actual musical culture of the early 21st century—the era of the iPod, the discotheque, the rapper and the fragmentation of anything resembling a shared, traditional, higher culture? Music theorists and sociologists in the early decades of the 20th century, such as Georg Simmel and the highly influential Theodor Adorno, already saw the urban industrial world of the 'late bourgeoisie' as overwhelming

---

173.   Kimerer L. Lamothe argues, in *Why We Dance: A Philosophy of Bodily Becoming* (Columbia University Press, New York, 2015) that life itself is movement; that, indeed, there is no such thing as 'matter', only movement. Hers, also, is a manifesto and an exuberant one. She posits that the 'materialists' have got us all into strife and that a radically new philosophy of movement is necessary for the good of humanity and of the ecosphere. Grappling with her epistemology would require a critical essay of considerable length. But at one point she quotes Isadora Duncan as having asserted:

> *The dance of the future will be a new movement, a consequence of the entire evolution which mankind has passed through.*

With this I can agree, since dance (at least as the term is customarily understood) has itself arisen out of human evolution and we have only come to understand that evolutionary process through the sciences which Lamothe both draws upon and throws into question with her freewheeling polemic against 'materialism'. Who knows what forms of dance might be prescribed by some self-appointed *avant garde* movement if we lose our grasp of the history and evolution of dance and our love for its classical forms? For me, Tchaikovsky and the Ballets Russe remain inspirational, almost the quintessence of dance; but there are many folk dances that more closely resemble what is needed on the everyday level, as a kind of existential psychotherapy.

and disorienting the human capacity for listening, for harmony, for coherent meaning, for anything resembling genuine autonomy. What are we to make of the vastly larger and more numerous cities and the endless cacophony of sound and 'information' in the early 21st century? The industrial urbanization of masses of human beings was thought, even ninety years ago, to be leading to the 'loss of echo'.[174] This had to do with radical changes in the built and acoustic environment; but it occurred, also, in a wider, metaphorical sense: the ancient rituals, beliefs, poetries and folk memories found less and less 'echo' in the *experience* of urbanized, industrialized, rationalized human beings. Now, in the 21st century world, they are disappearing entirely into 'entertainment'.

194

A profusion of musical possibilities: All these problems have, in a manner of speaking, been *amplified* since the first half of the 20th century—almost unrelentingly so. Yet, even as the cities of the human world have burgeoned and burst all prior boundaries and expectations over the past hundred years, so have the sciences broken open our knowledge in revolutionary ways and demonstrated that no Marxian historicism, no Freudian reductionism comes close to containing or describing the complexity of the human presence in the world. The overwhelming profusion of music in our time is no more an objection to the possibility of a higher culture than the profusion of languages and idiolects is a refutation of the science of linguistics or the possibilities for articulate expression—in many languages. What we need now is not some ideological cant about the oppression of the human spirit under capitalism, but recognition of the extraordinary creativity of which we are capable and which, in fact, we continue to exhibit. The future beckons.

195

Tapping into our humanity: To grasp the possibilities of music and dance in the 21st century, we must remind ourselves that rhythm and musicality are more deeply rooted in the emotional brain than language, reason or consciousness. This is central and, scientifically speaking, a very recent discovery. The relationship between the conscious self, the 'rational' mind or the *social* self and this deeper, primal experience of being cries out for our attention. Music, song, rhythmic movement are pre-eminently the ways in which human beings feel, remember and express meaning and belonging. Dancing on down from Toledo, therefore, stands for coming to feel and live our humanity, not in a *primitive* manner, but right down to the *primal core* of

---

174.   Veit Erlmann *Reason and Resonance: A History of Modern Aurality* (Zone Books, New York, 2014) p. 315.

our emotional and existential, not our ideological humanity.[175] St Augustine defined music, long before there was any modern science of the matter, as *the art of moving well*, but music is more than that. It *taps*, as it were, into our whole creaturely way of experiencing the world, from the simplest joys or fears to the most profound and complex apprehensions of the social and natural worlds.[176]

---

175. In writing this, I have in mind among other things, the remarkable findings of music therapy in very recent years. See Oliver Sacks *Musicophilia: Tales of Music and the Brain* (Revised and expanded edition, Picador, London, 2008). He wrote:

    For me, the first incitement to think and write about music came in 1966, when I saw the profound effects of music on the deeply parkinsonian patients I later wrote about in Awakenings. *And since then, in more ways than I could possibly imagine, I have found music continually forcing itself on my attention, showing me its effects on almost every aspect of brain function—and life.* (p. xiv)

176. Oliver Sacks published an autobiography, before his death in 2015, which, as it happens, has the title *On the Move*. He goes on, immediately after the passage from *Musicophilia*, cited in the previous footnote:

    'Music' has always been one of the first things I look up in the index of any new neurology or physiology textbook. But I could find scarcely any mention of the subject until the 1977 publication of Macdonald Critchley and R. A. Henson's book Music and the Brain, with its wealth of historical and clinical examples. Perhaps one reason for the scarcity of musical case histories is that physicians rarely ask their patients about mishaps of musical perception(whereas a linguistic problem, say, will immediately come to light). Another reason for this neglect is that neurologists like to explain, to find putative mechanisms, as well as to describe—and there was virtually no neuroscience of music prior to the 1980s. This has all changed in the last two decades with new technologies that allow us to see the living brain as people listen to, imagine and even compose music. There is now an enormous and rapidly growing body of work on the neural underpinnings of musical perception and imagery and the complex and often bizarre disorders to which these are prone.

    That, as he put it, 'there was virtually no neuroscience of music prior to the 1980s' is only one of many reminders that so much of what 'we' now know (in a vaguely collective sense) is of very recent provenance. If we were to draw a parallel between the rise of critical rationality and natural science in the Greek world two and a half thousand years ago and the era of modern science, the 5th century BCE would be the equivalent of the 17th century CE, while the 20th century CE would be the equivalent of the 3rd century BCE; and our own era the counterpart to the 2nd century BCE—the era immediately after the great scientists of Alexandria and before the crisis of the mid-2nd century BCE, which brought the golden age of Greek thought to an end. We have, of course, a vastly greater stock of knowledge than the Greeks could ever have imagined; but almost all of it has come in the past fifty to one hundred years—the 'Alexandrian' epoch of modern science.

196

Deep song and deep time: The pivotal idea in all of this is to see ourselves in the context of Deep Time in an unprecedented way. This should not be so difficult. Various religions, not least the Asian ones—Hinduism and Buddhism—or the old Mayan religion with its star observatories and mathematical calculations of long cosmological epochs, show that human beings are entirely capable of incorporating awe at immense periods of time or long cosmic cycles into their religious thinking. We now have a universal update on all of that: the science of cosmology has taken steps, in the past century particularly, transcending all the speculations of the old religions. We have that science—potentially—in common. We are all, regardless of our religious, ethnic or economic background, members of the species *Homo sapiens* and marooned on the small, blue planet we call Earth, tens of thousands of light years from the centre of the Milky Way; in a cosmos 13.7 billion years old and expanding. Our deep song begins right there—and our dance.

197

Primeval foundations and creative renewal: The doctrines, hymns and music of all the old religions begin with their cosmologies. So must ours. Moreover, our song—our Deep Song— will, of necessity, recall and acknowledge the many strands of human culture and speculation, belief and ritual which have preceded the state of scientific knowledge we have now reached. Just as Falla and Lorca found the *cante hondo* of Andalusia evocative and gathered together the folk songs of centuries, so shall we find the *cante hondo* of our cultural renewal in the songs and experiences of our human ancestors from around the Earth and across time. We shall, of course, gather and interpret all of them in the light of where we now stand; but that was *always* the case—for those earlier religions and cultures as it is for us. Think of the Benedictines building Monte Cassino on the site of a temple of Apollo; or Le Corbusier synthesizing Sun worship, goddess worship, Catholic tradition and his appreciation of both the Parthenon and the monasteries of Mount Athos into Ronchamp, in the 1950s. We have ample precedent for our great task.

198

Simplicity as well as orchestras: Deep Song is as much the feel for rhythm and song within the most 'primitive' human beings, the human appreciation of birdsong or whale song and the modern capacity to appreciate (and even feel nostalgia for) the plainchant of medieval monks, as it is anything 'sophisticated' or 'revolutionary'; perhaps more! Remember that it was the same Lorca who passionately loved the piano works of Beethoven that went out searching for and celebrating *cante hondo*. The renewal we are in need of is not a supercilious or destructive attack on the pieties of the past, but an attempt to creatively revitalize what serves human musical and ritual needs—in a manner consistent with what we now know to be the case about what we are and what the Earth and the Cosmos are. There are universal truths to respect, but there is no fierce persecution of heretics or unbelievers to carry out; no wrecking of Bamiyan Buddhas or sacking of venerable monasteries. There is simply an attempt to draw others into a common sense of the Deep Song of which we are part; into the dance on down from Toledo and into a whole new Axial Age of human awakening and civilization. The need is not to rush, but to think.

199

The saxophone and the future: There is no mention of the saxophone in Theodor Adorno's *Quasi Una Fantasia: Essays on Modern Music*, which was first published in 1963. This was a mistake on Adorno's part. The saxophone, it might be argued, is the quintessentially modern musical instrument. It is, of course, not one instrument, so much as a family of instruments, but it is pre-eminently a *jazz* instrument; one on which astonishing improvisations can be performed on even the simplest melodies. We should for all these reasons think of it as symbolic of where we now stand in relation to a theory of culture and religion in the 21st century. It is a wind instrument, dependent on breath control, whose ancestry takes us back to Palaeolithic bone flutes. It is also a marvel of modern technological engineering. It is an instrument of mood music and of popular culture. It is able to be used in elaborate musical ensembles, but can do splendidly as a solo instrument. It provoked laughter and derision among those who took themselves and their musical preferences rather too seriously a century ago. It does without pretentiousness and yet can gleam and soar with effects as sublime as those of any other instrument. It stands, in short, for much of what we seek in the future—much that free spirits have long been practising.

200

Likenesses to the shadow of God: The saxophone? That little note of libertarianism might scandalize all those who see religion as necessarily solemn in nature and who associate the saxophone with the perennial vaudeville of capitalism and the American dream.[177] It is not, of

---

177.   In his history of the instrument, Cottrell writes:

> ... *although the saxophone may have begun life as a European instrument, by the 1920s it was very clearly perceived as an American one, partly through the saxophone craze in which the*

course, intended as an instrument to be used exclusively by 'the devout'; only as an instrument that is symbolic of the freedom which is indispensable to any contemporary religion worthy of the name. For, lest there be any misunderstanding, all the old religions need to be 'naturalized' and, little by little, their synagogues, churches and mosques, their temples and shrines, made over into the abodes of a better informed reflection, remembrance and singing. Nietzsche, at the point where he first proclaimed the death of God, remarked:

> After Buddha was dead, his shadow was still shown for centuries in a cave—a tremendous, gruesome shadow. God is dead, but given the way of men, there may still be caves for thousands of years, in which his shadow will be shown.—And we—we still have to vanquish his shadow, too.

Do we have thousands of years in which to accomplish this task? It is certainly to be hoped so. Patience and good humour should certainly be among our virtues. We should not jump at shadows, but labour to naturalize the settings in which those of God and other more colourful deities continue to appear. And where crowds gather too seriously in awe of such shadows, we might have resort less to argument than to the saxophone in response—the music of freedom.

201

Concerning the red giant Sun: All the old religions had their notions about how the world began, what natural catastrophes portend and how the world as we know it will end. They were and are all in error. We now know with considerable confidence the life-cycle of habitable planets—of which ours is still the only one for which we have clear evidence. We have reason to believe that Ice Ages will recur and that they will have enormous and devastating consequences for any human civilization resembling ours or for that matter any extant form of human settlement. We have good reason to believe that much further in the future, as the Sun exhausts its supply

---

USA was by then immersed, but also because of the instrument's close identification with those styles of American popular music that were by now being rapidly disseminated throughout the world. As such the saxophone can be seen to denote the particular qualities that Caucasian Americans (at least) saw themselves as espousing: a democratic, inclusive, egalitarian society driven by the free market ... The saxophone wasn't weighed down by centuries of tradition, or enmeshed within the class-oriented structures prevailing in European art music. It was an instrument you could teach yourself, with minimal reliance on others and without the need, apparently, for extensive specialist education. It appealed to and could be played by all classes and ethnicities. It represented something of a fresh start, a new way of doing things, not unlike America itself with its newly immigrant population.

The Saxophone (Yale University Press, New Haven and London, 2010), p. 307.

of hydrogen, it will expand into a red giant star and obliterate life on Earth inexorably.[178] No religious ritual will save us from any of this; no prayer will affect it to the slightest degree. There is no deity in control of any of it. Therefore we must not blink at reality.

---

178.   Peter Ward and Donald Brownlee *The Life and Death of Planet Earth: How the Science of Astrobiology Charts the Ultimate Fate of Our World* (Piatkus, London, 2003). They point out that, well before the Sun swells into a red giant, life on Earth could face a colossal crisis owing to plate tectonics:

> *Our data and models predict that just as the world's continents once formed a super continent we call Gondwanaland a quarter billion years ago, they may drift together to form a successor to Gondwanaland a quarter billion years in Earth's future. And once again it may cause a mass extinction that kills off the majority of species on the planet ... What caused [the Permian mass extinction 250 million years ago] that greatest of mass extinctions [that killed off nearly 90 percent of all organisms on the planet]? It is one of the greatest mysteries of science. Was it caused by an impact of an asteroid or comet? Why some Earth scientists think so, there is still not conclusive evidence that that is the case. A prevailing view is that planet Earth did it to itself by clumping its continents together and our mathematical models of continental drift foresee a return to the same conditions. Perhaps the next such event will end all animal life, instead of nearly doing so.* (pp. 90-91)

They estimate (p. 106) that the expansion of the Sun will lead to the browning of the Earth and the long, inexorable retreat of life starting from as 'little' as 500 million years from now and eliminating at least all land-based life and perhaps all but bacterial life by about one billion years from now. These are not merely vaguely large numbers, but calculations based on the probable cycle of hydrogen combustion at the heart of the Sun. The most primitive forms of life, they estimate, could possibly survive up to another six billion years—'until almost the end of the Sun's life as a main sequence star.' (p. 143)

Long before things get to that point, however, something truly spectacular will have happened, which all of us should surely wish we could be alive to witness, simply because it will be so awe-inspiring a catastrophe as to dwarf anything of which we have record. The galaxy M31, commonly known as Andromeda, currently some 2.5 million light years from the Milky Way, will *collide* with the Milky Way. Andromeda is about twice the size of the Milky Way, with many hundreds of billions of stars. It is in free fall towards us at the rate of literally more than a million kilometres per hour and will crash into the Milky Way about three or four billion years from now. The sheer scale of such an event beggars the imagination. That we have been able to detect M31 and make such calculations is itself astounding. Who would seriously want to have lived in any prior era of human knowledge?

All these are not truths which exist *alongside* the claims of the old religions, as a separate and non-conflicting magisterium, in the language of the late evolutionary biologist and theorist of punctuated equilibrium, Stephen Jay Gould. They are the realities of the world and the cosmos in which we all live, whatever beliefs we might choose to cling to and whatever arcane rituals we might choose to practice and there is no other.

202

The task ahead of us: Our task is not to threaten any unscientific person with 'hellfire and damnation' for insisting that the future will be guided by the hand of God. It is to combine a more and more well-adjusted 'natural religion' with a better and better scientific capacity to do what we can to keep our planet hospitable to life. There is time enough for the present. In the long run, things don't look so good—but that is the *very* long run. That future will take care of itself. Our task is with the human world of the early third millennium CE. We have our work cut out for us in that regard, since our capacities for confusion and violent confrontation seem quite intractable. Yet we have made it to this point from what must surely have appeared—to an unconcerned, but observant extra-terrestrial eye—rather unpromising beginnings, a few million years ago. We have filled the world since the end of the most recent Ice Age and generated the most astounding technologies. The large question before us all now is simply: what do we want?

203

What do we want? Surely that is too broad, too vague a question!? How can it possibly be answered in a coherent and collective manner? In truth, there may not be any such answer. But the question, asked in the first person plural, is one which goes to the heart of our humanity. Robert Brandom's great (but largely unread) philosophical classic, *Making It Explicit*, begins with the observation that 'We are the ones who say 'we''—and in the process define and redefine ourselves.[179] This century, this new Axial Age, is a time in which we are called upon to redefine ourselves. That process is rooted in the question 'What do we want?' since it has to do not merely with individual appetites or perceived needs, but with the dialogue among human beings concerning the future of the Earth and the kind of being we ultimately see ourselves becoming. By pressing upon this question in that frame of reference, by making our ideas explicit, we will gradually create a new sense of collective identity within the biosphere and within the cosmological horizons we have opened up since the early 20th century.

204

Enlightenment and oxygen: Each individual who contributes something to that great questioning and redefinition plays the role of a simple and unpretentious prokaryote in the ancient days of the Earth: sucking in the light of the sciences, using it to fuel personal

---

179.   Robert Boyce Brandom *Making It Explicit: Reasoning, Representing, and Discursive Commitment* (Harvard University Press, 1998).

growth through a kind of intellectual photosynthesis; and giving off free oxygen in the form of creative work, constructive insight or informed assent. This is the Anthropocene and we are terraforming the Earth at a pace and to a depth that no species has done before—or at least not at such dizzying speed. It isn't simply 'fossil fuel companies' that are doing this. It is all of us as a species. The overall phenomenon is spectacular and has been overwhelmingly liberating for human beings—but it is time to take stock and rethink where we are going. We stand in need of redefining what 'liberation' is for and how it might be made more congruent with the intricacies of the biosphere under our free stewardship.

205

Me and my saxophone: I have made many observations and claims in this book. They have been my kind of free oxygen. You, the reader, will have made of them what you were able to. Perhaps it could be said that all I have been doing is playing a jazz tune called *Credo and Twelve Poems* on my saxophone; improvising on a series of themes.[180] I hope you have found yourself at times tapping your feet, clicking your fingers, even singing snatches of song as you went. If any or all of that has happened, I am content. Focus less on the claims than on the *mood*. Do the notes I have struck conjure up moods in you and your own questions? Good! Explore them! Take away what you will and hum it as long as you remember it. I'll be playing at another club in my next book—possibly on a different kind of instrument. See you there.

---

180.   In making this remark I have in my mind's eye the image of Dino Soldo playing his gleaming, golden saxophone at intervals throughout Leonard Cohen's wonderful 17 July 2008 concert at the O2 Arena, in London, as an accompaniment to the songs 'There ain't no cure for love,' 'Bird on a wire' 'Boogie Street' and 'I tried to leave you'. He was not playing solo and was not improvising; but the beauty of his instrument and the manner in which his playing lifted up and enhanced the melody in each case were exemplary of what I have in mind. Besides, my own playing here hardly takes place in isolation. As my abundant citations show, I am merely adding the sound of my saxophone to a chorus of singing voices and the artistry of many other instruments. So it is with all intellectual and creative endeavour. It may be that we exhale oxygen in our individuality, mimicking prokaryotes; but in a larger sense our minds work within 'eukaryotic' cultures of literary and technical, scientific and communicative divisions of labour.

Acknowledgements

This book began with a suggestion from John Spooner that we create a book together. Without his suggestion, it would not have come into being. He is, of course, absolved of all responsibility for what I have written. It was, however, a pleasure to have him respond with drawings to my poems and then watch as I filled out the book with my aphorisms and wrote my long critical essay on George Steiner and Friedrich Nietzsche. He has also contributed to stringent discussions about the aesthetic design of the book.

As this book was being written, another book that brings together much of my thinking over many years, *Opinions and Reflections* was going to press. This book, however, is both more original and creative than *Opinions and Reflections* and goes back to the very earliest years of my attempts to sort out my beliefs and orientations. Although its spells out from the start my explicit differences with both Steiner and Nietzsche, I owe each of those writers a vote of thanks for having written their pungent and learned books long before I became a reader of their work. My debt to each of them is considerable.

As the aphorisms make clear, I also owe a debt of thanks to countless other thinkers and scholars, biographers, scientists, artists and creative writers, many of whom are still alive and very much active. As I have paid tribute to a good many of them in both text and footnotes, I will not run through all their names here. If I was to single any one of them out for having had an influence over many years, through his writings and his life, it might be Boris Pasternak. The film by David Lean of *Doctor Zhivago* made an immense impression on me when I first saw it forty years ago and I would like to think that the influence of both the film and the novel are evident in the spirit of this book.

I wrote *Credo and Twelve Poems* while struggling with metastatic melanoma, often having to sleep twelve or even fourteen hours a day due to extreme fatigue and knowing that I could lose the battle and find myself spiralling downward into debility and terminal illness. That I was nevertheless able to write it rapidly and with very few revisions is due to the fact that the thoughts expressed here had been developing, piecemeal, for a very long time. The experience of writing them down was, therefore, not one of arduous research and reflection, but of creative release and self-expression. I was assisted, through those few months, by the generosity of family and friends and the attentions of my doctors and all deserve my gratitude.

The book is dedicated to my partner of eleven years and remarkable muse, Claudia Maria Alvarez Ortiz; because, more than anyone else, she has urged me, since we first met, to give expression at long last to all the thoughts accumulated through decades of reading, academic studies and reflection. Also because she is herself so passionately committed to thinking about how to change the world for the better by stimulating people in all walks of life to think critically and well. She has pursued that goal, with the good of her own country and the broader culture of Latin America in view, since she was a very young woman. We walk freely, hand in hand, in our approach to the world.

It is also dedicated to Joseph Lo Bianco, a fine scholar of languages and literature and a friend, whose gentle, cultivated conversation has been a constant delight since we first met at a talk I was giving about the prospects for Western civilization and he asked a question about culture and language, citing George Steiner. We struck an instant rapport and realized that we had to become better acquainted. Joe is the best kind of 'good European', but an Australian of unpretentious Italian immigrant stock and a worker in the vineyards of cross-cultural and inter-linguistic communication, both in the Indo-European and Asian worlds. On all these levels, this is a book offered to him, as my attempt to conceive unities and coherences in the human world of the 21st century.

Just as *Credo and Twelve Poems* was being typeset, I discovered and read Roberto Mangabeira Unger's *The Religion of the Future* (Harvard University Press, 2014). I rejoiced in what he was attempting and read his book very closely, but was unable to incorporate any reference to it into my own book. Instead, I have written an essay length response to it, which will be published at the same time as this book, under the title 'The Future of Religion'. Unger is an American citizen of Brazilian extraction and I expect to travel to Brazil early in 2016, with this book in my travel bags. I believe he and I are seeking broadly similar goals and look forward to dialogue and even collaboration with him in the years ahead.

Finally, I must acknowledge the passionate little team at Barrallier/Echo Books, who have converted a typed manuscript into a beautiful, durable and readable book. Ian Gordon and I first met well over a decade ago, over a dinner organized by the Chief of Army. This is our fifth book together. As one good friend of mine remarked this year, 'Every one of your books is a work of art!' Much of the credit for that belongs to Ian and his designer Peter Gamble. Before this book, we drew upon the art work of the late Jorg Schmeisser, with stunning effect. Here we have had the creative input of John Spooner. I thank Ian, Peter and John for their contribution to my self-expression; and hope that readers will appreciate it as much as I do.

Index

www.ingramcontent.com/pod-product-compliance
Lightning Source LLC
Chambersburg PA
CBHW050617110426
42813CB00008B/2587